CAPITAL AND EMPLOYMENT

STUDIES IN POLITICAL ECONOMY
edited by John Eatwell

Capital and Employment: A Study of Keynes's Economics,
    Murray Milgate, 1982
Gifts and Commodities, C. A. Gregory, 1982
The Economic Structure of Backward Agriculture, A. Bhaduri,
    1983

CAPITAL AND EMPLOYMENT

A Study of Keynes's Economics

MURRAY MILGATE

1982

ACADEMIC PRESS

A Subsidiary of Harcourt Brace Jovanovich, Publishers

London   New York
Paris   San Diego   San Francisco   São Paulo
Sydney   Tokyo   Toronto

ACADEMIC PRESS INC. (LONDON) LTD.
24/28 Oval Road
London NW1

United States Edition published by
ACADEMIC PRESS INC.
111 Fifth Avenue
New York, New York 10003

British Library Cataloguing in Publication Data

Milgate, M.
  Capital and employment.—(Studies in political
  economy; 1)
  1. Keynes, John Maynard   2. Keynesian
  economics
  I. Title   II. Series
  330.15′6   HB99.7
  ISBN 0-12-496250-5
  LCCCN 82-73227

Photoset in Great Britain by
Rowland Phototypesetting Ltd, Bury St Edmunds, Suffolk
and printed by St Edmundsbury Press,
Bury St Edmunds, Suffolk

Series Editor's Preface

The revival of the analytical principles of classical political economy that has gathered pace since the mid-1960s has been based on the firm foundation of a logically coherent theory of value and distribution. It was the failure to provide this foundation which for many years confined the classical approach to being, at best, a repository of useful ideas on growth and technological progress (Smith's discussion of the division of labour and Marx's dissection of the labour process being good examples), or at worst, identified with simple-minded devotion to the labour theory of value as the 'qualitative' expression of capitalist exploitation—the position to which Hilferding retreated in the face of Böhm-Bawerk's critique of Marx, so depriving the surplus approach of any quantitative significance as a theory of value and distribution. The publication of Piero Sraffa's *Production of Commodities by Means of Commodities* changed all that. Sraffa not only generalised the mathematical solutions to the surplus approach which had been advanced by Dmitriev and Bortkeiwicz, but also presented the analytical *structure* of the surplus approach with stark clarity. Moreover, Sraffa provided a critique of the neoclassical theory of the rate of profit and so of the entire neoclassical explanation of value, distribution and output—hence clearing the ground for the redevelopment of classical theory.

With the analytical core now secure, attention can be turned to the development of other facets of classical and Marxian theory and to the empirical insights which this theory provides. In stark contrast to the neoclassical approach, which reduces all economic activity to a single principle—the competitive resolution of individual attempts to maximise utility subject to the constraints of technology and endowment—classical theory is constructed from a number of analytically separable components. The core of the theory, the surplus approach to value and distribution, takes as data the size and composition of output, the technology in use (the conditions of reproduction) and the real wage (or, in some cases, the rate of profit). These data do not, however, lie outside the realm of economics (as, for example, the neoclassical economists' utility functions do). We need to provide theoretical explanations of their determination. Hence Smith, Ricardo and Marx advanced theories of the real wage and of the level of output (Say's law in the case of Ricardo), and Smith and Marx presented detailed analyses of technological change. Assembled around the core, these theories are the building blocks of a general theory of the operations of the capitalist economy. There is in all this a clear danger of constructing a disjointed *ad hoc* collage of theories and empirical generalisations. This is avoided by enveloping the entire edifice in a general characterisation of the economic system: the clear specification, that is, of the capitalist mode of production. This serves both to cement the elements of the theory together and to eliminate propositions that do not fit.

This series of books is devoted to studies which develop and extend the classical framework. Broadly, there are two jobs to be done.

First, the classical theory itself must be developed and generalised. All the elements surrounding the core analysis of value and distribution—theories of output and employment, of accumulation, of technology, of the wage, of competition and so on—require reassessment and 'modernisation' in the light both of Sraffa's results and of the many changing facets of the modern capitalist system. This will involve both theoretical development *and* empirical analysis. For one of the important characteristics of classical theorising is the manner in which theory is grounded in the socio-economic data of the system under consideration. The institutional environment is an essential part of the theory.

Second, the rejection of the now discredited neoclassical theory throws open a wide range of problems in international trade, development economics, fiscal and monetary policy and so forth, into which the classical approach can provide new insights. In part these will lead to the refreshing task of debunking the policy prescriptions of orthodox theory which revolve primarily around the fundamental theorem of welfare economics and the supposed 'efficiency' of competitive markets. But there is also a positive job to be done. The reconstruction of economic theory will inevitably precipitate a reinterpretation of economic policy and problems.

In this book Murray Milgate pursues the task of reassessing Keynes's theory of effective demand in the light of developments in the theory of value and distribution. The argument sweeps away the considerable accretion of confusion that has built up around the theory of output and employment since the publication of Keynes's *General Theory*, confusion which has stemmed primarily from vain attempts to integrate

Keynes's ideas into the corpus of neoclassical theory by means of a variety of arbitrary assumptions—'sticky' wages, the effects of uncertainty and expectations, short run rigidities and the like. Milgate not only presents a more coherent interpretation of the debates surrounding Keynes's ideas than has hitherto been available, but also points to the important theoretical compatability between the classical analysis of value and distribution and Keynes's theory of output.

John Eatwell
Trinity College, Cambridge
September, 1982

Preface

This work is offered as a contribution to a new and promising line of inquiry into Keynesian Economics opened up by the recent contributions of Pierangelo Garegnani. It has its roots in the economic theory of the old Classical Economists from Adam Smith down to Marx and, more recently, Piero Sraffa. Its essential ingredient is the rejection of the orthodox marginalist vision of the economic system operating according to the principles of demand and supply theory. This work seeks to show that not only is this the upshot of recent controversies in the theory of capital, but also that it is the course suggested by Keynes's contribution to the theory of employment. Its primary aim is to re-examine the nature of Keynes's contribution to economic theory and, following from this, to review critically dominant contemporary interpretations of Keynes's work. The work also seeks to isolate the linkages which exist between Keynes's theory of output and employment on the one hand, and the surplus approach to value and distribution of the old Classical Economists on the other. While the primary focus of the work is, so to speak, theoretical, its central conclusions embody important messages for the conduct of economic policy. In particular, while they suggest that the adoption of Keynesian policies is desirable, they also imply that this does not entail a return to those simplistic 'fine tuning' policies that became the norm after the Second World War. If the interpretation of Keynes's contribution that is given in this work is accepted, it implies the need for a much more interventionist stance than has hitherto been thought to be theoretically justified.

I should like to thank Dr John Eatwell for his aid and advice over the period which led up to the completion of this book. I should like also to thank Professors Pierangelo Garegnani, Luigi Pasinetti and Joan Robinson for their comments on earlier drafts of parts of this work. Though my reading of Keynes may not concur, on every point, with theirs, it will be obvious to the reader how profound has been their influence upon my thinking. It goes without saying that all errors and misinterpretations are my own responsibility.

MURRAY MILGATE
Cambridge, June 1982

Contents

Series Editor's Preface   v
Preface   ix

I. INTRODUCTION   I

    A. The contemporary position of 'Keynesian Economics'   2
    B. The problem of interpretation   5
    C. Outline of the argument   7

II. PRELIMINARY DEFINITIONS AND CONCEPTS   9

    A. A capitalist economy   10
    B. The 'object' and 'method' of economic analysis   11
    C. Theory *versus* method: the explanation of the object   11
    D. Long-period and short-period positions   12
    E. The traditional long-period method of economic analysis   12
    F. The method of 'intertemporal equilibrium'   12
    G. Some terminological conventions   13

PART ONE: THE PRE-1936 ORTHODOXY AND
           THE *GENERAL THEORY*

III. THE TRADITIONAL LONG-PERIOD METHOD OF
     ECONOMIC ANALYSIS   19

    A. Natural prices and the long-period method   19
    B. The representation of the persistent forces of free
       competition under the long-period method   23
    C. Monetary forces: persistent or transitory?   26
    D. The stationary-state and the long-period method   28
    E. Reasons for the supremacy of the long-period method   33
    F. Principal conclusions and remaining questions   34

IV. THEORETICAL SYSTEMS AND THE LONG-PERIOD
    METHOD   35

    A. The structure of classical economic theory   36
    B. The structure of marginalist economic theory   41
    C. 'Say's Law' and classical economics   46
    D. 'Say's Law' in marginalist economic theory   57

V.   THE ANALYSIS OF DEVIATIONS FROM
      LONG-PERIOD POSITIONS   59

      A. Short-period theory and long-period theory   60
      B. Movement away from the quantity theory in the analysis
          of deviations   63
      C. Wicksell's cumulative process   68
      D. Developments in England: Hawtrey, Lavington and
          Robertson   71
      E. The argument so far   75

VI.   THE PRINCIPLE OF EFFECTIVE DEMAND:
      THE POSITIVE PART OF THE *GENERAL THEORY*   77

      A. The principle of effective demand   77
      B. The long-period theory of output and employment   84
      C. Remnants of orthodoxy   91
      D. Keynes and marginalist economic theory   96
      E. Keynes and classical economic theory   98

VII. THE THEORY OF CAPITAL AND THE THEORY
      OF EMPLOYMENT: THE NEGATIVE PART OF
      THE *GENERAL THEORY*   102

      A. The inflexibility of money wages   104
      B. Keynes on the 'classical' theory of interest: I   111
      C. Keynes on the 'classical' theory of interest: II   113
      D. Reconstructing a critique   122
      E. Capital and employment   123

VIII. THE METHOD OF INTERTEMPORAL EQUILIBRIUM   125

      A. The trend in modern 'Keynesian' economics   125
      B. The method of intertemporal equilibrium   127
      C. The origin of the notion of intertemporal equilibrium 129
      D. Reasons for the emergence of the notion of 'intertemporal
          equilibrium'   136
      E. Historical reconstruction   140
      F. The stationary-state hypothesis   141

IX.   UNCERTAINTY AND EXPECTATIONS   143

      A. The 'method of expectations'   144
      B. Statics and dynamics   149
      C. The significance of the *General Theory*   151

PART TWO: THE *TREATISE ON MONEY* AND THE *GENERAL THEORY*

X. THE METHOD OF ANALYSIS IN THE *TREATISE* AND THE *GENERAL THEORY*   155

    A. Saving and investment: different decisions or new theory of employment?   156
    B. The conceptual framework of the *Treatise on Money*   163
    C. The 'length' of the short-period   167
    D. The conceptual framework of the *General Theory*   171
    E. 'Causal Sequences' and 'disequilibrium'   174
    Appendix: The Fundemantal equations: definitions and derivation   176

XI. THE THEORETICAL SYSTEM OF THE *TREATISE VERSUS* THE *GENERAL THEORY*   179

    A. The natural rate of interest and the level of employment: marginalist theory   179
    B. The theoretical structure of the *Treatise on Money*   180
    C. The principle of effective demand   184
    D. From the *Treatise* to the *General Theory*   187

APPENDIX 1: NATURAL PRICES, PERSISTENT FORCES AND THE CONCEPT OF SELF-ADJUSTMENT   189
APPENDIX 2: NOTES ON 'STOCKS AND FLOWS', 'SUPPLY-PRICE' AND 'QUASI-RENT'   193

References   198

Index   209

I. INTRODUCTION

It appears to me that one great cause of our difference of opinion . . . is that you have always in your mind the immediate and temporary effects of particular changes—whereas I . . . fix my whole attention on the permanent state of things which will result from them. Perhaps you estimate these temporary effects too highly, whilst I am too much disposed to undervalue them. To manage the subject quite right they should be carefully distinguished and mentioned, and the due effects ascribed to each. (Ricardo to Malthus, 1817, in Ricardo, 1951–1973, vol. VII, p. 120).

Controversy over the significance of Keynes's *General Theory* as a theoretical work has continued virtually undiminished since its publication in 1936. However, although a wide variety of themes have been aired, two basic issues have been central to the questions that interpreters of Keynes's work have sought to resolve. On the one hand, there has been the attempt to reveal the precise nature of the constructive theoretical contribution of the *General Theory* and, on the other, there has been the consequent attempt to provide an understanding of the significance of Keynes's ideas as a critique of received opinion. Of course, these two issues are not unrelated. Any interpretation of the *General Theory* must seek to resolve them both. But a separate treatment of these two topics provides a particularly clear and precise way of approaching the problem of the interpretation of the *General Theory*. For this reason the present examination of Keynes's contribution, and the associated critical analysis of subsequent interpretations of the *General Theory*, will be developed by addressing each of these issues in turn.

A. THE CONTEMPORARY POSITION OF 'KEYNESIAN' ECONOMICS

If one considers the dominant contemporary interpretations of the *General Theory*, two important sub-divisions may be isolated. There is one school that regards the constructive contribution of that book to consist exclusively of an examination of the short-period behaviour of the economic system. That is, the *General Theory* is seen to provide a detailed analysis of what Ricardo referred to in the passage quoted at the opening of this chapter as the temporary effects of particular changes. Accordingly, the significance of the *General Theory* as a critique of received opinion is, at most, that it draws our attention to the fact that the underlying forces working towards the establishment of long-period equilibrium, while always present, are only weakly felt. The basic idea is that the economic system may become 'stuck', so to speak, in a short-period position where certain frictions or rigidities prevent the systematic forces outlined by orthodox marginalist theory from producing those permanent effects that they ultimately have a tendency to produce.

This view may be associated, in particular, with the interpretations advanced by Hicks in his famous 'Mr Keynes and the classics' paper of 1937, and by Modigliani in his equally celebrated paper 'Liquidity preference and the theory of interest and money' of 1944. Interestingly, it was also the position adopted by Pigou in his self-styled recapitulation on the question of the significance of the *General Theory* in 1949, where it was argued that Keynes's purpose was to deal with "fluctuations over short periods" as distinct from questions about the "ultimate equilibrium" of the system (Pigou, 1950, pp. 3–4). Subscribing to the same school of thought, Schumpeter in his *History of Economic Analysis* was led to the conclusion that it would have been better had Keynes not objected to the *tendency* towards full employment "just as we do not object to the law of gravitation on the ground that the earth does not fall into the sun"; rather Keynes really meant "that . . . though it states a tendency correctly, [its operation] is impeded by certain facts" (1954, p. 624). Though it will be necessary later to define these terms more precisely (for the notion of equilibrium itself has changed in recent years), the general tenor of these interpretations is captured in the idea that Keynes's contribution was to 'disequilibrium' rather than to 'equilibrium' analysis.

So complete has been the triumph of this theme in the practice of Keynes's interpretation, that its presence is apparent everywhere in much more recent re-interpretations—despite the fact that one significant alteration (to the notion of equilibrium), which will be mentioned in a moment, has been introduced. Thus, for example, in the well-known contributions of Leijonhufvud the essential ingredient of the old view is still to be found. "Of course", Leijonhufvud writes, "Keynes used the term 'unemployment equilibrium'. [But] . . . it is not an 'equilibrium' in the strict sense at all. It is preferable to use some more neutral term which does not carry the connotation that no equilibrating forces at all are at work. The real question is why . . . the forces tending to bring the system back to full employment are so weak" (1969, p. 22, n. 1). Similarly, in his study of the development of Keynes's monetary thought, Patinkin (1976) concluded that Keynes's theory is not "strictly speaking" one of "unemployment equilibrium" (p. 114 *et seq.*). And James Tobin, in a recent exposé of the shortcomings of modern monetarist doctrines, although at one point recognising that Keynes "denies the existence of self-correcting market mechanisms . . . [even] in a competitive economy" (1980, pp. 1–2), refrains from drawing the radical conclusions that would follow from this assessment and falls back instead on the idea that Keynes showed (only) that "disequilibrium can be protracted and stubborn" (p. 19). Indeed, a list of the names of those writers in whose work this familiar theme is present would be enough to dominate, if not fill, the membership of an economics Hall of Fame.

However, the popularity of this view does not render it correct. The interpretation of Keynes's contribution that is presented in these pages breaks away entirely from this line of argument. Its starting point is to take seriously Keynes's claim, universally and disingenuously rejected as being not quite accurate by orthodox interpretations, that the dominant and systematic forces at work in market economies *do not* tend to produce the full employment of labour. Instead of arguing that Keynes *shared* with orthodox economics the same abstract characterisation of the mechanisms through which market economies operate and *differed* by claiming that these mechanisms were not always as beneficent in the actual world as they were in theory, it will be my central contention that Keynes in fact rejected the orthodox characterisation of the operation of the market mechanism. In short, in the *General Theory* Keynes provides us with a theory of employment different in character and content from anything that is to be discerned in the writings of his orthodox predecessors (where the argument that there exists an underlying tendency towards the full employment of labour is present), departing radically even from those of his forebears (and there were, as we shall see, not a few of these) who were suspicious of the likelihood of the swift operation of this tendency in practice.

The emphasis on short-period interpretations of the *General Theory* has been paralleled by developments in the orthodox theory of value and distribution which have culminated in the abandonment of the traditional notion of equilibrium itself and its replacement by the notion of equilibrium as a sequence over time of short-period positions. These developments, which will be discussed in detail later, have created an environment favouring the interpretation of the *General Theory* using this 'new' notion of equilibrium. This is the other main grouping into which contemporary interpretations of Keynes's ideas fall. This view, based on the notion of intertemporal equilibrium and the related concept of temporary equilibrium, finds its earliest champion in Hicks, in *Value and Capital* of 1939. It will be appreciated that the necessity of distinguishing this category of interpretation from its predecessors arises not because Keynes is no longer to be read as a 'disequilibrium' theorist—both groups adhere to this view. Rather, the distinction is required in order to highlight the fact that this 'new' approach to Keynesian economics entails as well the claim that the equilibrium (and, consequently, disequilibrium) concepts adopted by its proponents were also those of Keynes himself.

The single, most notable feature of both of these types of interpretation is that they facilitate, albeit in different ways, the re-assertion of the orthodox theoretical system of the marginalist school which holds that the full equilibrium configuration of relative prices and quantities is determined simultaneously by the mutual interaction of the forces of demand and supply. In no way do they challenge the orthodox characterisation of the operation of the market mechanism whereby, in the absence of frictions or rigidities, relative price variations (of a commodity or a 'factor of production' like labour) call forth a predictable, inverse response on the part of quantity demanded. This is not surprising, for it is from this very conception of the workings of a capitalist economy that orthodox economics derives the conclusion that there is a *tendency* towards full employment—a statement of tendency which, as has been indicated already, is nowhere questioned in mainstream interpretations of the *General Theory*. These paradoxically harmonious interpretations of the *General Theory*, a book that Keynes himself saw as being essentially revolutionary in character, raise an important series of questions as to the relationship between the theory of value and the theory of output and, as we shall see, are indicative of the difficulties that these relationships present for the interpretation of the *General Theory*.

B.   THE PROBLEM OF INTERPRETATION

In order to reduce the problem of Keynes' interpretation to manageable proportions, and in an attempt to penetrate the many confusions that surround the interpretation of the *General Theory* itself, use will be made of two fundamental dimensions in economic analysis—two dimensions which, it must be said, have themselves been obscured progressively during the century over which demand and supply economics has reigned supreme. Following a suggestion by Garegnani (1976), these are referred to as the dimension of *method* and the dimension of *theory* respectively. It may be said, reserving the details for subsequent consideration (see, especially, Chapters II and III below), that the method dimension refers to the specification of the *object* of economic analysis—that is, the abstract characterisation of what is to be explained. The dimension of theory, on the other hand, refers to the *explanation* of how the principal variables associated with the object are determined. A central task of the argument in the remainder of this volume will be to untangle these two dimensions, to trace their basis in economic thought, to apply them in the interpretation of Keynes's economics, and to explain with their assistance the confusions of his critics.

Furthermore, the present re-examination of the nature of Keynes's contribution has in no small measure been motivated by the promising new avenues for economic theory opened up by recent debates over the theory of value and distribution and, in particular, by the critique of the marginalist theory of distribution stimulated by Piero Sraffa's *Production of Commodities by Means of Commodities*. The relevance of these discussions to the question of coming to terms with Keynes's ideas derives from two facts.

The first is that there is no longer any excuse, if one ever existed, to presume that whatever Keynes had to say it must somehow have been related to the explanation of the determination of prices and quantities by the forces of demand and supply that forms the cornerstone of the economic theory invented by the marginalist school. An equally plausible possibility, and one that in this book I hope to show has a solid textual basis, is that Keynes's contribution to economic analysis, once isolated, fits less uneasily into the alternative account of value and distribution provided by the surplus approach as developed by Ricardo and refined by Marx and Sraffa.

The second reason which explains the relevance of the aforementioned debate derives from the fact that the marginalist explanation of distribution and the marginalist theory of employment are grounded on the same premise—the notion of capital as a 'factor of production' the proportion of which, to other 'factors' and output, varies inversely with the rate of profit. Thus, the critique of the marginalist theory of capital must also involve a critique of the marginalist theory of employment and be of consequential significance not only for the interpretation of the *General Theory* but also for a critical analysis of contemporary interpretations of that book. An approach via the theory of value and distribution, and the critique of the marginalist concepts of capital and labour as 'factors of production', enables some vital issues to be resolved; such as the division between the constructive contribution of the *General Theory* and its significance as a critique of received opinion, the reasons for the re-assertion of orthodox marginalist theory in subsequent interpretations of Keynes's work and the relationship that all of this bears to the theoretical system developed by the old classical economists from Adam Smith to Ricardo.

The interpretation of the nature of Keynes's contribution and of its relationship to his predecessors that will be offered here is quite straightforward. It can be summarised in two or three sentences. But its full significance, its critical force and its positive implications, cannot be understood properly until its basis in economic thought has been traced and some of the inaccuracies introduced in other interpretations of the *General Theory* have been thoroughly elaborated. An historical method of approach will therefore be adopted. However, the history of thought makes no claim to exhaustiveness. It is utilised in order to reveal analytical rather than historical conclusions and insights.

C. OUTLINE OF THE ARGUMENT

The argument is divided into two parts. Part I represents an attempt to compare and contrast the *General Theory* with a concrete picture of the pre-1936 orthodoxy. Part II seeks to re-affirm the results obtained there by undertaking a comparative examination of the *Treatise on Money*, viewed as part of that orthodoxy, and the *General Theory*.

It will be appreciated that the argumentation used to produce and sustain a re-examination of Keynes's work must face and resolve many controversial and difficult questions. Therefore the problem of interpretation is approached through a number of successive steps. But before the main argument begins, I have provided (in Chapter II) a preliminary outline of the central categories of *method* and *theory* that are utilised to develop my interpretation of the *General Theory*. This outline should not be understood as forming a part of the main argument. The concepts and categories with which it deals are only fully elaborated in subsequent chapters. Its sole purpose is to familiarise the reader with these concepts and to act, in this sense, as a point of reference as the main argument unfolds.

The first step in the main argument involves an examination of nineteenth century economic analysis in an effort to establish the traditional *method of analysis* within which the economic theories of that period were erected. The examination of natural or long-period normal conditions by the writers of this period is shown to define the traditional object of economic analysis, and it is argued that this object remained the same throughout the period even in the face of the substantial changes that were made at the level of theory in the final quarter of the nineteenth century. This discussion, although it is concerned with very basic issues underlying economic thought as a whole, is nevertheless especially significant for the interpretation of the *General Theory* in that it establishes the essential characteristics of the traditional method of analysis.

Having isolated the *method* dimension of the prevailing orthodoxy that faced Keynes in 1936, the discussion then proceeds to a consideration of the *theory* dimension of that orthodoxy. In order to trace to its source the received opinion, disputed by Keynes, that there exists a long-run tendency towards the full employment of labour, that body of economic theory developed by the old classical economists is examined and contrasted with the theory erected later by the marginalist writers.

It is only in the latter that one can find premises capable of justifying the conventional wisdom against which Keynes contended.

The next step in the argument involves confronting the orthodox picture with the content and implications of the *General Theory*. This is done in two stages. The constructive core of the *General Theory* is seen to consist of the provision of an argument that holds, unlike the orthodox marginalist position, that unemployment arises not through the operation of 'temporary phenomena', but rather that it is the outcome of the operation of more systematic and permanent forces at work in the system. The second step involves addressing the question of how one might go about reconstructing the critique of the received wisdom implied by this constructive contribution of the *General Theory*. The central conclusion, put very broadly, is that Keynes made no fundamental departure from his predecessors at the level of *method* but that he broke away radically from the orthodox marginalist *theory*.

The final step in the argument is to move beyond the *General Theory* to review critically contemporary trends in 'Keynesian economics' in an attempt to discover how accurately these represent the nature of Keynes's departure from the pre-1936 orthodoxy. The conclusions of Part I are confirmed in Part II by a comparative analysis of the *Treatise on Money* and the *General Theory*. It should be mentioned, however, that no attempt has been made in this study to relate each aspect of our argument to all other previous interpretations. For not only would this be a virtually impossible task (quantitatively speaking), but it would serve no real purpose. By relating the present argument and interpretation only to the most influential contemporary approaches to Keynes's economics (making wider comparisons only when the need arises), those points at which our analysis differs from the conventional views are more easily highlighted.

II. PRELIMINARY DEFINITIONS AND CONCEPTS

> The conclusions of Political Economy . . . are only true . . . *in the abstract*;
> that is, they are only true under certain suppositions, in which none but
> general causes—causes common to the *whole class* of cases under con-
> sideration—are taken into the account (J. S. Mill, 1874, pp. 144–145,
> italics in original).

The principal concepts and categories that form the basis of economic
analysis are not conjured from some magician's hat but are designed to
describe and characterise *actual* economic systems. The analytical
strength of an argument depends upon whether or not the level of
abstraction is appropriate to the problem under consideration. For this
reason the central concepts and categories of economic theory are
designed to facilitate the drawing of conclusions of general, as opposed
to particular or special, significance.* In the context of the present
examination of the analytical relationships between, on the one hand,
the theories of value and capital advanced by the two predominant
schools of economic thought (the classical and the marginalist or neo-
classical traditions) and, on the other, Keynes's theory of output and

---

* There would seem to be two quite distinct criteria by which to reach a judgement as to
whether the concepts and categories in question meet this particular requirement. One
is denotative and analytical—it must be asked in what objective sense the economic
system can be said to 'gravitate' to such a position in the absence of 'frictions'. The other
is cognitive and pre-analytical—an individual theorist may differ with another in that he
rejects the other's vision of 'what the world is really like'. It would seem to be obvious
that one would wish, in the first instance at least, to apply the former criterion, since
within its ambit it might just be possible to resolve the issue without resort to 'beliefs'
and 'visions' which surface when the second criterion is applied.

employment, a number of such abstract concepts and categories will be of decisive importance in delineating the general conditions under which these theories may be compared and applied. This brief chapter provides a short preview of the principal concepts involved. This preliminary discussion is not, however, meant to be at all exhaustive; rather it is meant to act as a guide to the difficult and sometimes controversial terrain that is to be covered in subsequent chapters.

A. A CAPITALIST ECONOMY

The theories which have been advanced to explain the operation of the forces that ultimately regulate relative prices, distribution, the level of employment and the level of output are concerned with the determination of the magnitudes of these variables in what, for the sake of brevity, will be referred to as a *capitalist economy*.* This concept had a clear and unambiguous meaning in the writings of the old classical economists where it referred to a generalised system of commodity production organised through markets and where the ownership of the means of production was concentrated in the hands of one class in society that met in the market with the labourer selling what Marx referred to as labour-power (see e.g. Smith, 1776, I. vii, pp. 73–74; Ricardo, 1951–1973, vol. I, pp. 89–91; Marx, 1963, vol. I, p. 72 and 1967, vol. I, pp. 169–170). The notion has, however, been somewhat obscured in subsequent literature so that although a capitalist economy still tends to be associated with some form of private ownership of the means of production (see e.g. Debreu, 1959, pp. 78–80), the nature of this ownership is not clearly specified.

It should be recognised that the classical notion is at once sufficiently flexible to admit so-called 'mixed economies' (which continue, of course, to be characterised by wage-labour) yet sufficiently discriminating as to exclude those economic systems within which no significant part of the means of production is privately owned.

---

* The term 'market economy' is sometimes used synonymously with 'capitalist economy', but this has been avoided here because the former encompasses some forms of economic organisation (for example, a system of 'free artisan' production) that should be excluded from a general description of 'capitalism' (cf. Marx, 1967, vol. I, ch. I *et passim*).

B. THE 'OBJECT' AND 'METHOD' OF ECONOMIC ANALYSIS

Since in an examination of a capitalist economy the aim of economic theory is first to provide statements of general applicability (or what used to be called 'statements of tendency'; Palgrave, 1963, vol. III, p. 140), one necessarily commences by specifying an abstract characterisation of the actual economy so as to isolate a well-defined set of phenomena upon which to concentrate theoretical endeavour. This abstract characterisation is meant to capture the systematic, regular and persistent forces at work in the system and thereby to permit the 'theory' (which is subsequently to be formulated to explain the circumstances determining the magnitude of the object) to exclude accidental, arbitrary and 'temporary' phenomena. This abstract characterisation of the actual system will be referred to as the object of the economic analysis or, more briefly, the *object of analysis*. It defines the conceptual framework within which subsequent theoretical discussion is conducted. This procedure involves no more than the application in economics of what John Stuart Mill referred to as the "scientific method" (Mill, 1874, pp. 121–123). We propose, however, to use the phrase *method of analysis* as a general description of the use of that conceptual framework implied by the adoption of a *specific* object of analysis (see Garegnani, 1976, where this terminology is suggested).

C. THEORY VERSUS METHOD: THE EXPLANATION OF THE OBJECT

Having specified an object of analysis the next task is to offer an *explanation* of the determination of the magnitude of the object and of the causal relationships that exist between its principal elements (variables). This explanation will be referred to as the *theory* so as to distinguish it formally from the object (and method). There will be, of course, some degree of interaction between method and theory, but because it is always possible to construct *more than one* theory to explain a single object (i.e. within the same method of analysis) they are sufficiently distinct to warrant separate consideration. In the context of theory, the minimum requirement that must be met is that of logical consistency.

D.   LONG-PERIOD AND SHORT-PERIOD POSITIONS

A capitalist economy is said to exhibit long-period characteristics (to be 'in' a *long-period position*) if, when the price of each commodity is uniform throughout the system, a *general* (uniform) rate of profit on the supply-price of capital associated with the dominant or, to use Marx's term, 'socially necessary' technique obtains. Conversely, the system is said to exhibit short-period characteristics (to be 'in' a *short-period position*) when there is no ruling general rate of profit—to put it another way, when the existing structure of the stock of capital equipment associated with the dominant technique is not appropriate to the demand for it. The significance of these two concepts becomes apparent when one considers the manner in which they may be used to specify an object of analysis.

E.   THE TRADITIONAL LONG-PERIOD METHOD OF ECONOMIC ANALYSIS

The *long-period method* of economic analysis identifies as its object the long-period positions of the system. There is a one-to-one relationship between the notion of a general rate of profit and that position of a capitalist economy which is viewed as being determined (or, perhaps more appropriately, 'governed') by systematic and persistent forces under the long-period method. The object is to provide an explanation of the manner in which relative prices, the wage-rate, the general rate of profit and the levels of output and employment are determined 'in' (or under) long-period conditions.

F.   THE METHOD OF 'INTERTEMPORAL EQUILIBRIUM'

The *method of intertemporal equilibrium* identifies as its object the examination of the determination of $n.t$ market-clearing prices (for n commodities over t 'elementary time periods' starting from an arbitrary short-period position) which establish an 'intertemporal equilibrium'. It is a property of such an equilibrium that not only will the price of the same commodity be different at different points of time but also that the stock of capital will not, in general, yield a uniform rate of profit on its supply-price. These 'intertemporal equilibrium' solutions are viewed as the states towards which, in the absence of other disturbances, the economic system is believed to 'tend' (see e.g. Hahn, 1965, p. 191).

G.   SOME TERMINOLOGICAL CONVENTIONS

There are now a number of points to which the reader's attention must be drawn. They concern exclusively matters of terminological convention. For unlike an exercise in pure theory, where the consistent application of a carefully defined terminology is both necessary and easily achieved, in an exercise in theory and the history of theory while it is possible to apply one's own terminology consistently, it cannot always be guaranteed that other writers used the same terms in exactly the same sense. When one is dealing with the Keynes of the *General Theory* this problem is magnified.

'Classical Economics' is probably the most basic of the labels being used in the present study, but by its use we mean to convey something much more specific, in terms of the body of theory known as classical economics, than Keynes meant to convey when he used the term in the *General Theory*:

> 'The classical economists' was a name invented by Marx to cover Ricardo and James Mill and their *predecessors*, that is to say the founders of the theory which culminated in the Ricardian economics. I have been accustomed, perhaps perpetrating a solecism, to include in 'the classical school' the *followers* of Ricardo, those, that is to say, who adopted and perfected the theory of the Ricardian economics, including (for example) J. S. Mill, Marshall, Edgeworth and Prof. Pigou. (*J.M.K.*, vol. VII, p. 3, n. 1, italics in original).*

In the present study we propose to exclude Marshall, Pigou and others of the marginalist school from classical economics (leaving aside, for the moment, the fact that to say, as Keynes does, that Marshall *et al.* 'perfected' the Ricardian system is incorrect—for what these writers did was to build a *different* theoretical system). Therefore, whenever in the remainder of this study the term 'classical economics' is used in

---

* Keynes added some further idiosyncratic 'twists' to his labels in a letter to Hawtrey after the publication of the *General Theory* (*J.M.K.*, vol. XIV, p. 24; see also p. 14).

Keynes's sense, we will adopt the convention of translating it into our own terminology (which is, of course, the more usual) by writing marginalist or 'classical' economics—the single inverted commas indicating that Keynes would at that point, on his own definitions, have been saying "classical economics". When we speak of that body of theory developed by Adam Smith and David Ricardo we will write Classical Economics.

Another convention of terminology that will be needed relates to the use of the terms rate of interest and rate of profit. The problem arises because the term rate of profit is replaced by the term rate of interest by most marginalist writers;* and when the discussion turns to Keynes's work the term rate of interest is used in a number of different senses. Now, what the marginalist writers meant to convey by the use of the term 'rate of interest' was exactly what the Classical writers had meant by the term 'rate of profit'; both were used to express the rate of return to capital in production under natural or long-period normal conditions. In *Interest and Prices*, for example, Wicksell defined the 'natural rate of interest' as that rate which equated the demand-and-supply for 'real capital' (see e.g. Wicksell, 1898, p. 102 ff., p. 122 ff., p. 146, p. 163, p. 171 and p. 174). Wicksell maintained this usage throughout his work on monetary theory, reserving the term 'market rate of interest' to denote the actual or money rate of interest (see Wicksell, 1901, vol. II and Chapter V below). Therefore, when by the term 'rate of interest' the writers mean the 'normal' return on the supply-price of capital, we will add, in brackets, the term 'profit'. The convention is therefore to write rate of interest (profit).

When the discussion turns to the *General Theory* it will become apparent that Keynes used the term 'rate of interest' in two quite distinct senses. In the positive or constructive core of the *General Theory* it referred exclusively to a *monetary* phenomenon whereas, as we shall see in Chapter VII below, in the negative or critical part it is often used

---

* It became the habit of the marginalist writers to use the term 'profit' to cover not just the return to capital in production but also to include windfall gains and losses and thereby to reserve the use of the term 'rate of profit' for discussions of the system under temporary (or market) circumstances. It depended "upon exceptional and not upon normal circumstances" (Walras, 1874–77, p. 423). Some of the confusions introduced by this change of terminology are discussed in Schumpeter, 1954, p. 1048 *et seq.* and in Hayek, 1941, p. 38. Interestingly, Keynes himself contributed to this confusion by using the term 'profit' in his *Treatise on Money* to refer to windfalls.

in the traditional sense of the rate of profit. Therefore, when it is possible to show that Keynes was using it in this latter sense we will again write rate of interest (profit).

PART ONE

THE PRE-1936 ORTHODOXY AND THE *GENERAL THEORY*

III.   THE TRADITIONAL LONG-PERIOD METHOD OF ECONOMIC ANALYSIS

English capital runs *surely and instantly* where it is most wanted, and where there is most to be made of it, as water runs to find its level. (Bagehot, 1873, p. 13, italics added)

In perhaps the most important chapter of the *Wealth of Nations*, entitled "Of the Natural and Market Price of Commodities", Adam Smith specified an abstract *object of analysis* and its relationship to actual economic circumstances that was to be adopted continuously and exclusively for at least the next one hundred and fifty years. The central task of this chapter will be to delineate the analytical characteristics of this object of analysis in order to establish the method dimension of the 'prevailing orthodoxy' from which Keynes's *General Theory* may be said to have emerged. Consideration of the theory dimension will be reserved for the next chapter. This discussion will ultimately lead to a point where it will be possible to confront and resolve a fundamental question: are the theoretical constructs of the *General Theory* offered as explanations of phenomena (the levels of employment and output) associated with the same object of analysis defined by Keynes's predecessors or does the *General Theory* depart from this traditional method?

A.   NATURAL PRICES AND THE LONG-PERIOD METHOD

It was with the formulation of the concept of natural price by the old classical economists that the object of economic analysis that was referred to in the previous chapter as forming the basis of the long-period method first acquired systematic expression. The theoretical arguments of Smith's *Wealth of Nations* are built entirely within this framework, expressed by Smith in terms of natural prices:

The natural price . . . is, as it were, the central price, to which the prices of all commodities are continually gravitating. Different accidents may sometimes keep them suspended a good deal above it, and sometimes force them down even somewhat below it. But whatever may be the obstacles which hinder them form settling in this center of repose and continuance, they are constantly tending towards it. (Smith, 1776, I. vii, p. 65).

This "center of repose and continuance" became the object of analysis and was characterised not only by a single price for each commodity but also by what Smith referred to as a uniformity between "the average . . . rates of profit in the different employments of stock" (1776, I. x, p. 125). In fact Smith argued that natural prices were associated *only* with a *general rate of profit*:

There is in every society . . . an ordinary or average rate of both wages and profits. . . . When the price of any commodity is neither more nor less than what is sufficient to pay . . . the wages of the labour, and the profits of the stock employed . . . , according to their natural [average] rates, the commodity is then sold for what may be called its natural price. (Smith, 1776, I. vii, p. 62).*

This is not to say that Smith was the very first writer to develop these concepts. Indeed, much earlier Cantillon had spoken of the notion in terms of a "perpetual ebb and flow in market prices" (1755, p. 31) and Massie in his essay on *The Natural Rate of Interest* of 1750 had employed essentially the same framework. The following passage, for example, manifestly embraces this framework:

For the Price which Money bears in Times of general Danger, or publick Necessity, cannot be call'd so, any more than the Price which a Man agrees to give for Wheat can be called the natural Price for it, when the Seller takes an Advantage of the Buyer's Necessity, or cannot have the Assistance of Law to oblige him to pay. (Massie, 1750, p. 21).

Turgot, too, used an analogy which was later to become quite fashionable; "the rate of interest may be regarded as a kind of water-level . . . it is like a sea spread over a vast region" (Turgot, 1973, p. 173; see also Meek, 1973a, p. 56, n. 4 on this point). The ultimate origin of the idea

---

* Rent, of course, is a component part of price in Smith and is mentioned in those sections of this passage which have been omitted. In excluding it here, no serious damage is done to Smith's message concerning the association of natural prices with a uniform rate of profit. (See also Ricardo 1951–1973, vol. I, p. 91.)

probably resides in the writings of the natural law philosophers of the sixteenth and seventeenth centuries.* However, Smith was the first writer to express these concepts in comprehensive and abstract terms and it is therefore more properly in his specification of the object of examining the determination of natural prices that the history of the long-period method of economic analysis begins. And this method was to dominate for the next century and a half, a continuity which, viewed against the backdrop of the fundamental changes that the theory of value and distribution was to undergo during that period, is certainly remarkable.

When Ricardo came to write his *Principles of Political Economy and Taxation* his first task was to acquaint his audience with the method of analysis of natural price which had been established by Smith (see e.g. Ricardo, 1951–1973, vol. I, chs 1 and 4). Ricardo, like Smith before him, examined the theoretical problems of value and distribution in terms of natural prices so as to isolate the forces that were, in his view, the more systematic and to exclude "accidental and temporary deviations of the actual or market price of commodities from . . . their primary and natural price" (Ricardo, vol. I, p. 88).

Preserving the same method, Marshall defined normal prices as excluding " 'market' or 'occasional' values . . . [upon which] . . . accidents of the moment exert a preponderating influence" (Marshall, 1961, p. vii) and focussed his attention upon the question of how these normal prices were determined. J. B. Clark followed suit and argued that " 'natural' or 'normal' prices . . . are the values . . . to which, in the long-run, market values tend to conform" (Clark, 1899, p. 16). Jevons, likewise, wrote that, "the use of an average . . . depends on the high probability that accidental and disturbing causes will operate, in the long-run . . . so as to neutralize each other" (Jevons, 1871, p. 86).

------

* The idea that there was a perpetual 'ebb and flow' in market prices is also older and can be found, for example, in Misselden (1622, p. 19). However, the mercantilists failed to notice that the 'central position' around which market prices fluctuated could constitute the object of a more systematic and general explanation of price determination. In this regard it should be noted that William Petty, in challenging the mercantilist doctrines, did argue for such a systematic analysis on the basis of 'natural' price so as to exclude "other accidents" (see, for example, Petty, in Hull (ed.), 1899, vol. I, p. 44 and p. 89). The general rate of profit concept emerged later, probably with Massie. For a further discussion of the origin of these concepts see Bonar, 1922, p. 106 n. 4; Marx, 1963, vol. I, pp. 373–377; and Meek, 1973a, ch. 1 *passim*.

Wicksell adopted the distinction "made by the older economists" (Wicksell, 1901, vol. I, p. 97) between market price and natural price "about which the market price always oscillated" (p. 97). Böhm-Bawerk argued that "local influences may for longer or shorter periods cause stocks to pile up and exceed the average . . . but such things are merely *secondary developments* which appear on the back, so to speak, of the *principal movement*" (Böhm-Bawerk, 1899, vol. II, p. 380, italics added). Finally, Walras borrowed Turgot's analogy to capture the same idea: "the market is like a lake agitated by the wind, where the water is *incessantly* seeking its level" (1874–77, p. 380, italics added). It was on the basis of this view of the persistent forces that were at work (likened by most of these writers to the principle of gravitation) that all significant nineteenth century theories of value and distribution were erected. This basis was in turn reflected in the overriding concern of all these writers with the explanation of a general, *uniform* rate of profit on the supply-price of capital in different lines of production. Walras stated the nature of the connection forcefully: "uniformity of . . . the price of net income [rate of profit] on the capital goods market . . . [is one] condition by which the universe of economic interests is automatically governed" (1874–77, p. 305).*

It is important to appreciate that while the operation of persistent forces occurs essentially in real time there is no concomitant guarantee that the 'long-period' or the 'short-period' will, as such, be associated with a definite interval of calendar time (cf. Opie, 1931, p. 199). The 'period' distinction refers rather to the nature of the causes that operate in the situation under consideration—and the distinction at this level is between 'fitful and irregular' causes and those of a 'permanent' nature. This usage reflects, of course, the manner in which 'long' and 'short' periods were seen to be related by the practitioners of this traditional long-period method. Natural, or long-period normal values were viewed as the centres around which market values tended to fluctuate†

---

* See also similar statements by Wicksell, 1901, vol. I, p. 149 and p. 171.
† Smith has already been quoted in this regard and Ricardo argues that the price of a commodity "will settle at or about its natural price" (1951–1973, vol. II, p. 38). Marx argues that the price of production (which is the same thing as natural price) is "the center around which the daily market prices fluctuate" (Marx, 1967, vol. III, p. 179). It is perhaps worth indicating at this point that deviations from free competition, in particular monopoly, might keep market price and natural price in a 'permanent' state of inequality.

and towards which, under the influence of more systematic forces, the latter were inexorably drawn.* Furthermore, the notion of 'centers of repose and continuance' was reinforced with the idea that changes in the factors affecting the elements that determined the long-period values were slowly changing ones.† That is, they were seen to embody the persistent forces that were at work in a capitalist economic system.

It goes without saying, of course, that the explanation (that is, the *theories*) offered for the determination of these natural, or long-period normal values diverged significantly among the practitioners of the traditional long-period method; differences to which the discussion will return in the next chapter.

B.   THE REPRESENTATION OF THE PERSISTENT FORCES OF FREE COMPETITION UNDER THE LONG-PERIOD METHOD

The specification of natural, or long-period normal conditions as the object of analysis entailed the translation of the idea that "society reflected the working of certain law-governed, mechanistic processes, 'autonomous' and 'objective' in the sense that they operated independently of the wills of men" (Meek, 1965, pp. 4–5, italics omitted) into a concrete but abstract representation of actual economic circumstances. But what are the reasons for associating these natural, long-period normal conditions with the outcome of the operation of the systematic, regular and persistent forces at work in the system? That is to say, on what objective basis do actual values 'tend' towards their long-period counterparts? It is in the answer given to this question that the rationale for the notion that categories other than those associated with natural, long-period normal conditions are inappropriate for the construction of general, as opposed to particular, theories about the operation of the

---

* See Appendix A below for a discussion of the relationship between this idea and that of the often misunderstood concept of 'self-adjustment'.

† Knight referred to long-period questions as being concerned with the influence of 'more slowly working forces' (Knight, 1921, p. 305) and in referring to long-period values Robertson argued as follows: "I shall often say that value is or does such and such, when what I mean is that it tends to be or do such and such when these slowly moving forces are taken into account" (Robertson, 1963, p. 94, italics omitted).

economic system is to be found. The reason is provided by the connection between the general rate of profit and the operation of 'free' competition.*

Underlying the operation of free competition in a capitalist economy is the competitive pressure that induces capitalists to seek the most profitable employment of their stock. This provides the formal basis of the presumption of a general tendency towards a uniform rate of profit and of its consequent association with the persistent forces operative in the system. Thus we find Marshall arguing that "it is to the *persistence* of the influences considered . . . that we refer when contrasting Market and Normal price" (Marshall, 1961, p. 348, italics added). Under all circumstances this tendency towards the equalisation of profit-rates will ultimately assert itself; only accidental or particular disturbances and frictions can prevent the assertion of this tendency and so such circumstances cannot constitute part of the abstract description of the 'center of repose and continuance' of the system. Thus, when general conclusions were sought, attention was focussed on those variables associated with this long-period position of the system.

Ricardo, for example, took great care to explain why the traditional long-period method involved the use of an object of analysis which satisfied this requirement: "It is then the desire . . . which every capitalist has, of diverting his funds from a less to a more profitable employment, that prevents the market price of commodities from continuing for any length of time either much above, or much below their natural price" (Ricardo, 1951–1973, vol. I, p. 91). This notion reappears frequently in Ricardo's writing. For example, he writes that "the profits of different employments have a tendency to conform to one another" (Ricardo, 1951–1973, vol. I, p. 129) and elsewhere, "I do not deny that the first discoverer of a new and better market may, for a time, before competition operates, obtain unusual profits . . . . But it is of the general rate of profit that we are speaking, not the profits of a few

---

* Free competition refers here only to competition among capitals and so requires only the condition that there is sufficient 'mobility of capital' to permit the channelling of investments into more profitable employments of stock (see Robinson, 1951–1979, vol. IV, p. 48). In particular it does not require, at this level, 'perfect knowledge' or 'perfect foresight' and so it is not equivalent to the notion of 'perfect competition' (we do not propose to explore this point any further at the moment; the reader can find an account of the tendency to uniformity of profit-rates in modern capitalist economies in Clifton, 1977, p. 138 *et seq.*).

individuals" (vol. IV, p. 24); and finally "this restless desire on the part of all employers of stock, to quit a less profitable for a more advantageous business, has a strong tendency to equalize the rate of profit for all" (vol. I, p. 88).

Marx was equally clear that the object of examining natural prices (he called them 'prices of production' but the concepts are equivalent; see Marx, 1967, vol. III, p. 198) was susceptible to interpretation as the centre of gravitation of the system precisely because "it is the competition of capitals in different spheres which first brings out the price of production equalizing the rates of profit in the different spheres" (vol. III, p. 180; see also Marx, 1975, p. 10 and p. 27). Wicksell saw the tendency implied by the operation of free competition as 'fundamental' (see Wicksell, 1901, vol. I, pp. 155–156 and p. 166) and Marshall did not hesitate in adopting it as basic to the general description of long-period normal conditions in the *Principles*:

> We . . . take it for granted that a very small difference between the rates of net interest to be got on . . . capital in two different modes of investment in the same . . . country will cause capital to flow, though perhaps by indirect channels, from the one to the other (Marshall, 1961, p. 591).

Similarly in the *Economics of Industry* we find that "Normal results are those which would be brought about by competition if it acted freely, and always had time to cause those effects which it has a tendency to cause" (Marshall and Marshall, 1879, p. 148). It might be added that Adam Smith's use of this doctrine of the equalising effect of competition was viewed by a contemporary of Marshall as "simple and obvious" (Cannan, 1893, p. 290).

The systematic and persistent nature of this tendency was attested to even by writers interested in actual market circumstances rather than purely theoretical questions. The passage from Bagehot's *Lombard Street* quoted at the beginning of this chapter is just one example of the widespread elaboration given to the general tendency towards equality in profit-rates in work on applied economics. A detailed discussion of its operation is given in Lavington's now almost forgotten study of the English capital market: "It is the business of the market", he wrote, "to facilitate the movement of . . . capital to the points of highest yield" (Lavington, 1921, p. 13). Lavington was not, however, as optimistic as Bagehot had been when he had argued that the tendency would assert itself "surely and instantly" (1873, p. 13); on the contrary, Lavington thought that the transfer of capital involved "much trouble and skill"

(1921, p. 13). But whether it occurs 'quickly' or 'slowly' in actuality does not alter in the slightest way this systematic tendency.*

This, then, is the formal basis for arguing that any situation exhibiting non-uniform profit-rates would be 'short-lived' and due to the operation of certain arbitrary 'frictions' and that persistent forces would ultimately make their presence felt by tending to equalise profit-rates and to pull prices back towards their natural level. Yet it was never a part of the traditional long-period method that such centres of gravitation would for any length of time, if indeed at all, be observable phenomena. They were instead thought to be embodied in each and every position in which a capitalist economy might find itself at different points in time. Like sea-level, the natural, or long-period normal position of the system had an objective meaning, even though at any given moment it might be disturbed by innumerable cross-currents.

C. MONETARY FORCES: PERSISTENT OR TRANSITORY?

This now leads us to confront two important, if somewhat more subtle questions about this traditional object of analysis.

The first is whether or not in the process of framing this abstract version of the actual system monetary forces have been automatically excluded from that set of forces which could be regarded as the more systematic, regular and persistent. That is, can it be said that simply by virtue of the selection of natural or long-period normal conditions as the object of analysis one has immediately (and necessarily) acknowledged that 'money is a veil'? The problem is: *Can* money matter under such conditions? It will be argued that the answer to this question is 'yes'. However, acceptance of this answer is prejudiced by the fact that there seems to be widespread tacit agreement that the answer is precisely the opposite: in long-period normal conditions money *is* a veil. † The

---

* The exact *mechanism* involved in the equalisation process depends on the *theory* not the specification of the object. It is only necessary to compare Walras's *tâtonnement* with Marx's M-C-M' chain to verify this.

† It can influence, at most, the general level of prices in the long-run (see Samuelson, 1968 and Patinkin, 1965, especially pp. 611–633). This is the idea that provides (or so it is erroneously thought) the foundation for the view that to find out what 'really' happens it is necessary to leave to one side monetary forces (see, for example, Robertson, 1947, p. 9) and that this is what is done in focussing on natural or long-period 'normal' conditions.

prejudice arises because the tenets of the quantity-theory (embodying the famous "classical dichotomy") and the so-called 'neutrality of money' doctrine are almost universally associated with the work of the writers of this period* (Marx being the notable exception). But by maintaining a firm grip on the formal distinction between object and theory it is possible to show that the answer suggested by the conventional wisdom is in fact to a rather different question. For it addressed not the question of *"Can* money matter?" but the substantively different question of *"Did* money matter?" This is not a word-game.

In defining the object of analysis nothing is said about the determining circumstances of the long-period phenomena (variables). Relative prices, the wage-rate, the general rate of profit and the levels of output and employment are not at this stage explained, the variables are simply isolated under conditions representing the centre of gravitation of the system. Whether 'monetary forces' or 'real forces' (or both) are relevant in these long-period normal conditions depends upon the explanation of the determination of the long-period variables. There is no exclusion of either type of influence at the level of abstraction at which the object is specified so that, indeed, monetary forces could be used as an integral part in the explanation of any one (or more) of the variables involved. They are, therefore, quite susceptible to being classed among the permanent rather than the short-period influences upon the behaviour of the system. † Thus, in framing the object of analysis one is assuming neither that there is no money (*vide* Robertson, 1963, p. 325) nor that monetary forces are necessarily excluded. Money *can* matter.

But while money *could* matter, it is certainly the case that in the *theories* offered for the determination of the long-period normal values

---

* Temporarily (in short-periods), of course, these could be 'modified' so that "money did matter" (witness the doctrines of 'forced savings' and hoarding). We may quote Samuelson on this point: "We believed that in the long [est] run . . . the amount of money did not matter . . . . To be sure . . . money . . . might cause substantive changes . . . But all this was at a second level of approximation, representing relatively transient aberrations" (1968, pp. 170–171). (See also Robinson, 1971, pp. 71–74.)

† As an example of how monetary forces might be used one could argue (at the level of theory) that the rate of profit is determined under the permanent influence of the financial system (even when the banking system follows so-called 'neutral policies'); a possibility which has been suggested by both Keynes and Sraffa and one to which we will return in a later chapter.

by, in particular, the marginalist school only real forces played a part—here money *did not* matter. One need only refer to Wicksell (1901, vol. II, pp. 159 *et seq.* and 1898, pp. 18–19), Marshall (1926, p. 323) and Jevons (1875, p. 3) to verify this. Even Ricardo's advocacy of the 'unimportance' of money would *appear* to exclude the possibility of monetary forces exerting a permanent influence. Ricardo seems to have seen the significance of money simply in terms of the manner in which it facilitated transactions; he was prone, like Smith, to compare its function to that of a 'highway' (Ricardo, 1951–1973, vol. III, p. 55). We will leave open for the moment the question of whether monetary forces can be grafted on to either of these formally distinct sets of long-period theory, and return to it later. Putting it this way makes it clear that this is really the essence of the point that the conventional wisdom was making in arguing that "money does not matter". It was referring to *theory* (and usually marginalist theory at that). The problem seems to have arisen because of a general failure to keep clearly in mind the formal distinction between *object* and *theory*, so much so that two or three generations of economists have apparently grown up believing that under any long-period normal conditions monetary forces were irrelevant. This is the implication of the conventional wisdom that is false.

The important point is that there is nothing in the specification of the object of analysis that would prevent monetary influences from being numbered among the persistent forces, so that they may indeed be made relevant to the determination of long-period phenomena. This fact is significant in itself and, moreover, when later we come to examine the implications of Keynes's contributions in this regard it will take on a decisive importance.

D.   THE STATIONARY-STATE AND THE LONG-PERIOD METHOD

The next question is whether or not specifying natural or long-period normal conditions as the essential object of analysis amounts to evoking an abstraction that can yield conclusions applicable only to the "famous fiction" of the stationary-state. Here, as in the case of the role of monetary forces, there exists a widely accepted opinion which holds that this restriction is, in fact, involved.* Furthermore, from this argument there follows a subsidiary proposition: given that arguments advanced in explanation of long-period positions refer only to stationary-states, it is not possible to deal adequately with issues relating to the dynamic behaviour of the system from such a standpoint.† However, closer inspection will reveal that this 'accepted view' and its corollary are mistaken. A mistake founded upon a series of analytical confusions and false historical analogies. To clear the ground for this argument it is essential to be precise in defining 'stationary' conditions. The pure stationary-state where "the general conditions of production and consumption, of distribution and exchange remain motionless" (Marshall, 1961, p. 367) is quite clearly one variety of 'stationarity' where the rate of accumulation of capital is zero.‡ But to this may be added the familiar steady-state conditions. Marshall, for instance, would appear to have embraced this slightly wider definition:

> The term 'relative rest' calls for notice: for it plays an important role in the so-called stationary-state of the economist. 'Absolute rest' is an unmeaning term, statical problems deal with relative rest (in Pigou (ed.), 1966, p. 312; see also Marshall, 1961, p. 367).

In the remainder of this discussion 'stationarity' will be interpreted as encompassing both of these two notions.

Now, consider the connection between stationary conditions so defined and natural or long-period normal conditions. The link between them derives from a shared characteristic—the uniform rate of profit. From what has been said earlier it is known that long-period normal conditions are associated, under the presumption of the equalising effects of competition, with a general rate of profit. To this may now be added a supplementary proposition concerning a stationary economy: stationarity implies the *existence* of a uniform rate of profit.

---

* The view has been popularised by Hicks (1946, p. 3, p. 115, n. 1, p. 117, n. 1; 1965, pp. 46–48; 1973a, chs 5 and 6 *passim.*) and taken up more recently by Bliss (1975, p. 55, pp. 69–70 and pp. 120–121) and Dixit (1977, p. 17).

† The usual justification for this argument is that in a stationary-state "we do not trouble about dating" (Hicks, 1946, p. 115) whereas in dynamics "every quantity must be dated" (p. 115).

‡ This does not necessarily imply that the rate of interest (profit) is zero (cf. Robbins, 1930, pp. 212–214; Schumpeter, 1934, pp. 34–38; Samuelson, 1943 and 1971; Whitaker, 1971).

That is to say, the competitive *tendency* towards uniformity of profit-rates is all that is required for the application of long-period normal conditions as the object of analysis. While it is quite possible for natural or long-period normal conditions to refer to stationary or steady-state economics (where the 'tendency' is realised in actuality), it is equally possible for them to refer to non-stationary economies. It is, of course, assumed that the factors affecting the forces which determine long-period normal values change slowly and not by frequent 'jumps' or 'jerks' (see, for example, Robertson, 1963, p. 60 and p. 325). An isolated change in any of these factors (for instance, in technology) would reveal the system 'gravitating' towards a different set of natural prices. Marshall referred to the examination of these slowly working changes under the heading of *secular* movements in value and price in order to distinguish it from the explanation of the persistent causes of value and price (Marshall, 1961, p. 380). The validity of directing theoretical endeavour towards the explanation of long-period normal phenomena rests upon the equalising tendency of competition as it affects profit-rates. The tendency to equality in profit-rates is systematic and persistent in both stationary and non-stationary economies. The difference being that in the "famous fiction" of the stationary-state the rate of profit is *always* uniform.

Indeed, Marshall's use of the traditional long-period method confirms exactly this point. Examining the *Principles* to establish the domain of application of this method of analysis one finds ample testimony to the fact that its applicability extended far beyond stationary economies. So that when Marshall argues that "every use of the term normal implies the predominance of certain tendencies which appear likely to be more or less steadfast and persistent in their operation" (Marshall, 1961, p. 34) he calls the reader's attention to the fact that other "intermittent forces" are not denied "but their disturbing effect is neglected" (p. 366) so as to isolate the forces which ultimately determine values.* In actuality, the unexpected may happen and "existing tendencies may be modified" (p. 347) but all this means is that it is essential to distinguish carefully between the forces isolated by

---

* Ricardo saw the application of this traditional long-period method in exactly the same way; his view is most clearly expressed in the passage from his correspondence with Malthus that was quoted at the opening of Chapter I above (Ricardo, 1951–1973, vol. VII, p. 120).

these 'existing tendencies' (which will reveal the fundamental determining causes) and those of a transitory nature "in applying economic doctrines to practical problems" (p. 347) where "the general conditions of life are not stationary" (p. 347). As Marshall goes on to argue forcefully:

> the hypothesis of a stationary state . . . is merely provisional, used only to illustrate particular steps in the argument, and to be thrown aside when that is done (1961, p. 366, n. 2).*

What is true in this regard for Marshall's use of the traditional long-period method holds equally for the use made of it by its other practitioners. Wicksell had argued, for example, that it was in order to resolve 'real world' questions concerning the fundamental causes of economic phenomena that "we . . . deliberately ignore conditions which are in themselves of great importance, because the problem in question is so complex . . . that it cannot be rationally treated in any other way" (Wicksell, 1901, vol. I, p. 10). Yet although "in all these cases the results [may be only] approximately correct, [and] are purely hypothetical" (p. 10) it was nevertheless true that "the inquiry is not, on that account, valueless" (p. 10). Having once isolated these ultimate determining causes it is necessary to examine both "disturbances of this equilibrium" (Wicksell, 1954, p. 165) and secular movements or "gradual changes" (Wicksell, 1901, vol. I, p. 207) in the factors affecting the ultimate causes themselves. These cornerstones of the traditional long-period method ensure its validity and applicability in the non-stationary capitalist economies in which we live. The reader

---

* We should not leave Marshall without mentioning a particularly celebrated footnote: "a theoretically perfect long-period . . . will be found to involve the supposition of a stationary-state of industry" (Marshall, 1961, p. 379, n. 1). It is no surprise that this passage has been used widely by those who argue that the traditional long-period method is applicable only in stationary economies (Hicks, for example, cites it; 1965, pp. 47–48). However, from the evidence presented above and from the general drift of Marshall's argument it would not seem that he saw the long-period method restricted in this way. Others have reached conclusions similar to ours on this point. Garegnani argues that "Hicks's quotation has to be read remembering the other passages where Marshall says that only in a stationary-state would the 'normal price' *coincide* with . . . the actual price . . . , and where this coincidence was evidently not held to be essential for the validity of 'normal price'" (Garegnani, 1976, p. 33, n. 11). A much earlier commentator on the same footnote states that "it is clear that Marshall's own analysis need not be pushed to such . . . an extreme" (Opie, 1931, p. 201).

may verify for himself that this position was widely held by referring to Walras (1874–77, p. 380), Clark (1891–2, pp. 111–112), Knight (1921, pp. 304–307) and Robbins (1930, p. 194). It should perhaps be stressed that we are speaking here of the general applicability of this *method* of analysis to non-stationary economies; nothing has yet been said about the explanations or *theories* provided for the determination of natural or long-period normal values where the question of the role of the stationary-state hypothesis will reappear. This issue is reserved for consideration in the next chapter.

By an unfortunate choice of terminology (that John Stuart Mill introduced after borrowing it from Comte) the traditional long-period method began to be referred to as the "static method" in the literature of this period (see Keynes, J.N., 1917, p. 146) and this has helped to support what is unquestionably a mistaken inference; that this method of analysis cannot adequately consider 'dynamic' questions.* However, it will be apparent from what has been said so far that this method was, on the contrary, designed precisely to facilitate the examination of such questions. As Marshall said of his *Principles*:

> the predominant attention paid in the present volume to the normal conditions of life . . . [has been taken to imply] . . . that its central idea is "statical" rather than "dynamical". But in fact it is concerned throughout with forces that cause movement; and *its key-note is that of dynamics rather than statics* (Marshall, 1961, p. 350, italics added).

Somewhat later, Knight was to be even more forthright on this point: "It is evident that a society might be ever so dynamic . . . and yet have all its prices 'natural' . . . . It is fallacious to define 'natural' conditions as 'static' conditions" (Knight, 1971, p. 36). Interestingly, Knight appears to charge John Stuart Mill with having made exactly this mistake (Knight, 1917–18, p. 68). In the *Principles* Mill had certainly written that the long-period method only provides "the economical laws of a stationary and unchanging society" (1871, p. 695), but this should not be read forgetting what Mill had had to say in his longer and more detailed essay on the subject: "conclusions which are correctly

---

* It was from this standpoint that Hicks argued that "although Marshall raised at least part of the general dynamic problem, it is curious to observe how reluctant he is to abandon the static conception even in dynamic analysis" (Hicks, 1946, p. 120). Hicks thereby incorrectly infers that the 'static method' has to go if one wishes to examine 'dynamics'.

deduced from the [assumed circumstances] constitute abstract truth; and when complemented by adding or subtracting the effect of the non-calculated [disturbing] circumstances, they are true in the concrete, and may be applied to practice" (Mill, 1874, p. 149, italics omitted). He goes on to argue that 'economic laws' are true in 'the concrete' as is the principle of gravitation in physical sciences even in the face of forces which 'modify' the 'tendency'.

What is required for a *method* of analysis to be capable of dealing with 'dynamic' questions is that the causes of the factors which determine, in this case, the natural or long-period normal values should incorporate the features of both the *process* in which the system is moving, and the *state* at which it finds itself at each point in this process. This is independent of the way in which any particular 'dynamic' question might be put and answered.

E. REASONS FOR THE SUPREMACY OF THE LONG-PERIOD METHOD

One has only to reflect upon these properties of the traditional long-period method to comprehend why this method of analysis dominated economics in the period under discussion. For it was by virtue of these characteristics that each of the formal requirements for an abstract object of analysis was satisfied by economic phenomena associated with natural or long-period normal conditions. No controversy surrounded this point (apart, perhaps, from the emergence of the historical school and the more influential institutionalists). However, a short digression into the broader significance of economic thought during this period may add further to an understanding of the continuity in the application of this method of analysis across the wide gap that separates the theory of the Classical school from that of the marginalists.

'Economics' was involved in establishing itself as a 'scientific discipline' on a par, or so it was argued, with the physical and biological sciences, so that having once settled upon the abstract category of natural or long-period normal conditions as the basis for elaborating ultimate 'laws' or 'principles' concerning the functioning of capitalist economies there was much work to be done *at the level of theory* where these 'laws' or 'principles' take on their exact form (as, for example, in the marginalists' principle that prices are determined by the mutual interaction of demand and supply). Controversy, some of which was substantial and some not, centred therefore on questions of theory, not method. In the historical process to which successive generations of economists saw themselves as contributors the substantive disputes surrounded the formulation of adequate theories first for 'ultimate causes' under long-period normal conditions and subsequently with theories explaining 'disturbing causes' in the short-run. The details of these theories will be considered in the following two chapters.

F.   PRINCIPAL CONCLUSIONS AND REMAINING QUESTIONS

The principal contentions of this chapter are three. First, it is formally possible to separate the analytical issues concerning the specification of the *object of analysis* form issues that will subsequently surround the provision of *theories* to explain the object. Second, in isolating the systematic, regular and persistent forces the traditional method deferred to the equalising effects of competition and focussed upon natural or long-period normal conditions as the basis for providing statements of general validity (i.e. statements of 'tendency'). Third, the specification of this object of analysis involves no necessary exclusion of monetary forces from the general class of systematic forces nor any limitations in the application of statements about it to stationary economies. According to this traditional programme one isolates 'ultimate causes' under long-period normal conditions, examines 'disturbing causes' in the short-run and examines 'secular movements' in those broad factors that effect the 'ultimate causes' themselves.

However, nothing has yet been said about the theory dimension of this prevailing orthodoxy; it has yet to be established which parts of the completed picture of this orthodoxy the *General Theory* may require us to abandon (i.e. method parts, theory parts, or both); and we have still to account for and examine critically the conspicuous trend in modern economics towards replacing the traditional long-period method itself.

IV. THEORETICAL SYSTEMS AND THE LONG-PERIOD METHOD

> The distinction made by the classical economists between the study of value and the study of forces governing distribution goes together with a separation between the study of value and that of levels of output (Garegnani, 1970a, p. 279).

> The refined pleasure of contemplating the Many in the One is afforded by the spectacle of the economic system—the prices of all commodities and all factors of production—deduced from one simple principle, that which underlies the action of supply and demand (Edgeworth, 1925, vol. III, p. 268).

The traditional long-period method is only one aspect of the economic thought of the nineteenth and early twentieth centuries that was handed down to Keynes. The other involved the explanations or theories offered for the determination of the elements of the natural or long-period normal position of the system and of the principal causal relationships that connected these elements. At the level of theory, however, the story is not the one of strong continuity that is apparent at the level of method (and object) in the period prior to the appearance of the *General Theory*. Rather, it is change that is the dominant feature—the essential distinction being that which must be drawn between the theoretical system of the old Classical economists on the one hand and that of the marginalist or neo-classical economists on the other. When subsequently we offer an interpretation of Keynes's claim that the principal error of the conventional wisdom lay in its assertion that, in the long run, there was a tendency towards the full employment of labour, we will need to be clear about the reasoning (theory) upon which this conventional wisdom was founded. To put it another way, in order to isolate Keynes's point of departure from orthodoxy, we will need to know from which economic theories the conventional wisdom was derived. As is well-known, Keynes did not help to clarify matters by grouping together under the one heading, "The Classical Economists", not only Ricardo, but also Marshall, Edgeworth and Pigou (*J.M.K.*, vol. VII, p. 3, n. 1). Since our concern is with those *common* theoretical elements that link the writers in each of these respective schools of thought (and so formally separate the schools from each other) we will not give much prominence to the differences within the Classical school between, for instance, Ricardo and Marx on the determination of the natural wage-rate or the differences within the Marginalist school between, say, Böhm-Bawerk and Clark on the appropiate measure of the 'quantity of capital' or between Marshall and Walras over partial versus general equilibrium analysis.

A. THE STRUCTURE OF CLASSICAL ECONOMIC THEORY

The most striking feature of that body of economic theory outlined by Adam Smith and developed subsequently by Ricardo is that it envisages the provision of separate explanations of the determining circumstances of the various elements of the natural or long-period normal position of the system. Taking the theory of value (i.e. the study of the determination of relative prices) as a starting point it is possible to explain this 'separability' in a more concrete fashion.

The Classical theory of value takes as data the physical specification of the technology, the structure and level of output and the manner in which the surplus is distributed in order to determine the natural prices of commodities associated with the general rate of profit under long-period conditions. In a simple circulating capital model (with wages being viewed as part of circulating capital) relative prices and the rate of profit will be found as solutions to the following set of equations:

$$(1+\pi)\left[\Sigma_j k_{ij} p_j + \omega l_i\right] = p_i y_i, \qquad\qquad i,j = 1 \ldots n$$

where ω = $p'w$ = the 'natural' wage-rate;

    k_{ij} = the amount of the jth activity's output used-up in the ith activity. The matrix $[k_{ij}]$ is the matrix of means of production other than labour;

    y_i = gross output of the ith activity;

    l_i = direct labour employed in the ith activity.

The formal structure of this approach to the theory of value and its connection, in the first place, with the theory of distribution, reflects the distinguishing characteristic of Classical economic theory. Without altering the characterisation of the forces which determine the natural prices of commodities, it is possible to explain distribution proper (in this case the wage-rate, since the general rate of profit is determined along with the relative prices of commodities) in a number of different ways. This is one aspect of the 'separability' previously mentioned.

For example, the so-called 'subsistence wage' theory of the Classical economists masks some quite important differences. In Smith the idea of a subsistence wage is seen to derive from an inequality (reflecting inequalities in the wider social framework) in bargaining strengths between 'workers' and 'capitalists' so that:

> though in disputes [over wages] with their workmen, masters must generally have the advantage, there is however a certain rate below which it seems impossible to reduce for any considerable time, the ordinary wages even of the lowest species of labour.
> A man must always live by his work, and his wages must at least be sufficient to maintain him (Smith, 1776, I. viii, p. 76.)

Whereas in Ricardo, Malthusian population theory played a prominent part in the determination of the subsistence wage—the natural price of labour being that which maintains a given population. "The natural price of labour is that price which is necessary to enable labourers . . . to subsist and perpetuate their race, without either increase or diminution" (Ricardo, 1951–1973, vol. I, p. 93). Its operation is apparent also in Ricardo's description of the gravitation of the market price of labour to its natural price: ". . . when the market price of labour exceeds its natural price . . . [then] by the encouragement which high wages give to the increase of population, the number of labourers is increased, [and] wages . . . fall to their natural price" (Ricardo, 1951–1973, vol. I, p. 94).

The strength of this analytical structure of Classical Economics is reflected by the fact that it is possible to accept or to reject either of the above theories of distribution (as Sraffa, 1960, suggested might be necessary when wages share in the surplus) without having any effect upon the explanation of value (relative price determination). This, of course, does not mean that it is possible to have *any* theory of distribution whatsoever; a demand-and-supply explanation along the lines that were later to be developed by the marginalist writers cannot be adopted because then, as will be shown in the following section, the theory of distribution is one and the same thing as the theory of value. Ricardo, in summing-up a much broader set of issues for McCulloch, emphasises this separation of theories: "After all, *the great questions of Rent, Wages and Profits* must be explained by the proportions in which the whole produce is divided between landlords, capitalists and labourers, and which *are not essentially connected with the doctrine of value*" (Ricardo, 1951–1973, vol. VIII, p. 194, italics added).

Before leaving the theory of distribution it would not be out of place to mention the basic property of the Classical concept of profits. This is, of course, their calculation in terms of the *surplus product* of the system. In Ricardo's now famous terminology, the rate of profits is given by "the proportion of production to the consumption necessary to such production" (Ricardo, 1951–73, vol. VI, p. 108; but see also vol. I, p. 126.)

In the corn-economy model of the *Essay on Profits* this was the *physical* ratio of surplus net of rent (a given quantity of corn) to capital advanced (i.e. wages in terms of corn plus seed input).* It is when this ratio must be expressed in terms of *value* (i.e. when there is more than one commodity and *relative prices* enter into the calculation†) that the problem of defining a suitable standard of value arises (this problem has

---

* Algebraically we have,

$$(1+\pi)K_c = Y_c$$

which yields a solution for the single unknown π, the corn rate of profit;

$$\pi = \frac{Y_c - K_c}{K_c}$$

where K_c = circulating capital (including subsistence wage)
             a quantity of corn
and Y_c = gross output
             a quantity of corn.

† Reverting to the general algebraic description of the system presented earlier, the general rate of profit is given by the expression:

$$\pi = \frac{p_i y_i - [\Sigma_j k_{ij} p_j + \omega l_i]}{\Sigma_j k_{ij} p_j + \omega l_i}, i,j = 1 \ldots n$$

(for all i). And as Sraffa emphasises, in this case "[the rate of profit] must be determined through the same mechanism and at the same time as are the prices of commodities" (1960, p. 6).

been discussed extensively in Garegnani, 1958, pt. I; but see also Eatwell, 1975a). The only point that should be noted is that this problem of measurement is quite distinct from the problem of defining the 'quantity of capital' that, as we shall shortly see, is required in the demand-and-supply explanations of the general rate of profit offered by the marginalist economists. Garegnani (1960) has taken great care to point out that these apparently similar 'measurement' problems arise in 'different forms' and present 'different difficulties' in each theoretical system. The apparent similarity of the problems should not be taken to imply that similar theories lie behind them.

Turning next to the relationship of the theory of value to the theories of output and employment we find the same 'separability' which differentiated the study of value from the study of distribution. In fact, the Classical writers offered no substantive theory of the forces determining the level of output other than the assertion that 'saving is spending' (Ricardo, 1951–1973, vol. II, p. 449). This doctrine cannot correctly be called a 'theory of output' since it fails to pose the essential question that such a theory must answer: by what process, to use a more modern terminology, is planned investment brought into equality with planned saving. More will be said about this in Section C of this chapter. For the present two points need to be noted, the full significance of which can only emerge after an examination of the corresponding marginalist theories in the following section. The first is that the Classical theory includes the proposition that capacity will 'normally' be fully utilised.* The second is that although capital is fully utilised this does not imply that labour will be fully employed (i.e. that there will be no involuntary unemployment).

Indeed, the only statement about employment is the one entailed in the idea that the level of employment will be adjusted to the results of past accumulation (given the 'efficiency' of undifferentiated labour). Thus Ricardo had maintained that "the quantity of employment in the country must depend . . . on the quantity of capital . . . [and] upon its advantageous distribution"† (1951–1973, vol. V, p. 501). But this

---

* 'Full-capacity' is used here in its customary sense, so that at full-capacity utilisation there will always be some slack to be taken up in the face of small unanticipated changes in demand (warehouse stocks, variations in shift-work etc.).

† That is, upon it being 'distributed' in such a way as to realise the general rate of profit in all its employments (cf. Ricardo, 1951–1973, vol. IV, p. 35).

condition is not sufficient to guarantee the *full* employment of labour at that stock of capital. Again we may quote Ricardo: "to say that there is a great abundance of labour, is to say that there is not an adequate capital to employ it" (1951–1973, vol. II, p. 241). This is the very situation to which Ricardo referred in his celebrated discussion of the machinery question: "[whenever] the discovery and use of machinery [is] attended with a diminution of gross produce . . . it will be injurious to the labouring class, some of their number will be thrown out of employment, and population will become redundant, compared to the funds which are to employ it" (1951–1973, vol. I, p. 390).

The fact that it may be concluded from this that as far as Ricardo was concerned natural or long-period normal circumstances would not necessarily be associated with the full employment of labour is highly significant not only because an opinion to the contrary has firmly taken root in the history of economic thought (cf. e.g. Blaug, 1968, p. 151), but also because an error of interpretation on this point partly explains Keynes's attempt to unite Ricardo with Marshall and Pigou and to accuse Ricardo of having overlooked "the fact that even in the long-period the volume of employment is not necessarily full" (*J.M.K.*, vol. VII, p. 191). Moreover, when Ricardo did contemplate means of increasing employment he did so by referring to the broader, secular movements of the system as a whole. That is, to those movements induced by accumulation and/or changes in population (cf. Ricardo, 1951–73, vol. I; p. 390, *et seq.*). And it will be recalled from the previous chapter that these movements do not number among the determining circumstances of the long-period normal variables, rather they are statements about the future development of the economic system. Thus one will not find in Ricardo's long-period theory the idea that a decrease in the wage-rate will lead to greater employment with an unchanged 'quantity of capital' (but of different physical composition) because of the possibilities for 'substitution' in production and consumption opened up by the change in relative prices consequent upon the fall in wages. If one wished to draw a connection between a decrease in the wage-rate and the level of employment while remaining faithful to Ricardo's theory, it would be necessary to move beyond long-period theory and appeal to the secular implications such a change might hold—either by the stimulus it gives to accumulation (since, according to Ricardo, a fall in wages implies an increase in profits) or by the check to population that it might entail.

B. THE STRUCTURE OF MARGINALIST ECONOMIC THEORY

The case is quite different with the long-period theory that was erected by the marginalist (or neo-classical) economists during the final quarter of the nineteenth century. The principal characteristic of this theory is that long-period normal values are explained in terms of the mutual interaction of 'demand-and-supply'. Marginalist theory takes as data the technology of production, the preferences of individuals and the endowments of the system. It determines the relative prices of commodities and 'factors of production' and their levels of output and utilisation through a process of substitution (i.e. 're-allocation' and 'transformation') among endowments in accordance with the maximising behaviour of the individual agents in the system. Under appropriate assumptions about technology and preferences an agent's planned supply (of commodities and 'factors') can be expressed as a function s_j (p,e_j) and planned demand as a function d_i (p,e_i) where, for any given vector of relative prices (p), the planned supply will be technologically feasible and profit maximising and the planned demand will both be feasible (in the sense that it is within the budget constraint, $p.e_i$) and utility maximising. This given, it is possible to show that there will be a set of relative prices and an input-output vector such that utility is maximised for all consumers, profit is maximised for all producers, and the market 'clears'. In the context of the present investigation the property of this equilibrium that is most noteworthy is the fact that it implies both full-capacity utilisation ('normal' capacity) and full employment of labour. Were it to be otherwise, entrepreneurs would not be maximising their profits and/or workers would not be maximising their utility. There would, therefore, exist another set of relative prices and net outputs for the system that would simultaneously give higher profits and greater utility. Hence the original situation could not have been an equilibrium. To put it in the more familiar terms of later Keynesian controversies, in equilibrium planned saving equals planned investment at the full-employment level of output.

Yet this is not all that should be noted about this property of the long-period equilibrium of the system. To begin with, in the manner in which the marginalists' approach to the theory of value was applied to the determination of 'factor prices' (that is, to the explanation of distribution proper) is to be found an explanation of a process through which planned saving and investment were thought to be brought back into balance in the face of a divergence between them. This mechanism was, of course, just a particular example of the familiar idea of relative price variation in the face of an imbalance between the demand for, and the supply of any commodity. In the case of the market for capital in its 'free form' the equilibrating 'price' is the rate of interest (cf., Walras, 1874–77, pp. 390–391; Wicksell, 1901, vol. I, p. 150; Böhm-Bawerk, 1899, vol. III, p. 9; Clark, 1899, p. 375; Jevons, 1871, pp. 239–240; Marshall, 1961, p. 534). By focussing upon the operation of the markets for 'free capital' and labour (for the moment, in isolation from the markets for other commodities) it is possible to obtain a fairly clear understanding of the grounds upon which the marginalist school based its assertion that there was a tendency for planned investment to be brought into equality with planned saving so as to produce full employment.

To begin with, consider the market for 'free capital'. At any given rate of interest the demand curve tells us the demand for a *stock* of capital at that rate of interest. Together with the 'quantity of capital' available (given as a value-measure, but seen to be free to change its physical 'form') the equilibrium or natural rate of interest (profit) can be determined. But if the stock of capital (which results from past investment) is to be free to alter its 'form' through a process of scrapping and re-investment as the rate of interest (profit) varies, so that it may ultimately assume the appropriate physical composition compatible with equilibrium, this simple picture has to be supplemented with the idea that the demand for capital as a *flow* (i.e. the investment demand function) has the same properties as the demand for capital as a stock. In particular, planned investment must vary inversely with the rate of interest.* This hypothesis is in fact no more than an implication of the marginalist explanation of distribution in the sense that it derives directly from the latter (cf. Garegnani, 1978–1979, pt. 1, p. 347, and

----

* A more detailed discussion of the connection between the stock and flow aspects of the demand for capital will be found in Appendix B below. There are, however, two points concerning this theory that should be mentioned here. The first is that this relation between the rate of interest (profit) and the amount of capital (demand for investible resources) implies not that the demand curve is 'highly' elastic with respect to the rate of interest (profit). However, the idea that the magnitude of this elasticity may be zero is not compatible with the idea that the demand for investment depends on the

Kaldor, 1955–1956, pp. 362–363). The hypothesis that planned investment adjusts to planned savings in this manner is just an expression of the marginalist theory of distribution.

The same hypothesis underlies the argument that the operation of the forces of demand and supply in the labour market leads to full employment. Given any wage-rate, the demand curve for labour tells us the amount of employment entrepreneurs will be willing to offer. Together with the available supply, the equilibrium real wage-rate can be determined and there will be no involuntary unemployment. But to suppose that entrepreneurs respond to a change in the wage-rate by varying employment in the opposite direction so that ultimately an equilibrium in the labour market is reached, it is also necessary to suppose that there will be forces operating that will be capable of restoring the balance between saving and investment that would have been upset by the change in the level of income induced by the original change in the level of employment. It is in this way that the idea that there exists a long-run tendency towards full-employment relies upon the notion that the rate of interest acts as an equilibrator between decisions to save and decisions to invest and hence upon the marginalist explanation of distribution.

It is clear, moreover, that in so far as this theory of distribution is concerned, the 'principle of substitution' operates through a downward sloping demand curve for 'capital' in its 'free form'. In this way it is ultimately based on the conception of capital as a 'factor of production' that will be employed (as in the case with labour in the face of changes in the real wage-rate) in decreasing proportions (to labour and to output) as the rate of interest (profit) rises.* Indeed, in drawing demand and supply 'curves' in the market for 'capital' and in outlining the mechanism by which variations in the rate of interest (profit) establish an equilibrium, one is simultaneously implying the mechanism by which the wage-rate varies so as to ensure equilibrium in the labour market. In

---

cost of funds in any meaningful way. Indeed, in this case the level of investment will be explained not by demand-and-supply but by the reasons for the constancy of its level. The second point is that the associated idea of the supply curve of savings is likewise a function of the rate of interest. Although some marginalist writers thought that savings might respond only 'insensitively' to changes in the rate of interest (cf. e.g. Marshall, 1961, p. 534), this *relative* inelasticity of the supply curve does not change the theory in any way.

* This is what Pasinetti (1969) referred to as the 'unobtrusive postulate'.

fact, this is what the so-called 'principle of substitution' as applied in marginalist economic theory is all about (cf. e.g. Knight, 1935, pt. I).

But a well-known and fundamental problem of logical consistency arises from this very property of the marginalist theory of distribution. In order to maintain that there exists an inverse relationship between the 'price' of a 'factor' and the quantity of its services demanded one must be prepared to specify, when the 'factor of production' is capital and its 'price' the rate of interest, a 'quantity of capital'. Furthermore, to speak of changes in the proportions in which such 'quantities' of 'factors' will be employed as the price of their services varies requires that these 'quantities' themselves be defined in such a way as to ensure their independence from relative prices. In the case of the 'quantity of capital' this is not so straightforward a matter. In a one-commodity world we could speak about the 'quantity of capital' in *physical* terms quite unambiguously, but in any other situation capital consists of a heterogeneous collection of reproducible commodities not susceptible to aggregate measurement in physical terms. However, if in this case a *value* measure of the 'quantity of capital', is proposed, as was done for example by Marshall,* it is no longer possible to achieve the required independence of the 'quantity of capital' from relative prices.† In all such cases it is not possible to determine the general rate of interest (profit) along marginalist lines since the inverse relationship between 'factor price' and 'quantity' employed that is the basis of this explanation of distribution will no longer hold in general.‡

It is crucial to realise that this problem applies to any attempt to explain a *general* rate of interest (profit) in terms of demand-and-supply. It applies not only to aggregate production function models of the J. B.

---

* The 'flow' equivalent of this procedure is to take as exogenously given the steady-state growth rate; but this does not appear to be the way Marshall and his contemporaries set about the problem (see, for example, Garegnani, 1976, p. 33, n.11, for a discussion of this point).

† As Sraffa has shown this 'quantity of capital' cannot "be measured independently of, [or] prior to, the determination of the prices of the products [and the rate of profit]" (1960, p. 9).

‡ The same problem arises in Wicksell's theory where the 'quantity of capital' is measured by the average period of production. We do not propose to go over the formal demonstration of this result; suffice it to say that it depends on the usual possibilities of reswitching and reverse capital-deepening. These issues have been discussed exhaustively in the literature; but see especially, Garegnani, 1958, 1960 and 1970 and the *Q.J.E.* 'Symposium', 1966.

Clark type and to the 'average period of production' models of the Austrian or Wicksellian type, but also in a theory like that of Walras, where 'capital' is conceived of as a collection of heterogeneous objects, the same problem is present. In this case the marginalist approach, conducted in terms of demand-and-supply, leads to a different rate of net income (interest) for each produced item among the means of production. But this, in turn, is inconsistent with Walras's attempt to explain the uniform rate associated with the long-period position of the system. This rate cannot be deduced without first specifying the 'quantity of capital' (see Garegnani, 1958, p. 119 and pp. 138–139; and 1976, pp. 36–37).*

In the light of what has been said above, it becomes clear just what Edgeworth was driving at in the passage quoted at the beginning of this chapter when he borrowed Marshall's motto 'the many in the one' (1920, title page) to describe the structure of marginalist theory. The point is simply that the *same* explanation (the mutual interaction between demand and supply) serves to determine not only the relative prices of commodities, the rate of interest (profit) and the wage-rate, but also the levels of output of commodities and the levels of utilisation (employment) of 'factors of production'. In striking contrast to the vision of the older Classical economists there is no separability of theories to be found here. The explanation of value, distribution, output and employment is provided at one and the same time by one and the same principle. The full significance of this fact will become apparent when we undertake an examination of the attempts that have been made since to reconcile this principle with the contribution of Keynes.

If the foregoing discussion correctly isolates the formal distinctions between the respective theoretical systems of the Classical economists, on the one hand, and the marginalists, on the other, then it is apparent that a reconsideration of the interpretation of 'Say's Law' in these theories is called for. In particular, a rather large class of interpretations which derive from Keynes' assertions that Malthus' 'defeat' at the hands of Ricardo in the celebrated 'general glut controversy' was a

---

* This will be elaborated in Chapter VIII. For the present it is sufficient to note that Walras' conception of capital is inconsistent with his attempt to determine a general rate of interest (profit) (cf., Garegnani, 1978–1979, p. 345, n.2).

"disaster to the progress of economics" and "constrained the subject for a full hundred years in an artificial groove" (*J.M.K.*, vol. X, p. 98 and p. 87) would appear, in the light of what we have argued, to obscure more information than is revealed.* For although it would be correct to argue that a proposition like 'an act of individual saving inevitably leads to a parallel act of investment' (which was one of Keynes's short-hand characterisations of 'Say's Law' in the *General Theory*, p. 21) has a place in both Classical and marginalist economic theory, it is a mistake to go on from this to conclude that the proposition that 'there is a long-run tendency towards the full employment of labour' also has a necessary place in each. Briefly stated, the error incurred by drawing the second conclusion involves a failure to distinguish the Classical notion that 'saving is spending [investment]' from the substantively different idea of the marginalists that 'the rate of interest is the balancing factor which brings investment into equality with saving'. Only the marginalists' version of 'Say's Law' carries along with it the implication that under long-period normal conditions there will be full employment. But before examining the premises used by the marginalists to support this conclusion, it is necessary to consider in more detail the use of 'Say's Law' in the Classical economic theory.

C. 'SAY'S LAW' AND CLASSICAL ECONOMICS

In view of the fact that it is widely agreed that the usual mnemonic attached to 'Say's Law', that "supply creates its own demand", means different things to different people (*vide* Schumpter, 1954, pp. 624–625), our present purpose will be served best if we refrain from adding to an already long list of elaborations of the 'law' and allow those who used it (and criticised it) to speak for themselves.

J.-B. Say, himself, does not offer much of an advance on the textbook mnemonic. In the *Traité* he says simply that it "is production which

---

* Apart from Keynes, see Klein (1968, p. 44) and O'Leary (1942) who claims that Malthus "was led to adopt and develop . . . the same line of approach which Keynes has made . . . to the problem of involuntary unemployment" (p. 919). There has always been a tradition which rejected this strong assertion by Keynes (cf., Robbins, 1952, p. 30 n.2; Schumpeter, 1954, p. 481; Blaug, 1968, p. 176; Corry, 1959, p. 718).

opens a demand for products" (Say, 1880, p. 133).* It seems fairly clear, however, that Say produced this 'paradoxical' conclusion (as he called it) in order to make two points. First, that "money is but the agent of the transfer of values" (p. 133)†—an assertion that, in this context at least, has less to do with the so-called 'classical dichotomy' between monetary and real forces (as is claimed, for instance, by Blaug, 1968, p. 149 and by Baumol, 1977, pp. 153–154 and pp. 158–159) than it has to do with disputing what Adam Smith had earlier regarded as the mercantilist heresy that a nation's wealth depended on its total stock of money.‡ Second, that while it was quite possible for one commodity to be "raised in too great abundance in relation to all others" (Say, 1880, p. 136, n. 3) a general overproduction of all commodities was not possible.§ On this issue Say explicitly aligned himself with Ricardo and against Sismondi and Malthus.

James Mill differs little from Say at this level. He argued that "the whole of what is annually produced is annually consumed" (Mill, 1844, p. 226) and that "it is, therefore, impossible, that there should ever be in any country . . . commodities in quantity greater than the demand, without there being, to an equal amount, some other . . . commodities in quantity less than the demand" (p. 235).¶ Mill's sole purpose in these

---

* This quotation comes from the chapter "Des Débouchés" of the English translation of the 4th edition—the celebrated chapter in this connection and one which was to be revised and expanded in successive editions of the *Traité*. In the 1st edition the same idea is expressed. (See Stigler, 1965, p. 312 for a translation of that part of the text which makes this point. The entire chapter of the 1st edition is translated in Baumol, 1977, pp. 147–148).

† In the 1st edition: "money performs no more than the role of a conduit" (Baumol, 1977, p. 148).

‡ A fact noted by Blaug (1968, p. 150) but subsequently dismissed by him. Sowell (1972), on the other hand, makes a point of it (p. 16).

§ Say does not appear to have made this point in the version of this chapter in the 1st edition. It is made, however, elsewhere in that edition (see Baumol, 1977, pp. 155–156 for a translation of ch. 5 of the *Traité*).

¶ 'Supply' and 'demand' must be understood here (as, indeed, they must in Classical economics as a whole) in Adam Smith's sense of 'quantity brought to market' and 'quantity demanded' (his 'effectual demand') respectively and not in the marginalist sense of functional relationships ('schedules') between price and quantity. We may quote Smith to illustrate this point: "the market price of every particular commodity is regulated by the proportion between the quantity which is actually brought to market and the demand of those who are willing to pay the natural price of the commodity" (Smith, 1776, I. vii., p. 63, italics added). (See the discussion of this matter in Groenewegen, 1973.)

statements taken from his *Elements* was to combat Malthus's opinion on the question of a general glut of commodities; the very same possibility Mill had been led to deny in his earlier *Commerce Defended* (1807).

Leaving aside for the moment the version of the quantity theory of money that may be deduced explicitly from the emphasis Say gives, following Smith, to the 'means of exchange' function of money (together with the attendant idea that the only permanent reason for the holding of money balances derives from its use for transactions purposes★), it is not immediately apparent which of the analytical issues of the subsequent 'Keynesian' controversies over 'Say's Law' are entailed by these propositions of Say and Mill. In this connection there would seem to be only one contentious point. Both Say and Mill maintain that aggregate demand cannot set a permanent limit to production whereas Keynes holds that a lack of effective demand would, indeed, constrain output ('production'). Yet without a discussion of the saving-investment process underlying these different results as well as a consideration of the theory of employment and, in particular, some reference to the full-employment condition that Keynes always associated with 'Say's Law' (see *J.M.K.*, vol. VII, p. 26), the full significance of this opposition of conclusions cannot be ascertained unambiguously. To accomplish this task it is necessary to turn to Ricardo and his famous controversy with Malthus.

'Say's Law', or what Ricardo himself preferred to call 'Mr. Mill's Proposition' (Ricardo, 1951–1973, vol. VI, p. 142; see also p. 134 and p. 148), led Ricardo to pronounce that "demand is only limited by production" (1951–1973, vol. I, p. 290 and vol. IV, p. 178) and on the basis of this proposition to advance the following argument:

> There cannot . . . be accumulated in a country any amount of capital which cannot be employed productively . . . [and] whether these increased productions . . . shall or shall not lower profits depends solely on the rise of wages (1951–1973, vol. I, p. 290 and p. 292).

★ 'Hoarding' might certainly occur during fluctuations in trade, or be undertaken by 'timid people' in the face of fluctuations in the value of money as Ricardo noted (Ricardo, 1951–73, vol. III, p. 172) and 'idle money' would appear during a crisis (Marx, 1963, vol. II, p. 494), but there was no permanent motivation for hoarding: "few people . . . lock up their money in a box" (Malthus, 1827, p. 238).

And furthermore:

> Productions are always bought by productions . . . money is only the
> medium by which the exchange is effected. Too much of a particular
> commodity may be produced . . . but this cannot be the case with respect
> to all commodities (1951–1973, vol. I, p. 292).

From this evidence it is possible to begin to say something quite specific
about Ricardo's use of 'Say's Law'. It is apparent that there were two
grounds upon which Ricardo invoked 'M. Say's Principle'. The first,
which is illustrated in the first of the two passages quoted above, was in
an attempt to dispute the claim that too rapid an accumulation of capital
would precipitate a fall in the rate of profit. Ricardo asserted, contrary
to Adam Smith,* that the only permanent cause of a lowering of the rate
of profit was an increase in the natural wage-rate. In proposing this, of
course, Ricardo was quite correct (at least in terms of the logic of his
own theory of value and distribution). He then invoked 'Say's Law' for
the critique of the internal logic of Smith's position.

It is, therefore, not without interest to note that a major part of
Ricardo's dispute with Malthus was over the same question†—the
circumstances under which there would be a permanent fall in the rate
of profit. So when Malthus maintained that "under a rapid accumulation of capital . . . the demand, compared with the supply of material
products, would prematurely fail, and the motive to further accumulation be checked" (Malthus, 1820, p. 463), the same reason that
caused Ricardo to oppose Adam Smith's views on the effects of
accumulation led him, necessarily, to question Malthus's similar views
on the subject. The argument that Malthus advances in the above

---

* To quote Smith: "The increase of stock . . . tends to lower profits. When the stocks
of many rich merchants are turned into the same trade, their mutual competition . . .
tends to lower its profit; and when there is a like increase in stock in all the different
trades . . . the same competition must produce the same effect in them all" (Smith,
1776, I. ix., p. 98). Ricardo complains: "Adam Smith . . . uniformly ascribes the fall of
profits to accumulation of capital . . . [but] no accumulation of capital will permanently
lower profits, unless there be some permanent cause of the rise of wages" (Ricardo,
1951–1973, vol. I, p. 289; the order of the sentences has been reversed here without, I
contend, any alteration of Ricardo's meaning).
† Ricardo's annotations to Malthus' *Principles* are most extensive for the chapter "On
the Immediate Causes of the Progress of Wealth". Of a total of 315 notes 119 are
attached to this chapter; in a letter to McCulloch, Ricardo referred to it as "perhaps the
most objectionable chapter in Mr. Malthus' book" (Ricardo, 1951–73, vol. VIII, p.
180).

passage, that under accumulation lack of 'effectual demand' would cause a fall in the rate of profit, together with the idea that a boost given to this demand by a "body of unproductive consumers" (1820, p. 463) would be the only way this decline could be prevented, is little more than an elaboration of Adam Smith's idea that profits are determined by the 'competition of capitals' (see n. *, p. 49 for Smith's view; see also Malthus, 1820, pp. 310–311 where he associates himself explicitly with Smith). This theory of profits Ricardo could not embrace. On the contrary, Ricardo held that "profits . . . depend on high or low wages, and on nothing else" (Ricardo, 1951–1973, vol. II, p. 252) so that the Ricardian theory of distribution (unlike Malthus's version of Smith's theory) did not accept that the general rate of profit could be determined under the influence of 'aggregate demand'.

But Ricardo was not content to allow his opposition to Malthus's position to stand or fall simply on a positive statement of his alternative theory of the rate of profit. He was concerned also to bring out the flaw in the argument of the opposing camp. Ricardo traced the basis of their argument concerning the effects of accumulation on the rate of profit to the idea that there could be an over-abundance of capital in the sense that there could be an amount of a country's total stock of capital (which results from past levels of accumulation) that would be unable to find productive employment. It was at this juncture that Ricardo invoked 'Say's Law' (as the first of the two passages from the *Principles* quoted above illustrates) to show that there could be no permanent over-supply of capital, so disproving the Smith–Malthus argument.

It is interesting to observe that Marx, who as we shall see presently criticised Ricardo's use of 'Say's Law' in another context, was perfectly in agreement with Ricardo on this point. Marx argues: "When Adam Smith explains the fall in the rate of profit from an over-abundance of capital . . . he is speaking of a *permanent* effect and this is wrong" (Marx, 1963, vol. II, p. 497, n. 1, italics in original). When later Marxist scholars took up the criticism of 'Say's Law' this particular use of it by Ricardo was similarly accepted as correct (see, for example, Bukharin, 1972, p. 204 who approvingly quotes the above passage from *Theories of Surplus Value*).

In relation to the subsequent 'Keynesian' critique of 'Say's Law', this aspect of Ricardo's use of the notion that 'demand is only limited by production' does not seem to involve the errors towards which that critique was directed. For while Ricardo denies that aggregate demand can permanently influence the rate of profit, there is nothing in his argument as outlined above that would necessitate a rejection of Keynes's idea that effective demand determines the level of output or (as we have already had cause to remark in Section A of this chapter) that under the 'full utilization of capacity', in the meaning that Ricardo's theory would assign to it, the attendant level of employment of labour would necessarily be 'full'.

Of course, Ricardo's doctrine that "to save is to spend" (Ricardo, 1951-1973, vol. II, p. 449; see also vol. VIII, p. 181 and vol. X, p. 409) is embodied in this argument. For Ricardo, an act of individual saving constituted, *pari passu*, an act of investment. 'Savers' were 'investors' who, if they did not use their savings to hire productive labourers directly, would lend it to others who would. In this matter Ricardo was simply following Smith, who held that: "whatever a person saves . . . he adds to his capital, and either employs it himself in maintaining an additional number of productive hands, or enables some other person to do so, by lending it to him for an interest" (Smith, 1776, II. iii, p. 358). To Ricardo this amounted to no more than recognising the simple fact that 'capitalists' were 'capitalists'. But it would be an error to infer from this either that since this was Ricardo's view, Malthus must have adhered to a different view and had analysed a process by which investment was brought into equality with saving in the face of a divergence between them,★ or that Ricardo's view could be said to constitute a theory of output. †

As regards the first point one need only observe that Malthus defined 'parsimony [saving]' as 'the conversion of revenue into capital" (Malthus, 1820, p. 369 n.1), to see that Malthus too had identified decisions to save with decisions to invest. Indeed, although I have attached the modern term 'saving' to the older term 'parsimony' in order to make the point that saving is investment, in fact, the term

---

★ In his search for precursors Keynes made just such a claim. Malthus, wrote Keynes, "[posed] the whole problem of the balance between Saving and Investment" but "the brilliant intuitions of his . . . far reaching *Principle of Effective Demand* have been forgotten" (*J.M.K.*, vol. X, p. 102, italics in original). We will return to Keynes's claims in this regard in the detailed analysis of the *General Theory* in Chapter VI below.
† By lumping Ricardo in with Marshall and Pigou, Keynes not only succumbed to this by ascribing to Ricardo a theory of output but also to the error of attributing to him the theory of *full-employment* output of the marginalist school. This, too, is a point to which we will return in Chapter VI.

'parsimony' as used by Malthus did not just mean 'saving'—it meant 'saving that was matched by an equivalent investment'. The extent to which no distinction was made between decisions to save and decisions to invest is shown by the fact that these writers used one term to describe both acts. When Adam Smith declared that "capitals are increased by parsimony" (Smith, 1776, II, iii, p. 358) he used the term in exactly this sense. (See Schumpeter, 1954, p. 641 n.40; Corry, 1959, p. 719; Blaug, 1968, p. 164; Bleaney, 1976, p. 222; and Garegnani, 1978–9, pt. I, p. 339, for the same conclusion.) The second point is that in order to be in possession of a theory of output one has first to specify a *mechanism of adjustment* that describes the operation of the saving-investment process in the face of a divergence between planned investment and saving. It is precisely because no such mechanism is to be found in Ricardo that it can be said that his theoretical apparatus is 'open' in the sense that there is room for the provision of an explanation of the determination of the level of output* (see Garegnani, 1964–1965 and 1978–1979, pt. I, p. 340, for a similar conclusion).

This brings us to the remaining aspect of the dispute between Ricardo and Malthus; the question of general overproduction. Here we discover the other major theoretical issue which helps to explain Ricardo's use of 'Say's Law'. The second of the two passages from the *Principles* quoted earlier in this section illustrates Ricardo's views on the subject. As is well-known, Ricardo admitted that it was quite possible for an oversupply to occur in *one* sphere of production but for Ricardo, unlike Malthus, a general overproduction of *all* commodities simultaneously was another question entirely. In a debate in which both men had taken up their respective positions well before either had published a *Principles* text, their correspondence in 1814 provides an unambiguous picture both of Malthus's argument and of Ricardo's reasons for rejecting it.

In September that year Malthus wrote to Ricardo saying simply that "if we were to grow next year half as much corn again as usual, a great part of it would be wasted, and the same would be true if all com-

---

* Maurice Dobb (1973) lapses from his usual clarity when discussing this point. During a consideration of 'Say's Law' in the face of a divergence between planned saving and investment he mentioned Ricardo's name in a context where it might imply an adjustment mechanism (and so a theory of output) was in fact present: "the economists' answer . . . was that interest rates were the equilibrating mechanism" (1973, p. 217). This was not Ricardo's answer, but the marginalists'.

modities of all kinds were increased one half" (Ricardo, 1951–1973, vol. VI, p. 132). This is Malthus's position in a nutshell. Starting from the premise that an increase in production implied an increase in income, Ricardo found Malthus's argument highly suspect. He agreed that there was no foundation for the idea that the additional income created by an increased output of a particular commodity would be spent in such a way as to absorb all of that increased output; without, that is, the price of the commodity whose output had increased falling below its natural price. In reply to Malthus, Ricardo wrote that "if half as much corn again as usual were produced next year, a great part of it would undoubtedly be wasted, and the same might be said of any commodities which we might be ingenious enough to name" (1951–1973, vol. VI, p. 134). However, Ricardo disagreed with Malthus's attempt to extend this argument to cover the case of an increase in the ouput of all commodities simultaneously (without a change in the proportions in which the commodities appear as elements of gross output). In the first place Ricardo correctly insisted that in this case the question was whether the increase in aggregate income necessarily equivalent in magnitude to the increase in aggregate output, would or would not be sufficient to provide the demand for that output (assuming that there was no change in the purchasing power of money). The answer was obviously 'yes'. "The real question is this; if money should retain the same value next year, would any man (if he had it) want the will to spend half as much again as he now does" (1951–1973, vol. VI, p. 134). In the second place, since Ricardo made no distinction between an act of saving and an act of investment, the rest of his argument followed immediately: "and if he did want the will, would he feel no inclination to add the increase of his revenue to his capital, and employ it as such" (p. 134).

Given that Malthus had also not distinguished between decisions to save and decisions to invest, it is not at all easy to see in what way his argument on general overproduction can amount to anything more than a restatement of earlier arguments by Adam Smith* or in what context it could be said that Ricardo had rejected Malthus's claims on the basis of an argument that was analytically unsound. In fact precisely the reverse

---

* See Adam Smith's argument as quoted in n*, p. 49, of the present chapter. Garegnani has argued that this was Ricardo's assessment as well: "In the 3rd edition of the Principles (1821), published after Malthus's Principles, Ricardo does not explicitly refer to Malthus's ideas. . . . He seems to have thought that the criticism of Smith in ch. XXI was sufficient" (Garegnani, 1978–9, pt. I, p. 340).

is true given the theoretical framework within which the Ricardo–Malthus debate was conducted; a logically consistent argument triumphed over an inconsistent one. This is not to say that there is no criticism of Ricardo's position available; indeed there is more than one course open to the critic, as we shall presently see. The point is that effective criticism must rely upon tracing the problem in Ricardo's exposition to the 'saving is investment' doctrine. But in presupposing this very doctrine, Malthus's critique is lacking in precision and consistency.*

It would not be out of place to consider the arguments of some of the other early critics of Ricardo's position. Here the two foremost names are those of Sismondi and Marx. Initially in *Richesse Commerciale* (1803) and later in more detail in his *Nouveaux Principes* (1819), Sismondi advanced the idea that a 'lag' between the receipt of income and the purchase of commodities for consumption purposes might cause there to be a shortfall in 'effective demand' for commodities (at their natural price).† Sismondi's thesis was simple: "C'est le revenue de l'année passée qui doit payer la production de cette année" (1819, vol. I, p. 120).

This argument leads to the admission of a divergence between 'planned' and 'actual' investment when capitalists find that due to a lack of 'effectual demand' they are unable to realise in current production the general rate of profit (that is, that rate which in the past they anticipated would be realised in the present).‡ It needs to be stressed, however, that Sismondi viewed this as only a short-period deviation

---

* A tradition seems to have become established that Malthus stuck to his position because of his superior practical intuition (see for example, Stigler, 1965, p. 324 and Bleaney, 1976, p. 55). A joke by Marx seems to be the origin of this tradition (Marx, 1963, vol. III, p. 53)!

† Leaving aside Marx, our appreciation of Sismondi's contribution derives from Schumpeter (1954, pp. 493–496). Sismondi receives only a single mention in Haberler's survey of underconsumption theories (1958, p. 118); a single mention in Birck (1927, p. 22); and no mention at all in Neisser (1934). The balance has been restored more recently by Sowell (1972 and 1974) and Bleaney (1976).

‡ It should, perhaps, be remarked that while it has been argued here that Malthus's opposition to Ricardo did not lead him to consider possible divergences between planned saving and investment, others have linked Malthus's name with Sismondi. In another context, for example, Marx claimed that Malthus had simply plagiarised Sismondi's *Nouveaux Principes* (Marx, 1963, vol. III, pp. 53–54)—a claim which the evidence in Sraffa's edition of Ricardo's *Works* reveals to be unfounded (vide Malthus's position in the 1814 correspondence). Moreover, it requires a very generous reading of Malthus's *Principles* (verging on a misreading) to establish the presence there of a Sismondi-like 'lagged income' model (see the lengths to which Sowell, 1972, pp. 58–59 has to go to impart to Malthus's statements such a meaning).

from the natural or long-period normal position of the system.*
Therefore, it would be wrong to consider this modification of Ricardo's
position on general overproduction as constituting a long-period theory
of output of the kind that is missing in Ricardo. We will elaborate on the
significance of this when we examine the long-period implications of
Keynes's theory of effective demand in Chapter VI below.

An argument of a related kind was advanced by Marx in his critique
of 'Say's Law'. However, Marx's criticism of Ricardo's position is at
once more subtle and more powerful than Sismondi's. To begin with
money, and not just 'time', plays a crucial part in Marx's argument.
According to Marx, money is not just a medium through which
exchange is facilitated (as Say and Ricardo would have it), but it is "at
the same time the medium by which the exchange of product with
product is divided into two acts, which are independent of each other,
and separate in time and space" (Marx, 1963, vol. II, p. 504). For Marx,
it is this separation of purchase and sale, "the general nature of the
metamorphosis of commodities" as he called it, that "contains the
possibility of a general glut" (1963, vol. II, p. 504; see also Marx, 1971,
p. 98). Furthermore, this separation will be reflected in the saving-
investment process: "purchase and sale get bogged down and unemployed capital appears in the form of idle money" (Marx, 1963, vol. II,
p. 494). But, as in the case of Sismondi's critique, Marx confines this
argument to situations where the general rate of profit cannot be
realised at prices of production (i.e., to short-period positions of the
system as we have defined them). As Marx says, "transitory over-
abundance of capital . . . [is] something different [from a permanent
over-abundance of capital]. Permanent crises do not exist" (Marx,
1963, p. 497 n. 1).†

---

* Following Schumpeter's lead (1954, p. 695) many writers comment on Sismondi's
use of the term 'equilibrium' to describe this position (cf., e.g. Sowell, 1972, p. 39). So
that such remarks should not be interpreted to imply that Sismondi has some priority in
the origin of this term, the reader should note its earlier use in Steuart, 1767, vol. I, p.
189.

† It is true that Marx argued that crises were an inherent feature of capitalism, but his
theory of crises can no more be turned into a long-period theory of output than the
associated argument that market prices usually deviate from prices of production
(and are determined by 'demand and supply') can be turned into a theory of prices of
production (i.e., into a long-period theory of relative prices). Marx's insistence on the
possibility of crises merely parallels his insistence on the necessary deviation of market
prices from prices of production.

The central element of these criticisms of Ricardo's position is the idea that planned saving and investment may diverge from each other during temporary disturbances of the actual system from its long-period normal position. In this regard it is interesting to observe that while Malthus also saw his debate with Ricardo in these very terms ["the question of a glut is exclusively whether it may be general, as well as particular, and not whether it may be permanent as well as temporary" (Malthus, 1827, p. 62)], the extent to which Ricardo saw the issue in this way is more difficult to judge. It is well known that apart from Ricardo's adoption of the traditional long-period method (which explicitly allows for temporary deviations), he devoted a chapter to 'sudden changes in the channels of trade' where "temporary reverses and contingencies" (Ricardo, 1951–1973, vol. I, p. 263) may give rise "during the interval while [capitals] are settling in . . . situations which new circumstances have made the most beneficial" (p. 265) to a situation where "much fixed capital is unemployed, perhaps wholly lost" (p. 265). And it was, after all, in a letter to Malthus concerning their dispute over 'Say's Law' that Ricardo suggested "that one great cause of our difference . . . is that you have always in your mind the . . . temporary effects of particular changes—whereas I . . . fix my whole attention on the permanent state of things which will result from them" (vol. VII, p. 120). In this light, together with what we have already found to be at the base of Ricardo's opposition to Smith and Malthus on permanent over-abundance of capital, it would be erroneous to assert that Ricardo had denied by his use of 'Say's Law' the possibility of crises.*

But this aside, the modifications made by Sismondi and Marx to 'Say's Law' did not involve a theory of how planned investment is adjusted to saving to determine the levels of output and employment. Indeed, on this point they were very 'Ricardian'. The question of how the balance between saving and investment was re-established just did not arise. An appropriate understanding of the role of 'Say's Law' in Classical economics would appear, therefore, to hinge upon recognising that while its use led to the denial of any permanent causal influence of

---

* In this context, we may note the ease with which Ricardo's heirs were able to accept temporary 'modifications' (cf., e.g., McCulloch, 1864, pp. 144–145 and p. 149; see also Sowell, 1974, pp. 47–48, for a discussion of how Say himself had admitted this by the 5th edn. of his *Traité*).

aggregate demand on the rate of profit and, when modified, to the admission of a temporary but not permanent influence of aggregate demand on production, it certainly did not constitute in itself, or produce when it was modified, a long-period theory of output; nor did it carry with it any premises capable of justifying a belief that there was a long-run tendency towards the full employment of labour.

D.   'SAY'S LAW' IN MARGINALIST ECONOMIC THEORY

When one considers the role of 'Say's Law' in marginalist economics a quite different picture emerges. For here the analysis underlying the proposition that 'an act of individual saving inevitably leads to a parallel act of investment' differs in content and character from that which underlies the same idea in Classical economics. Not only did marginalist analysis commence with the idea that 'Say's Law' applied only to those conclusions that followed from a consideration of long-period problems, so that short-period 'modifications' to the proposition were admitted (about which more will be said in the next chapter), but marginalist theory also specified a *mechanism of adjustment* that would operate, in the absence of 'frictions', to restore a balance between planned saving and investment in the face of a divergence between them. This meant that not only was a long-period theory of output present, but also that the substance of that theory provided both premises to support the conclusion that there existed a long-run tendency towards the full employment of 'factors of production' (capital *and* labour) and reasons for enforcing a rigid dichotomy between monetary and real forces. These results follow, of course, from what was said in Section B of this chapter. But before moving on to a consideration of the 'modifications' that were made to these properties when short-period deviations were examined, there is one point that can usefully be made in conclusion.

Some recent discussions of 'Say's Law' in marginalist economic theory have chosen to draw a distinction between two notions labelled 'Say's Identity' and 'Say's Equality' (cf. e.g. Baumol, 1977, p. 146). The former referring to those expositions which, or so it is claimed, did not admit even 'temporary' modifications and the latter referring to those expositions which *did* consider these. Furthermore, 'Say's Equality' is then regarded as a 'weaker' proposition than 'Say's Identity' (cf. e.g. Baumol, 1977, p. 146). To illustrate the distinction, a contrast is then drawn between Walras' *tâtonnement* process and Wicksell's cumulative process. Since the *tâtonnement* implies that trading only occurs at equilibrium prices, it is an example of the 'identity' (we need not consider recontracting models at present); since in Wicksell's theory things happen 'in time' (i.e. out of equilibrium) it is an example of the 'equality'. On such a basis, Schumpeter asserted that Wicksell was the patron saint for all those who abandon 'Say's Law' (Schumpeter, 1954, p. 1117, n.1). It is, however, obvious that while such ideas are appropriate ways of capturing the differences between, say, the *tâtonnement* model and any other model, they are patently useless for discovering which marginalist writers adopted 'Say's Law' (and the 'real forces'—'monetary forces' dichotomy). Because a short-period 'modification' to the 'law' does not constitute its abandonment—the 'law' relates to the conclusions of long-period theory where the ultimate governing forces are discussed. And here, the conclusions of Wicksell and Walras are precisely the same.

V. THE ANALYSIS OF DEVIATIONS FROM LONG-PERIOD POSITIONS

At any moment . . . there is always a certain rate of interest, at which the exchange value of money and the general level of commodity prices have no tendency to change. This can be called *the normal rate of interest*; its level is determined by the current natural rate of interest, the real return on capital in production, and must rise or fall with this.

If the rate of interest on money deviates *downwards* . . . from this normal level prices will, as long as the deviation lasts, rise continuously; if it deviates *upwards*, they will fall indefinitely in the same way (Wicksell, 1969, pp. 82–83, italics in original).

Of the two theoretical systems examined in the previous chapter it was the marginalist theory that was to take over as the orthodox theoretical position by the close of the nineteenth century. So complete was this dominance that scarcely anyone (with the notable exception of Marshall who maintained the pretence that there had been a complete continuity at the level of theory in economic thought since Adam Smith* regarded Ricardo's economic theory as any more than a detour. Thus Jevons was led to claim that "when at length a true system of economics comes to be established, it will be seen that that able but wrong-headed man, David Ricardo, shunted the car of economic science on to a wrong line" (1871, p. 72; see also Böhm-Bawerk, 1899, vol. I, p. 242 for a similar remark). As far as the theory and method dimensions of the turn of the century are concerned, the combination of the traditional long-period method

---

* Wicksell, of course, was a keen supporter of Ricardo, but not for the reasons that are relevant here: it was the theory of population that had won him to Ricardo's cause. Marshall's view is once again enjoying widespread, though unjustified, support.

with the marginalist theory was all-pervasive. However, the first quarter of this century saw 'new' developments in terms of the analysis of short-run monetary theory—the passage from Wicksell quoted above is illustrative of this trend—and it is therefore necessary to consider the extent to which, if at all, these developments should be regarded as a break with orthodoxy. This examination forms an essential prerequisite for that part of the following chapter which is devoted to an assessment of the connections between these developments and the contribution of the *General Theory*.

A.   SHORT-PERIOD THEORY AND LONG-PERIOD THEORY

The basis of the traditional long-period method had always been the distinction between permanent, systematic forces operative in the economy and temporary or accidental disturbances. But in view of the fact that no attempt to produce an ordered discipline of 'economics' had been made much before 1776, it was quite proper, indeed inevitable, that early attempts to do so should have concentrated their efforts first upon isolating the systematic forces and subsequently upon explaining their operation in terms of cause and effect. This meant that most studies were devoted to the specification of the traditional object of analysis (the natural or long-period normal position of the system) and to the provision of an adequate long-period theory to explain it. However, this was by no means the complete programme that these writers had in mind. Ricardo for example, defined quite clearly the overall programme: to separate out the persistent from the temporary causes and to ascribe the due effects to each. These sentiments were echoed again and again throughout nineteenth century economics, culminating in a celebrated passage of Marshall's *Principles*:

> markets vary with regard to the period of time which is allowed to the forces . . . to bring themselves into equilibrium . . . . This element of Time requires . . . careful attention . . . . For the nature of the equilibrium itself, *and that of the causes by which it is determined*, depend on the length of the period over which the market is taken to extend (Marshall, 1961, p. 330, italics added).

It would be fair to say that the whole territory of short-period theory, the detailed examination of deviations between the actual position of the system and its corresponding long-period normal position, was left largely unexplored until around the turn of the century*—with one notable exception.

The exception was Marx's analysis of the possibility of crisis—mentioned in the earlier discussion of 'Say's Law' and to which it will be instructive to return in order to highlight, by way of example, the formal relationship between short-period theory and long-period theory. The two principal characteristics of this relationship are revealed in Marx's analysis.

The first is that the conclusions of the short-period theory temporarily modify but do not change the conclusions of the underlying long-period theory. In fact, an example of this in Marx's analysis has already been examined in the previous chapter where it was noted that Marx could simultaneously launch a vigorous attack on Ricardo, charging him with repeating "the childish babble of Say" (Marx, 1963, vol. II, p. 502) in denying general overproduction or the possibility of crisis, yet declare with his usual forthrightness that 'permanent crises' do not exist in reference to a passage from Adam Smith that Ricardo had found equally unsatisfactory (Ricardo, 1951–1973, vol. I, pp. 289–290). There is, of course, no contradiction here. Marx was perfectly correct to maintain the two positions side-by-side; the first is a conclusion of short-period theory while the second is that of long-period theory. The same is true, of course, of the relationship between the theory of market prices (short-period) and the theory of prices of production (long-period).

A second characteristic of the relationship between short-period theory and long-period theory likewise gains expression in Marx. It is that short-period statements relate to long-period statements in the same way as the 'particular case' relates to the 'general case'. To claim that 'deviations' occur frequently and/or hold especially undesirable implications for the well-being of some or all members of the society should not be mistaken for the claims either that the systematic forces isolated by the long-period theory have ceased to be operative or that the forces that initiate the disturbance can be regarded as anything other

---

* The early underconsumptionists can hardly be said to have provided any clear and consistent short-period theory (though Schumpeter, 1954, pp. 494–495, singles out Sismondi for special mention), Wicksell's *Geldzins und Guterpreise* did not appear until 1898 and Hilferding's *Das Finanzkapital* not until 1909. However, Clement Juglar's *Des Crises Commerciales et de leur Retour Périodique* of 1862 (2nd edn, 1889) did attempt to do just this.

than 'secondary'. Marx, of course, made the first claim, but correctly and consistently refused to draw either of the two mistaken inferences from it.* Thus in his discussion of deviations between market prices and prices of production, Marx argues that while 'demand' and 'supply' (recall n.¶, p. 47 above) are relevant to the determination of market prices, "natural price . . . is . . . determined independently of demand and supply" (Marx, 1967, vol. III, p. 192). Likewise with crises: "crises are always but momentary . . . solutions of the existing contradictions" (Marx, 1967, vol. III, p. 249).

Marx's analysis, of course, only serves to illustrate the general principles involved. The same principles apply to the short-period theory of the marginalists (beneath which lies a long-period theory that differs from that of the Classical economists upon which Marx was building). What is of paramount importance in the present context is the fact that the manner in which these questions were posed was entirely within the framework provided by the traditional long-period method. That is, in terms of the analysis of deviations between the actual position of the economic system and its long-period normal position. Whatever explanation was offered for the determination of natural or long-period normal conditions, it was not left behind by moving to a consideration of short-period deviations. The former remained always as the point of reference; the general, as opposed to a particular case. Furthermore, this connection was not altered by the way in which a deviation arose; i.e. whether it arose due to a *movement* to a new long-period normal position or an oscillation about an unchanged long-period position. Maurice Dobb, for example, accurately commented upon the nature of the relationship for the 'oscillation' case: "while [this] may have the effect of weakening or delaying the operation of certain of the determining influences, and so of retarding the working of the equilibrating forces after an initial displacement has occurred, *it may be held to . . . [leave] unaffected the nature of the determining forces*" (Dobb, 1937, p. 188, italics added). It was, however, primarily the oscillation-type deviation upon which the marginalist literature of the early twentieth century concentrated. The causes of such deviations

---

* It does not seem possible to attribute the same consistency to all of his interpreters, especially in their discussions of 'crisis theory'. A more correct account is given in Green (1982).

being ascribed to the presence of certain 'rigidities' or 'frictions'. In particular, uncertainty (with anticipations that went unfulfilled) and the rigidity of certain prices (like the market rate of interest or the wage-rate) began to play a prominent and formal role in the explanation of how the system behaved in the short-run.

B. MOVEMENT AWAY FROM THE QUANTITY THEORY IN THE ANALYSIS OF DEVIATIONS

This section is devoted to a consideration of how, in the analysis of deviations, certain of the properties associated with the long-period marginalist theory are able to be temporarily suspended or modified and how, at the same time, this does not mean that the general case, to which the long-period theory refers, has been left behind. At the risk of oversimplification, we intend to concentrate on just one property that was modified in the analysis of deviations: the quantity theory of money.* Moreover, since many writers undertook such an analysis in their own (and so slightly different) way, we propose to take Wicksell's monetary theory as representative of the approach—because by common consent his contributions contain the clearest and most complete discussions of this issue available among the writings of the marginalist school as a whole.

Quite early on, Wicksell had spoken of the quantity theory of money in very definite terms: "I . . . am convinced that this theory is fundamentally sound and correct . . . but it [is] too narrow, it [is] not immediately applicable to concrete reality" (Wicksell, 1969, pp. 68–69). And a little later: "It is not possible . . . to throw the old quantity theory overboard . . . with all its weaknesses it is still the only theory that *rests on a sound, logical basis.* What is in fact required is an attempt to develop its fundamental idea, which in itself is correct, so that it conforms completely with reality" (Wicksell, 1969, p. 73, italics added).

---

* The reader will recall the nature of the connection between the quantity theory, 'Say's Law' and the tendency towards full employment deduced by marginalist theory (Chapter IV, Section D above). There are short-period 'modifications' for all of these conditions.

These remarks confirm that there was never any question of changing the long-period theory when setting forth to make it 'conform with the reality' of the day-to-day behaviour of the economy (see also Wicksell, 1901, vol. II, pp. 159–208). Indeed, Wicksell went on to attempt a reconciliation of the dispute between the proponents of Ricardo's monetary theory, on the one hand, and the empirical results obtained by Tooke, on the other, by arguing that the former had been speaking of the 'general' case while the latter's empirical results referred to 'particular' circumstances (see, especially Wicksell, 1969, p. 74 *et seq.*).

The details of Wicksell's attempted reconciliation of the great debate between the so-called Banking School (of Tooke and Fullarton) and the Currency School (of which Ricardo was regarded as the founder) are highly significant because they illustrate quite precisely the connection between what marginalist theory held to be *generally* true in the long-run (the quantity theory) and what experience showed could happen in the short-run.★ Wicksell began this discussion with the remark that 'Ricardian theory' was "too one-sided . . . it was too narrow, it was not immediately applicable to concrete reality" (1969, pp. 68–69). On the other hand, according to Wicksell, Tooke had "set out to fight the Ricardian theories and to prove that their conclusions in many cases did not tally with reality" (1969, p. 69). From here Wicksell's argumentation was straightforward. Borrowing an example from Hume, Wicksell agreed that if everybody's cash-balances were doubled overnight "prices would soon be doubled" (1969, p. 74). Likewise he agreed that if cash-balances were cut in half there would be a movement in the general level of prices "until in time another equilibrium was attained . . . by a fall in prices to a level compatible with the reduced cash holdings" (1969, p. 75). These are the same conclusions that would be derived from the application of the familiar equation of exchange, $M V = P T$. However, and this point is fundamental, Wicksell applied this only to discover the *ultimate* effect

---

★ It should be noted that there are certain 'historical' inaccuracies and confusions embodied in Wicksell's interpretation of this debate. We do not propose to consider these here, as to do so would take us beyond the scope of the present study. However, the reader might refer to Laidler, 1972, for a more accurate 'historical' discussion. It might also be noted that Marx, starting from the long-period theory of the Classical economists, reached a different conclusion—he said simply that the Banking School was right (Marx, 1968, vol. III, ch. XXXIV). See also Green (1982).

of a change in the money-supply (an equi-proportional change in the general level of prices). In complete accordance with the long-period method, at no time did Wicksell dispute the long-period validity of the quantity theory of money (see e.g. Wicksell, 1898, pp. 38–39, p. 41 and p. 50).

The real source of Wicksell's quarrel with Hume's version of the quantity theory has therefore to be sought elsewhere. It is to be found in its characterisation of the day-to-day workings of the monetary system. For according to Wicksell, "the rise in prices required by the Quantity Theory from an increased supply of money is in fact *not* reached in *this* manner" (Wicksell, 1901, vol. II, p. 161, italics in original).

It was therefore the short-period theory of the exchange value of money and the general price level entailed by the mechanism of operation of the quantity theory in its traditional form to which Wicksell objected. According to Wicksell's perception of the debate, the problem was that the Currency School ignored the role of credit as a highly liquid cash substitute and concentrated instead upon a system of individual cash balances for which the demand (a transactions demand) was thought to be approximately constant (cf. Wicksell, 1901, vol. II, p. 135; 1898, p. 41; 1969, p. 75). In Wicksell's view, this effectively amounted to the assumption of a constant velocity of circulation. It was Wicksell's belief that this way of viewing the short-run problem did not stand-up to the statistical evidence mounted against it in Tooke and Newmarch's *History of Prices*. Indeed, when one considered the influence of credit upon the general price level (Wicksell refers to Tooke in this connection), so admitting other short-term motives for holding money (cash and credit) balances than simply transactions, a more adequate way of explaining the short-run behaviour of the system was required. Wicksell's 'positive solution' (1901, vol. II, p. 190 *et seq.*) is embodied in his distinction between the natural and market rates of interest. In this matter, however, Wicksell was no more than elaborating upon the orthodox combination of the traditional long-period method and marginalist theory. His work on short-run monetary processes certainly extended this, but cannot be regarded as a departure from it. Here Wicksell had recognised correctly that the analytical foundations of the quantity theory of money (as a long-period theory derived from the framework of the marginalist explanation of value and distribution) did not necessitate the rejection of the idea that the short-run burden of adjustment between alterations in the conditions of money supply and the general level of prices could operate via changes in the velocity of circulation. It is certainly the case that the characterisation of the short-run adjustment process may be subject to differing emphasis. It is also true that depending upon the emphasis rather different policy prescriptions will follow. However, in none of this is there a matter of principle upon which any issues of long-run theory depend. In particular, Wicksell's short-run monetary theory does not provide any basis for rejecting the quantity theory in long-run analysis.

Nor, it seems, would Wicksell have disagreed with this assessment. In a passage that parallels many remarks that Keynes was later to make in his *Treatise on Money*, Wicksell outlined the framework within which his monetary theory was to be conducted:

> Every rise or fall in the price of a particular commodity presupposes a disturbance of the equilibrium between the supply of and the demand for that commodity . . . What is true *in this respect* of each commodity separately must doubtless be true of all commodities collectively. A general rise in prices is therefore only conceivable on the supposition that general demand has for some reason become . . . greater than the supply. This may sound paradoxical, because we have accustomed ourselves, with J. B. Say, to regard goods themselves as reciprocally constituting and limiting the demand for each other. And indeed *ultimately* they do so; here, however, we are concerned with precisely what occurs, *in the first place*, with the middle link in the final exchange of one good against another, which is formed by the demand of money for goods and the supply of goods against money. Any theory of money worthy of the name must be able to show how and why the monetary . . . demand for goods exceeds or falls short of the supply of goods in given conditions (Wicksell, 1901, vol. II, pp. 159–160, italics in original).

From what has been said already about persistent forces (and statements of tendency) as opposed to temporary deviations, it is scarcely surprising to find Wicksell emphasising 'ultimately' and 'in the first place' in the above passage.

Wicksell's argumentation on this matter highlights some important principles that lie behind the respective positions taken up in the Currency School-Banking School debates as well as in the subsequent interpretations of that controversy. Leaving aside the confusions which were introduced into the debate by certain members of the Banking School who did not fully appreciate that having once accepted the Say's Law basis of the quantity theory of money (a basis they shared with the Currency School) the objections they raised against it were confined to the analysis of deviations (see Green, 1982, pp. 76–83), the absence of any necessary incompatibility between the two positions re-affirms the stance taken by John Stuart Mill on the subject. In fact, Wicksell himself, in charging Mill with having failed "to be altogether clear and self-consistent" (Wicksell, 1898, p. 43) seems to have adopted an interpretation of Mill's contribution that is not entirely satisfactory.

It is well-known that in his *Principles* Mill had acknowledged the presence of an element of 'truth' in the positions taken by each of the two schools in the debate (see e.g. Mill, 1871, III, vii, §1 and III, viii, §6). But in this case Mill was surely correct rather than inconsistent. After all, in claiming that "other things being the same, an increase of the money in circulation raises prices, a diminution lowers them" (III, vii, §1) and that chief among the other things was the 'rapidity of circulation' (III, viii, §3), Mill was simply stating what Wicksell was to argue himself: "the Quantity Theory is *theoretically* valid so long as the assumption of *ceteris paribus* is firmly adhered to . . . [and] among the other "things" that have to be supposed to remain "equal" . . . [is] the velocity of circulation" (Wicksell, 1936, p. 42, italics in original). As Schumpeter observed, "Mill's conceptual arrangement achieved the same end that others achieved by making velocity an economic variable" (1954, p. 705).

Wicksell's remarks are all the more perplexing given that the very distinction upon which Wicksell had propounded his 'reconciliation' between the protagonists in the debate—that of the separation between the acts of purchase and sale—was an integral part of Mill's own contribution. As early as 1830, Mill had maintained that "the effect of the employment of money . . . enables . . . one act of interchange to be divided into two separate acts" and that therefore "buying and selling become separated" in time (Mill, 1874, p. 70). Any criticism that might be due to Mill on this matter could at most be directed at his failure to develop these ideas in as thorough a manner as Wicksell. But to charge him with inconsistency or even lack of clarity, as Wicksell did, was to deny the correctness of Mill's distinctions—distinctions which, in the context of his own approach, Wicksell had adopted wholeheartedly.

John Stuart Mill, like Wicksell, was perfectly clear about the general relation between long-period theory and the analysis of deviations:

> disturbing causes have . . . laws, as causes which are thereby disturbed have theirs; and from the laws of the disturbing causes, the nature and

amount of the disturbance may be predicted *a priori*, like the operation of the more general laws which they are said to modify or disturb, but with which they might more properly be said to be concurrent (Mill, 1874, p. 151).

It is difficult to see how, in this particular context, Mill can be charged with any inconsistency. That the principal implications of marginalist economic theory when applied to long-run analysis need not necessarily apply in an unmodified form to short-run analysis is a conclusion of considerable importance. Since the long-period theory itself is not incompatible with anti-quantity theory conclusions in the short-run (nor, it may be said, with the existence of unemployed resources) and since the analytical foundations of any short-run analysis of this sort are to be found in the marginalist explanation of value and distribution, the mere fact of a difference of opinion over short-run questions cannot be taken to indicate a break either at the level of theory or at the level of method. The regularity with which one can discern in modern controversy over the quantity theory of money the mistaken belief that some ultimate theoretical principle is at stake if the so-called transmission mechanism were to be characterised by output responses rather than by purely price level responses, serves only to reinforce the importance of this message from the history of economic thought. Just how misleading a failure to heed this message can be, is especially apparent in the interpretation of the *General Theory*.

C.   WICKSELL'S CUMULATIVE PROCESS

Wicksell's discussion of the quantity theory of money forms part of what is widely recognised as the first sophisticated analysis of deviations undertaken in orthodox marginalist circles prior to the publication of the *General Theory* (see e.g. Schumpeter, 1954, p. 863 and Marget, 1966, vol. II, p. 90, n. 1 and pp. 92–93). Directly or indirectly it provided the inspiration for all similar discussions that appeared on the subject until the early 1930s.* The formal basis of Wicksell's apparatus

---

* Haberler, for example, took Wicksell's approach as the basis for a comparison of the short-period theories of Hayek, Robertson, Pigou and Schumpeter (Haberler, 1958, p. 34). We will make specific reference to the Wicksell connection in this literature when we come to examine it a little later on (and we will postpone an examination of the connections with the *Treatise on Money* until pt. II below).

is the distinction between the natural rate of interest (profit) determined, as already shown, by "the supply of and demand for *real capital**" (Wicksell, 1901, vol. II, p. 190, italics in original) and the market (money) rate of interest which represents the current terms of borrowing in the market.† Wicksell also uses the term 'normal rate of interest' to refer to that value of the market rate at which the demand for and supply of loans balance (i.e. where planned saving and investment are equalised), but this rate is just the natural rate of interest (profit) as previously defined (see e.g. Wicksell, 1901, vol. II, p. 192 and 1898, p. 102). Whenever there is a divergence between the market and the natural rates of interest a cumulative process of deflation or inflation is set in motion and continues until once again equilibrium is restored and the two rates coincide.

In the present context, the important characteristics of the analysis of this process are first, that it is accomplished within the framework of the traditional long-period method and second, that at any point during such a process forces exist that will operate so as ultimately to bring the system back into a situation consistent with the properties of the underlying long-period equilibrium. Thus any properties exhibited by the system during such a process that apparently do not conform with the conclusions of the underlying long-period theory must be regarded as having their origin in the operation of 'momentary' or 'particular' forces that temporarily prevent the immediate expression of the tendencies implied by the operation of the permanent and systematic forces upon which the general description of the system's functioning ultimately depends. A brief example may serve to illustrate this in a more concrete fashion.

Consider the case where for some reason the market rate of interest (r_m) is below the natural rate (r_n) that defines the position of equilib-

---

* That is, "it is . . . mobile capital in its free and uninvested form with which we are concerned" (Wicksell, 1901, vol. II, p. 192).

† There is a slight complication that should be mentioned. In the financial market the terms of borrowing will differ as between short-term loans (where the 'bank-rate' is relevant) and longer-term loans (associated with the 'bond rate'). But if we wish to speak unambiguously about the 'market' or 'loan' rate we have to choose between the above rates. Wicksell's solution involved the assumption that the difference between long and short rates reflected a 'risk premium' (1901, vol. I, p. 161) so that a variation in the bank-rate would ultimately induce a variation in the bond-rate. In this way it was possible for Wicksell to see the terms of borrowing as being regulated by the bank-rate.

rium.* Thus instead of $r_m = r_n$ we now have $r_m < r_n$. In this situation planned investment, $I(r_m)$, is greater than planned saving, $S(r_m)$. Now, if banks act 'neutrally' in the sense that the only function they perform is that of an intermediary between savers and investors, the resultant excess demand for loans will drive up the rate of interest to a point where $S(r) = I(r)$. That is where once again $r_m = r_n$. The short-period deviation from equilibrium is thus eliminated relatively quickly (though not, of course, instantaneously). However, as Wicksell observes, there is no reason to assume that banks will only behave in this way (cf. e.g. Wicksell, 1901, vol. II, p. 198). If, on the contrary, banks were simply to meet investors' demands for funds at the rate r_m ($<r_n$) then there would be a further obstacle (not just a time-lag) to prevent the market rate of interest from gravitating back towards the natural rate under the influence of the systematic forces of marginalist theory; demand and supply. In this case, with $r_m < r_n$, there will be an excess demand for commodities (measured by the excess of investment over saving at r_m) which will not quickly disappear since the forces which might have acted in the loan market to raise the market rate of interest have been nullified by the behaviour of the banking system in meeting all demands for loans at r_m. What follows, therefore, is a cumulative inflation of the general level of prices. Sooner or later, however, banks deplete their reserves because of their policy of meeting the demands of investors without having received corresponding deposits from savers:

> The condition on which the banks could maintain a rate of interest permanently below the real rate would therefore be an incessant flow to them of new gold . . . [or] . . . for gold we [may] substitute banknotes, fictitious deposits, or other bank credit (Wicksell, 1901, vol. II, p. 198).

The obstacle that was originally placed in the way of the operation of the equilibrating mechanism is then removed and the market rate will tend back towards the natural rate.† This only serves to illustrate what has

---

* Wicksell himself considered the effects of an increase in the natural rate, the market rate remaining at the initial position where it had been equal to the old natural rate (cf., Wicksell, 1901, vol. II, p. 193 and 1898, p. 138 *et seq.*). From an analytical point of view it does not matter whether the deviation between r_m and r_n arises because of a rise in r_n or because of a fall in r_m.

† Closely related to this analysis is the so-called monetary over-investment theory of crisis. In this theory the expansion of credit by banks is seen to lead to a 'maladjustment in the structure of production' (Haberler, 1958, p. 71) which precipitates a crisis. The argument is that at the market rate of interest ($< r_n$) entrepreneurs would begin to adopt

already been said about Wicksell's contribution. It is a model example of the orthodox position of the time; a combination of the traditional long-period method and marginalist theory.

D. DEVELOPMENTS IN ENGLAND: HAWTREY, LAVINGTON AND ROBERTSON

Wicksell's analysis of deviations was paralleled by a set of developments in England. Though differing in detail, these analyses all focussed on the modifications to long-period marginalist theory that were required to bring it into closer touch with the day-to-day behaviour of the system. Short-period theories were offered to explain the operation of the economic system in the presence of frictions or rigidities.

Hawtrey, in *Good and Bad Trade*, had found a straightforward, humane rationale for the study of deviations:

> . . . fluctuations of trade are important on many grounds, but *it is on account of their bearing upon the unemployed problem* that an explanation of their causes and true character is most urgently called for (Hawtrey, 1913, p. 3, italics added).

For him the deviation from the full-employment state that was at the heart of long-period marginalist theory was explained simply:

> . . . producers of commodities depend for their profits and for the means of paying wages . . . , upon the money which they receive for the finished commodities. *They supply in response to a demand, but only to an effective demand.* A want becomes an effective demand when the person who experiences the want possesses . . . the purchasing power necessary to meet the price of the thing which will satisfy it (1913, p. 4, italics added).

---

more 'roundabout' methods of production, increasing the production of investment goods at the expense of production for final consumption (i.e., there is 'forced saving'). The crisis occurs when the banks' expansion of credit ceases. The flow of investment required to complete programmes already undertaken and to maintain intact those already completed that had previously been supplied by virtue of the 'forced saving' consequent on banking policy now dries up. There is a 'capital shortage' (i.e., an excess *flow-demand* for capital—there is, of course, an excess *stock-supply* of capital simultaneously) and the system collapses since it must now move back to that 'structure of production' (less 'roundabout') required for restoring equilibrium at the natural rate of interest (cf. e.g. Hayek, 1935). This doctrine of 'forced saving' was to confuse Keynes in a manner (and for reasons) that will be elaborated in Chapter VI, Section E below.

In the short-run 'desired' and 'actual' results need not coincide, rigidities and frictions interfere with the tendency to full employment, plans go astray and expectations are disappointed. Hawtrey looked for the causes of these disturbances in the organisation and operation of the monetary system and at this stage explicitly used the distinction between the market and the natural rate of interest (1913, p. 66, *et seq.*★) to analyse the problem. The generic similarity between this approach and that of Wicksell is evident in Hawtrey's summary statement of the causes of a downward movement in the level of activity:

> A Depression of Trade occurs when the amount of credit money in existence is more than the bankers think prudent, having regard to their holdings of cash, and they raise the [market] rate of interest in order to reduce the excess (1913, p. 267).

In short, the market rate of interest rises above the natural rate, there is a contraction of credit and activity and employment falls off, subsequently to recover, of course, under the influence of the dominant tendency towards full employment. As Hawtrey later argued: "the alternation of expansions and contractions would be comparatively harmless but for the dislocation and distress which accompany the contraction" (Hawtrey, 1923, p. 422). The entire analysis again reflects the combined application of the traditional long-period method and marginalist theory. It is perhaps worth mentioning, however, that Hawtrey saw the cause of disturbances in purely monetary terms in the sense that they originated in changes in the flow of money. Unlike Wicksell, Hawtrey considered only oscillations around an unchanged equilibrium (cf. e.g. Hawtrey, 1923, pp. 42–43) and did not discuss the deviation that would arise due to a change in the natural rate of interest (profit) itself.

Lavington approached the problem in an analogous fashion. His explanation of the trade cycle relied upon four properties of the actual system that in an objective way kept it from settling into its long-period normal position:

> *first*, . . . the responsibility for production is assumed by a special class of business men, each acting on his own judgement and at his own risk; second, that, as production takes time, its present activity depends on

---

★ See also Hawtrey, 1923, pp. 42–53. Hawtrey seems to have introduced this terminology independently of Wicksell (cf. Haberler, 1958, p. 15, n.2 and p. 36, n.1).

estimates of future conditions, on forecasts liable to error; third, that the market for the output of each firm is dependent on the output of all others; finally, that as business estimates are based, not on prospective needs but on prospective prices, they are liable to further error from arbitrary variations in the price index (Lavington, 1922, pp. 26–27).

Uncoordinated decisions about investment and saving (see also Lavington, 1922, p. 18), uncertainty and lags, were the 'frictions' in the system. They caused the perpetual oscillation of market values about their natural or long-period normal levels; what Lavington called 'the rhythmical variations in the activity of business' (1922, p. 7). None of this is either extraordinary or unorthodox.

Lastly, and very briefly, it is apparent that Dennis Robertson used the same theory/method combination in his analysis of deviations (though, of course, what he called 'real' forces played a greater role than they had done for many others*). It was *only* during the trade cycle that the implications of long-period marginalist theory could be temporarily modified:

> The most obvious external manifestations of the trade cycle . . . are a quasi-rhythmical movement in the level of prices, in the level of money profits, and in the level of employment (Robertson, 1949, p. 6).

Robertson's analysis of such deviations though based, on the surface at least, upon the concept of saving (or 'forms of lacking' in the terminology of *Banking Policy and the Price Level*), resolves itself into a similar form as that used by Wicksell—the deviation between the market and the natural rate of interest. †

It is not necessary to penetrate very deeply to see why this is so. Saving (whether defined as including hoards or not) is at all times influenced by the rate of interest in Robertson's model (hoards may or may not be affected, it makes no difference because the existence of hoards is a short-run factor). When planned saving gets out of step

---

* See Robertson, 1949, pp. 1–2, for example. Of course, from the present point of view, whether 'real' or 'monetary' is not important, their short-run character is what matters.

† In 1934 Robertson produced a paper designed to show precisely the connection: "The following [is] . . . an attempt to bring together (1) [my] concept of saving . . . and (2) the attempts which have been made to analyse cyclical fluctuation in terms of a divergence between the 'natural' and the 'market' rates of interest" (Robertson, 1966, p. 64).

with investment there is a divergence between the market and natural rates of interest that will be eliminated, in the absence of frictions, by variations in the rate of interest. Changing the definition of saving does not alter the fact that it is regulated via a rate of interest adjustment mechanism, it simply alters the precise way in which the mechanism works. Robertson, of course, realised that this was the implication of the particular theory/method combination he was using and, as we shall see in more detail in Chapter X, based his entire controversy with Keynes over the *General Theory* upon this proposition. He thought that Keynes had switched to a new definition of saving (see Robertson, 1966, pp. 150–159 and Robertson, 1948, p. 208, *et seq.*). However, as will be argued in the next chapter, Keynes had effectively switched to a new theory and Robertson had missed the point.

The traditional character of these analyses is highlighted by the fact that both Marshall and, even earlier, John Stuart Mill had recognised that frictions would operate through objective mechanisms from day-to-day in the economic system.

In the *Economics of Industry* the Marshalls had argued that an important 'friction' was to be found in incorrect anticipations:

> Producers and dealers endeavour to anticipate every fluctuation of market value . . . . Thus their action . . . is the same as it would be if their object were to restrain the oscillations of the market value on either side of the Normal value. When they succeed, supply is said to be closely adjusted to demand; *but the market price is likely to deviate far from the Normal price when they err in their calculations* (Marshall and Marshall, 1879, p. 158, italics added; but see also pp. 154–155).

This of course was viewed by the Marshalls as just one possible, objective cause of a disturbance. Apart from bad harvests, a factor emphasised by Jevons (1884, pp. 194–205), money market disequilibria were also important disturbing influences:

> When we come to discuss the causes of alternating periods of inflation and depression of commercial activity we shall find that they are intimately connected with . . . variations in the . . . rate of interest (Marshall, 1961, p. 594).

Mill, likewise, whilst adhering to the wholly orthodox opinion that "the general theory of over-production implies an absurdity" (Mill, 1976, p. 560), was always prepared to admit that the actual system would deviate from the position determined by his long-period theory (i.e. the 'general theory' to which he referred). In 'particular' cases he was quite clear that 'frictions' would arise:

> . . . Those who have the means [to purchase] may not have the wants, and those who have the wants may be without the means (1871, p. 558).

In fact in a similar way in which Wicksell later tried to reconcile the debate between the Currency and Banking schools, Mill argued that it was a failure to perceive that actual circumstances (where overproduction may be seen) need not always reflect reality in terms of the dominant and persistent forces that had led to what he thought was a false general statement of tendency:

> What then is it by which men . . . have been led to embrace so irrational a doctrine? I conceive them to have been deceived by a mistaken interpretation of certain mercantile facts. *They imagined that the possibility of a general over-supply of commodities was proved by experience* (1871, p. 560, italics added).*

But all of this analysis of deviations (and one can find it in some form in almost every general treatise on economic theory) was just that and no more: the system would gravitate towards an underlying long-period position that had its characteristics set by the theory offered for the determination of the magnitudes of its constituent variables. In the case of the marginalist writers these characteristics involved full employment and the quantity theory of money.

E.   THE ARGUMENT SO FAR

Thus our picture of the pre-1936 orthodoxy is complete. The argument so far may be summed-up as follows: orthodox opinion in economics at the time of the appearance of the *General Theory* consisted of the

---

* Wicksell criticised J. S. Mill for failing on this point to be "altogether clear or self-consistent" (1898, p. 43)—a criticism that may stand up when directed against Mill's theory. But the charge is surely unwarranted when levelled against Mill's ability to embrace the abstract relationship between the conclusions of long-period theory and the conclusions of short-period theory, towards which Wicksell apparently directs it. For here he is behaving in the same way as Wicksell himself. Wicksell quotes a remark by Marx (Marx, vol. I, 1967, p. 124 n.2) that he interprets as support for the view he takes of Mill—but Marx was agreeing with Mill's position when he said that Mill "understands how to hold at the same time the view of his father . . . , and the opposite view."

long-period method of analysis and the marginalists' explanation of the associated long-period variables. The analysis of deviations which had begun to assume more importance did not depart in any significant respect from this orthodoxy. Such analysis marked, in fact, its embellishment not its overthrow.*

---

* It will be shown in Chapters X and XI below that Keynes's *Treatise on Money* falls into this category. On this characteristic of Keynes's early work, see also Milgate (1983a).

VI. THE PRINCIPLE OF EFFECTIVE DEMAND: THE POSITIVE PART OF THE *GENERAL THEORY*

What distinguishes the *General Theory* is . . . the crucial role that it assigns to [changes in the level of income] as an *equilibrating force* . . . with respect to saving and investment. Indeed, this is what Keynes' theory of effective demands is all about (Patinkin, 1976, p. 14, italics in original).

From the point just days after the publication of the *General Theory* when Austin Robinson reviewing it for *The Economist* wrote that "in equilibrium . . . saving must equal investment . . . if these two tend to be unequal, the level of activity will be changed until they are restored to equality" (E. A. G. Robinson, 1936, p. 471) to the present, when the passage from Patinkin quoted at the head of this chapter was written, this much seems to have been agreed. But this apparent agreement masks substantive differences. Indeed, Keynes himself not only did not give any really detailed indication of all of the aspects of his departure from the orthodox position, but he also adopted (as we shall see) many elements of that orthodoxy itself in the *General Theory*. Before attempting to produce an interpretation of his work one therefore requires a fairly accurate picture of what went on before the *General Theory*. This explains the time spent in the foregoing chapters establishing the theory and method dimensions of the pre-1936 orthodoxy. It is on the basis of what was established there that the arguments of the next two chapters are founded.

A. THE PRINCIPLE OF EFFECTIVE DEMAND

The central arguments of the *General Theory* revolve around one straightforward, analytical argument:

The reconciliation of the identity of saving and investment with the apparent 'free will' of the individual to save what he chooses irrespective of what he or others may be investing, essentially depends on saving being, like spending, a two-sided affair. For although the amount of his own saving is unlikely to have any significant influence on his own income, the reactions of the amount of his own consumption on the incomes of others make it impossible for all individuals simultaneously to save any given sums. Every such attempt to save more by reducing consumption will so affect incomes that the attempt necessarily defeats itself. It is, of course, just as impossible for the community as a whole to save less than the amount of current investments, since the attempt to do so will necessarily raise incomes to a level at which the sums which individuals choose to save add up to a figure exactly equal to the amount of investment (*J.M.K.*, vol. VII, p. 84; see also pp. 63–64 and p. 178).

The formal proposition is that *saving and investment are brought into equality by variations in the level of income (output).*★ This is the principle of effective demand. Leaving aside for the moment the fact that this adjustment between saving and investment will not occur instantaneously (after all, the principle of effective demand does not refer to the *ex post* equality between saving and investment that holds in any theory but rather to the process through which decisions to save are adjusted to decisions to invest) the manifestly unorthodox idea that gains expression in Keynes's theory is that the economic system will generally find itself a position with planned investment equal to saving without there being any guarantee that the level of employment of labour is full. This theory is to be contrasted with that of the marginalists which requires, for reasons already outlined, that such an equilibrium will be characterised by the full employment of the 'factors of production'.

Before attempting to trace this difference in theory to its source it will be useful to make a slight digression in order to consider the connection between the principle of effective demand and the 'multiplier analysis' introduced well before the *General Theory* by Kahn (1931). This digression is not undertaken with any intention of dating the origin of Keynes's theory (as is attempted, for example, in Patinkin, 1976, pp.

★ Few would dispute the fundamental nature of this proposition. Harrod refers to it as being "at the heart of Keynes's quarrel with traditional theory" (Harrod, 1972b); Garegnani refers to it as the 'constructive core' of the *General Theory* (1976, p. 41); see also Pasinetti, 1974, pp. 31–33.

68–71) but rather with the intention of understanding better the relationship between the two arguments. For it will be argued here that there is not a one-to-one correspondence between Kahn's 'multiplier argument' and Keynes's subsequent principle of effective demand.*

A comparison between Kahn's advocacy of the case for government expenditure based on the 'multiplier analysis' and Keynes's similar advocacy on the basis of the principle of effective demand† reveals important differences. Kahn set out to provide a 'stronger case' for public works than that which 'had always been recognized' (Kahn, 1931, p. 1) for the relief of the unemployment experienced in the depths of depression (1931, p. 11). He did this by providing one 'positive' argument and two 'negative' ones. The 'positive' case was built upon the method outlined to calculate the exact impact on employment (primary and secondary) of a given increase in investment expenditure; the famous 'multiplier' (1931, p. 12). To support the case two 'negative' arguments were added. On the one hand, there was a rebuttal of the view that expenditure by government would draw investible funds from the private sector hence 'crowding-out' private investment (1931, pp. 2–3 and p. 18)‡ and on the other, there was an argument designed to show that the effect on the general level of prices of such a policy would be no worse than that experienced by the "return of prosperity by a more natural route" (pp. 5–6). The first thing to be noted about these arguments is that they refer to the manner in which an increase in investment expenditure, either private or public (cf. pp. 1–2), leads to an increase in 'primary' employment and to an increase in the demand for output as a whole (and so 'secondary' employment etc.). Since this refers essentially to the relationship between investment and employment it is quite compatible with the orthodox picture where the same relationship would be observed in the face of a fall in the rate of interest

---

* This appears to be the way Keynes saw it (cf. e.g. *J.M.K.*, vol. XIV, p. 85). A contrary opinion seems to be implicit in the arguments Klein (1968, pp. 36–41) and Leijonhufvud (1968, p. 205, n.1).

† We refer to the argument contained in the *General Theory*. It seems clear that Keynes's *Means to Prosperity* of 1933 (in *J.M.K.*, vol. IX, pp. 335–366) is just a lay-person's guide to Kahn's multiplier analysis (*vide* Moggridge, 1976, p. 103) and Patinkin, 1976, p. 79, n.23). Keynes's pre-*Treatise* pamphlet *Can Lloyd George Do It?* (in *J.M.K.*, vol. IX, pp. 86–125) will not be considered for similar reasons.

‡ Kahn regards this as one of the main features of his paper (cf., Kahn's letter to Patinkin, in Patinkin and Leith (eds), 1977, p. 147).

which opened up new avenues for profitable investment (cf. p. 26). Secondly, the starting point of the analysis is a case where investment falls short of that level which would ensure full employment because, in the case Kahn considers, the cost of production of new investment goods exceeds savings. The situation can be expressed in more familiar terms as follows: $I(r_m)<I(r_n) = S(r_n)<S(r_m)$. Although Kahn noticed that from his basic relationship between investment and output (employment) it was possible to conclude that an *increase* in investment and hence output would lead also to an *increase* in saving, he did not apply this idea to an analysis of the original discrepancy between investment and saving (and so did not notice that this would have been eliminated in the first place by variations in the level of output). Indeed, Kahn concluded that "under certain circumstances employment can be increased *without any significant alteration in the difference between savings and investment*" (1931, p. 10, italics added). It is quite clear that Kahn, at that time, believed that in only one case would saving and investment balance: "this is the case to which Mr. Keynes's [fundamental] equations apply in their full simplicity . . . it occurs when the whole of the factors of production are employed" (1931, p. 10).

The reference here is, of course, to the *Treatise on Money*. It is interesting to consider Kahn's argument in relation to an argument advanced by Joan Robinson not long afterwards that has also been cited as an early example of the use of the principle of effective demand (Robinson, 1951–1979, vol. I, pp. 52–58; see Klein, 1968, p. 39 who claims that "Mrs Robinson . . . was actually writing one of the first expositions . . . of the really essential parts of the *General Theory*").

Kahn's argument was based upon the first 'fundamental equation' of the *Treatise* (see below, Appendix to Chapter X, Section (b) ii), when $I'>S$. In these circumstances, the supply of consumption goods is perfectly elastic. Kahn maintained (1931, p. 10) that the second term of that equation, $(I'-S)/R$, would remain constant in the face of government investment in 'roads'. While this entails the recognition that an *increment* of investment will be matched by an equal *increment* of savings (or, more properly, that $(\triangle I-\triangle S)/\triangle R$ = constant), Kahn had clearly not seen that the mechanism that produced this conclusion would have operated 'earlier', so to speak, and eliminated the discrepancy between I' and S originally postulated. This would have led him to the conclusion that an 'equilibrium' $(S=I')$ would exist at less than full-employment and so to the principle of effective demand. But he just did not go this far. On the other hand, Joan Robinson approached the same question in a different way. She considered the second 'fundamental equation' (see below, Appendix to Chapter X, Section (c) iii) when $S = I$. She then advanced the proposition that "[an] increase in output must bring about an increase in savings equal to the original increase in investment" (Robinson, 1951–1979, vol. I, p. 56). This, of course, is just Kahn's argument applied to output as a whole rather than to the output of consumption goods. But to hold true it requires that the supply of output is perfectly elastic and this violates, in terms of the *Treatise*, her initial condition that $S=I$ (Kahn had guaranteed the necessary elasticity in the supply of consumption goods by starting from $I'>S$). It is quite clear that Joan Robinson did not notice this and so, like Kahn, did not have in hand at that point a version of the principle of effective demand. The upshot of this appears to be that both were in what might be described as a 'half-way house' with the *Treatise* too close behind them and the *General Theory* as yet out of sight. Indeed, one gets the feeling in reading these arguments that they are not totally consistent with the theory advanced in either of those books (see also n.* p. 86 below).

The contrast between this way of arguing and the position taken by Keynes in the *General Theory* on the same issue is marked. To begin with, the circumstances in which Keynes advocates public expenditure are differently conceived. There is certainly involuntary employment (*J.M.K.*, vol. VII, p. 128) but this neither reflects, as it does in Kahn's example, an imbalance between investment and saving (quite the reverse, saving having already been adjusted to investment) nor is there any 'more natural route to prosperity'* that Kahn agrees is present in the case when the argument is conducted within the more orthodox framework of the Fundamental Equations (*vide* Kahn, 1931, pp. 5–6). Indeed, Kahn's 'natural route' is the orthodox one, variations in the rate of interest: "the whole point of a policy of public works is that it enables an increase in the rate of home investment . . . without that *fall* in the rate of interest that would be necessary if we were relying on private enterprise" (1931, p. 26, italics in original).

---

* Since Keynes maintains that it is 'natural tendencies' which produce the problem, there can be no 'natural' remedy (*J.M.K.*, vol. VII, p. 254). We will have a little more to say on this subject in Appendix A below.

But perhaps even more important is the fact that to Kahn's 'multiplier' argument (than an increase in investment expenditure leads to an increase in employment and output) a new dimension is added by Keynes. The proposition now becomes that an increase in expenditure on investment *generates* an excess of income over that required for consumption (*via* the marginal propensity to consume) so that the volume of savings will increase until saving once again equals investment and there need not be full employment.* This proposition can find no place in the orthodox picture; it stands apart as an alternative view of the connection between saving and investment.

The problem of tracing to its source the difference of opinion between Keynes's position and the orthodox position with respect to the level of employment now becomes straightforward. It resides in the very premise upon which the marginalist writers based their assertion that there existed a long-run tendency towards full employment: that variations in the rate of interest ensured the equilibrium of saving and investment. This is not the way Keynes conducted his argument in the *General Theory*. There, variations in the level of income (employment) ensure this equality. The two theories stand side-by-side as alternative explanations of the same process.

On the evidence contained in the *General Theory* it would seem that Keynes too regarded this as being at the centre of his departure from the orthodox position. The whole of Chapters 6 and 7 of the *General Theory* are based upon it,† as are Chapters 11 and 12,‡ and it is returned to in Chapter 16 where it is reflected in the following 'negative', so to speak, statement of the principle of effective demand:

> The . . . idea that an act of individual saving is just as good for effective demand as an act of individual consumption, has been fostered by the fallacy . . . that an increased desire to hold wealth, being much the same

---

* We cannot, therefore, entirely agree with Joan Robinson's subsequent assessment of Kahn's paper and the state of affairs that prevailed in the early 1930s: "R. F. Kahn, who was at the time involved in explaining that the multiplier guaranteed that savings equals investment, asked [Hayek] in a puzzled tone 'is it your view that if I went out tomorrow and bought a new overcoat that would increase unemployment?' 'Yes' said Hayek" (Robinson, 1951–1979, vol. IV, p. 94).

† Cf. *J.M.K.*, vol. VII, pp. 64–65 and pp. 84–85. If, instead of saving, consumption is considered, then it is obvious how significant was the idea that it depended on income.

‡ These two chapters parallel the two mentioned in the previous footnote, but are concerned with the determinants of investment.

VI. THE PRINCIPLE OF EFFECTIVE DEMAND

thing as an increased desire to hold investments, must, *by increasing the demand for their investment, provide a stimulus to their production* (*J.M.K.*, vol. VII, p. 211).

Thus Keynes sets himself in opposition to the "tradition [that] has regarded the rate of interest as the factor which brings the demand for investment and the willingness to save into equilibrium with one another" (*J.M.K.*, vol. VII, p. 175).

Something of a tradition has grown up, however, which traces Keynes's differences with the orthodox position to another source altogether. This line of argument claims that Keynes's fundamental proposition signals a departure from earlier theories in one major respect; it recognises that saving and investment are in general carried out by 'different individuals' at 'different times' and for 'different reasons'.* However, an interpretation of Keynes that stresses only the distinction between an act of saving and an act of investment (which, as we shall see in Chapter X below, stems ultimately from the *Treatise on Money*) appears to obscure rather than to clarify the source of Keynes's departure for two important and not unrelated reasons. On the one hand, it is quite clear that Keynes was not simply concerned with the fact that such acts were undertaken 'by different people, at different times and for different reasons', but, much more importantly in the context of his departure from earlier theory, with what *adjusted* saving to investment (the passages already cited provide ample evidence of this). When Keynes referred to 'different activities' and 'motives' he did so to illustrate the rôle of the level of income in this adjustment process. On the other hand, if one subscribes to the 'different decisions' interpretation one then faces a serious problem of consistency. For it is quite apparent that the marginalist position did not require (and was not thought to require†) the idea that the act of saving and the act of investment were carried out by the same individual. What would have been argued, however, was that variations in the rate of interest adjusted the

---

* In Keynes's obituary notice, E. A. G. Robinson wrote that Dennis Robertson's *Banking Policy and the Price Level* "was first to bring home to us in Cambridge . . . the essential distinction between the act of saving and the act of investment . . . [and it] . . . forced Keynes to re-examine a number of the fundamentals of monetary theory" (E. A. G. Robinson, 1947, p. 36). More recently this argument has been expounded by Kregel (1973, p. 10) and by Moggridge (1976, p. 78).
† Cf. e.g. Wicksell, 1901, vol. II, pp. 24–25.

one to the other. Here is the problem of consistency in a nutshell: how does one square the asserted importance of this distinction with the fact that the one school of thought, that of the marginalists, which provided premises to support a claim that there was a tendency towards full employment could also embrace this distinction? This inconsistency dissolves into absurdity when we recall that the one school, the Classical school, that *failed* to draw this distinction *did not* provide such premises.

To recapitulate, it can be said that in adopting the principle of effective demand as an alternative to the orthodox marginalist theory of the equilibrium of saving and investment Keynes was placing himself at odds with the received wisdom of the day. But strictly speaking this substitution is a 'positive' achievement only, it does not itself constitute the basis for a *critique* of the older orthodoxy. However, a consideration of the grounds upon which such a critique can be erected will be postponed until the next chapter, for there are other aspects of Keynes's theory that have yet to be considered.

B. THE LONG-PERIOD THEORY OF OUTPUT AND EMPLOYMENT

Having shown how the operation of the principle of effective demand determines a level of output that will not usually be that which guarantees the full employment of labour, it is now essential to face and resolve an important question. Does the principle of effective demand equip us with a long-period theory of output? It is necessary to know whether the levels of output and employment so determined correspond to the long-period normal levels towards which actual levels may be regarded as constantly tending (though the tendency may be disturbed at any given moment by innumerable 'accidental' forces). It will be appreciated, of course, that this question is not only a complicated one but also controversial. Indeed, subsequent interpretations of Keynes's theory in mainstream circles have confined it in one way or another to the short-period.

For example, according to one line of argument, Keynes's theory is best viewed as a development of the orthodox approach to the 'analysis of deviations' that was examined in the previous chapter. From this standpoint it can be argued that "to complete [Keynes's] theory, we

must be able to explain what determines the level of long-run equilibrium . . . [and this] . . . can only run in terms of . . . more fundamental
[real] factors . . . technol[ogy] and psychol[ogy]"* (Modigliani, 1944,
pp. 87–88). † In this way Keynes's theory is relegated to a consideration
of that class of circumstances where certain frictions or rigidities
prevent the systematic forces outlined by marginalist theory from
'actually' producing the results that they 'ultimately' have a tendency to
produce. Another line of argument, enjoying a wave of popularity at
present, is that which interprets Keynes with the aid of the framework
provided by the method of intertemporal equilibrium. From this
standpoint, Keynes's contribution is viewed as constituting the abandonment of the traditional long-period method itself. ‡

Partly because of this climate of opinion and partly because our
question is a complicated one in any case, it will be approached in a
number of stages; commencing with a consideration of the weight
Keynes wished to attach to his theory of output and employment. A
letter from Keynes to Kahn often quoted by those interested in dating
the origin of the principle of effective demand in Keynes's thought §
provides the first clue.

In this letter (*J.M.K.*, vol. XIII, p. 374) Keynes refers to a position
of the system with 'long-period unemployment' and maintains that this
constitutes "an equilibrium position short of full employment" (p.
374). While it cannot be claimed that the argument which led Keynes to
this conclusion was based on a clear and consistent application of the

---

* The order of Modigliani's sentences has been reversed without, I submit, altering his
intention. Robertson was to employ a similar argument in order to justify a return to
"our old friends productivity and thrift" (Robertson, 1963, p. 388).

† The basis upon which such interpretations are erected will be considered later. For
the present it is necessary only to note that this generic form of interpretation underlies
many apparently different species of 'Keynes criticism'. For example, it is at the bottom
of Dennis Robertson's disputes with Keynes (cf. e.g. Robertson, 1937, *passim* and
1966, pp. 150–23; Johnson, 1951–2, p. 9); Schumpeter similarly thought that "it would
have been more natural [for Keynes] not to object to [the tendency towards full
employment], just as we do not object to the law of gravitation on the ground that the
earth does not fall into the sun, but to say simply that . . . though it states a tendency
correctly, [its operation] is impeded by certain facts" (1954, p. 624; see also n.2 on that
page); Hick's celebrated IS-LM is another of its species (Hicks, 1937); and to this list
may be added Pigou (1950), Harrod (1937), Haberler (1958) and Modigliani (1963).

‡ This interpretation will be elaborated in Chapter VIII below.

§ Cf. e.g. Patinkin, 1976, p. 69 and Moggridge, 1973, p. 79, n.24.

principle of effective demand,* Keynes does appear to regard the
position of the system referred to in his letter not simply as one where
the economy has reached a 'stationary point' in the course of a cycle due
to the presence of some obstacle that prevents at that moment the more
systematic long-period forces from asserting themselves. But rather,
although in a not too clearly defined sense, as a position produced by the
operation of systematic long-period forces themselves so that there will
be no 'tendency' to change at all. † This would seem to be at least one
way to account for his associating this position with 'long-period'
conditions.

Leaving aside for the moment the fact that Keynes's exposition of the
principle of effective demand in the *General Theory* is usually regarded

---

* In fact the argument is based on an inconsistent application of the Fundamental
Equations not unlike those of Kahn and Joan Robinson discussed on pp. 80–81 above.
Keynes builds his argument on the second 'fundamental equation': "[if there is
already unemployment] an increase of I makes Q positive, O increases and S increases
but Q/O gradually diminishes. If Q/O reaches zero before O reaches maximum we
have . . . an equilibrium short of full-employment" (*J.M.K.*, vol. XII, p. 374). But
a problem is already apparent in this argument. To be consistent with *Treatise* arguments Keynes's initial condition requires that $I - S = Q <$ zero, so that what he has in
fact shown can be expressed as follows:
$$(I + \triangle I) - (S + \triangle S) = Q + \triangle Q$$
$$\text{i.e.} \quad (I - S) + (\triangle I - \triangle S) = Q + \triangle Q,$$
but even if $\triangle Q =$ zero (as Keynes shows) we still have $I - S = Q <$ zero. And this is not
an equilibrium in the *Treatise* sense at all. The inconsistency between this argument and
the *Treatise* arises because Keynes thought he had started from a *Treatise* 'equilibrium'
(the word he actually uses for the condition appended in square brackets above) when in
fact he had not done so. (There is no doubt about the initial condition, the words we
added in square brackets were used by Keynes at the beginning of the letter containing
this argument.)
† Barring accidental disturbances of course. Keynes's long-period is not to be thought
of as a stationary or steady-state, it corresponds to the level of employment consistent
with a given state of long-term expectations: "it follows that, although . . . the actual
level of employment . . . never [has] time to reach the long-period employment . . .
every state of expectation has its definite corresponding level of long-period employment" (*J.M.K.*, vol. VII, p. 48). To this passage Keynes adds a footnote: "long-period
conditions are not necessarily static" (p. 48, n. 1). Joan Robinson has taken this to mean
that while the long-period is not necessarily a stationary-state, correct foresight is
required so that the only generalization is to the case of steady growth: "Mr. Keynes's
position of long-period equilibrium . . . is a situation in which the equilibrium position
is moving ahead of the actual position at a steady foreseen rate" (Robinson, 1947, p. 77,
n. 1). But *correct* foresight (rather than just the taking of a 'long-view') does not
obviously underlie Keynes's statement: "the only condition is that the existing
expectations should have been foreseen sufficiently far ahead" (p. 77, n. 1).

as having been conducted within a short-period framework, there are numerous statements in that book which indicate that Keynes was convinced that his theory was capable of providing an explanation of the determination of the long-period normal levels of output and employment. Perhaps the clearest example of this comes in a statement made at the end of Chapter 18 in which Keynes summarised his main argument.

> we oscillate . . . round an intermediate position *appreciably below full employment* . . . [this] mean position [is] determined by 'natural' tendencies, namely by those tendencies which are likely to persist (*J.M.K.*, vol. VII, p. 254, italics added).*

It is difficult to see how a reading of this passage could be made to support an analysis of deviations interpretation of the *General Theory*. To be consistent with that type of analysis there would have to be at every moment 'natural', long-period forces at work tending, however slowly, to pull the system back into a state compatible with long-period normal circumstances. No such idea underlies Keynes statement. On the contrary, the position to which he is referring here and its characteristics are held to reflect the outcome of the operation of those long-period 'natural tendencies' themselves. There are no 'more general', 'systematic' forces on which to pin hopes of an escape from unemployment in this case.† It is also worth noticing that the framework of the

---

* The idea that in a long-period position there need not be full employment is also embodied in the discussion of Chapter 5 of the *General Theory* (especially pp. 48–50). The argument there is of the traditional long-period type. Keynes even speaks of the 'economic machine' (p. 50)—a term which comes direct from Adam Smith who used it as an analogy for the operation of 'natural' forces.

† Leijonhufvud has argued otherwise: "Keynes, of course, used the term 'unemployment equilibrium'. Even cursory examination will reveal, however, that it is not an 'equilibrium' in the strict sense at all. It is preferable . . . to use some more neutral term which does not carry the connotation that no equilibrating forces at all are at work. The real question is why . . . the forces tending to bring the system back to full employment are so weak" (1969, p. 22, n.1). One way of reading this passage would allow us to summarise Leijonhufvud's argument as follows: 'Keynes's theory was/is not capable of bearing the weight he clearly assigned to it' (this is an analytic issue to which we will return). But if Leijonhufvud is claiming that Keynes did not give his theory this weight it is almost as if we are not being referred to the *General Theory* at all. The idea that Keynes was thinking in the traditional way (recall Chapter III above) of forces that act permanently and systematically (i.e. those associated with 'natural' tendencies as this concept was traditionally used) is in fact embodied in Keynes's discussion of 'involuntary unemployment' (see Chapter X, Section E below). This begins on p. 5 of the *General Theory*.

argument contained in this passage bears all the hallmarks of the traditional long-period method: the choice of the term 'natural' to describe the tendencies of a market economy and of the term 'persist' to describe their long-period character is the standard fare of the traditional method. The idea that the system oscillates around such a position completes that picture. So even in the long-run Keynes felt that the principle of effective demand would operate so as to determine the normal levels of output and employment. In the long-period, variations in the level of income would continue to ensure the equality between saving and investment. Keynes's 'long-period theory' (in the terminology of Chapter III above) of output and employment was embodied, as far as he was concerned, in the fundamental proposition of the *General Theory*.★

Subsequent critics attempting to counter Keynes's claim to have 'generalized economic theory' with the argument that Keynes's theory applied only to the analysis of deviations† (i.e. it applied to 'particular' not 'general' cases) apparently accept what has already been said above about the way Keynes's himself viewed the significance of the principle of effective demand in a long-period context (cf. e.g. Pigou, 1936, p. 115 and Schumpeter, 1954, p. 624, n.19). |Furthermore, Keynes explicitly offered his theory as an alternative to the idea that the rate of interest is the balancing factor which brings saving and investment into equilibrium|‡ and this idea is no more than an expression of the orthodox, marginalist long-period theory of output and employment. If we are to take Keynes's claim literally and regard effective demand as a serious contender to the place occupied by marginalist theory then it must compete with that theory in its most abstract, 'general' form and this, as we have already shown, is to be found at the level of long-period theory.

This brings us to the next stage in our argument; the implications of Keynes's choice to develop his theory on the basis of the assumption

---

★ As far as I am aware only two full-scale attempts have been made to consider Keynes's theory in this particular way. One was made by Joan Robinson (1947, pp. 75–100) the other by Garegnani (1964–5 and 1978–9).

† Here the 'analysis of deviations' camp subdivides conveniently into two groups: one views it as a positive strength of the theory (e.g. Modigliani, 1944), the other holds that it makes all of Keynes's arguments misleading, if not downright fraudulent (Pigou and Dennis Robertson were subject to irritation in this way).

‡ Cf. e.g. *J.M.K.*, vol. VII, p. 175.

that "the existing quality and quantity of available equipment [is given]" (*J.M.K.*, vol. VII, p. 245). It is necessary to discover whether the views he held about the validity of his theory under long-period normal conditions are consistent with this assumption or whether, as Pigou put it, "we have watched an artist firing arrows at the moon . . . whatever be thought of his marksmanship, we can all admire his virtuosity" (1936, p. 132). We may begin by considering this assumption in relation to the Marshallian short-period with which it is often equated.

The relevant property of a Marshallian short-period, the one that would give rise to the unemployment of labour, is not that the stock of equipment is inadequate in 'quantity' but rather that its physical composition has not yet assumed a 'form' compatible with long-period conditions in the sense that it will yield a uniform return on its supply-price. A process of saving and investment, releasing capital in its 'free form' to be re-invested in a different physical form, is necessary before full employment can be re-established. The 'natural tendency' working to promote this necessary re-adjustment is expressed through variations in the rate of interest. Now, Keynes's assumption is similar to this in one respect in that it does not maintain that the stock of capital is inadequate in quantity to employ the entire labour force. Indeed quite the reverse is true, much of Keynes's argument is conducted in a framework where unemployment and excess capacity exist simultaneously. But the important point is that it is not the composition of this stock of equipment that is 'wrong'.*

According to Keynes's theory of employment the full adjustment of the system to the normal level of output (determined by effective demand) will not involve the re-emergence of the same 'quantity of capital' with a different physical composition but rather will involve the appearance of long-period (or structural) unemployment (cf. *J.M.K.*,

---

* Keynes was quite explicit about this in his definition of 'involuntary unemployment'—the phenomenon his theory set out to explain. Keynes excludes from this fundamental category all those cases of unemployment admitted by orthodox theory in the analysis of deviations (*J.M.K.*, vol. VII, pp. 15–16). In particular, the definition of 'involuntary unemployment' excludes 'frictional unemployment' (p. 16) so that the theory explaining the former cannot depend on conditions which admit the latter. And we have only to turn back a few pages to find that one of the orthodox 'causes' of unemployment thereby excluded from Keynes explanation is the inappropriate 'organization' of production (p. 7; see also p. 279).

vol. VII, p. 204, pp. 217–220 and p. 254). Capacity utilisation will become 'full' in the face of this adjustment (since certain items of equipment inherited from the past will not be reproduced) but unemployment will persist. An interpretation of Keynes's 'given equipment' assumption more in line with his own theory and less likely to lead to errors of interpretation would therefore appear to hinge on the recognition that it was designed not to limit the analysis to a Marshallian short-period but rather to allow the analysis to proceed without the need to consider "the results of far reaching social changes or . . . the slow effects of secular progress" (*J.M.K.*, vol. VII, p. 109) due to changes in technology, accumulation and the like.

The effect of a misinterpretation of this point partly explains the origin of the view that Keynes's *General Theory* was *not* examining the properties of the 'centre of gravitation' of the system but rather that it was examining particular forms of deviations from its natural or long-period normal position. However, there seems to be little doubt that the whole of the innovative core of the *General Theory* is best regarded as dealing with the 'centre of gravitation' of the system. Keynes was after a theory with which to explain what he referred to as *persistent* unemployment. That is, it was towards the systematic forces which tended to determine the level of (un)employment that Keynes turned his attention in the *General Theory*. The use of the 'given capital equipment' assumption does not modify this (see Eatwell and Milgate, 1983, ch. 1).

To the above assessment of Keynes's positive contribution one final point may now be added. It is that the fundamental proposition of the *General Theory*, that decisions to save are adjusted to decisions to invest *via* changes in the level of income (output), is entirely independent of the existence of uncertainty and expectations. This, of course, is not to say that these phenomena are unimportant in the 'real world' or, for that matter, that Keynes's notions of 'risk' and 'probability' formulated much earlier in his *Treatise on Probability* are not significant in themselves. But it does indicate that it is not in these ideas that one finds the basic departure made by the *General Theory* from the prevailing marginalist orthodoxy. Keynes thus himself observed that:

> the theory of effective demand is substantially the same if we assume that . . . expectations are always fulfilled. [. . .] I now feel that if I were writing the [General Theory] again I should begin by setting forth my theory on the assumption that . . . expectations were always fulfilled; and then have a subsequent chapter showing what difference it makes when . . . expectations are disappointed (*J.M.K.*, vol. XIV, p. 181).

In view of the confusions that have been incorporated into the literature of economics in the name of 'uncertainty and expectations' (the confusions will be elaborated in Chapters VIII and IX below), we propose to leave them to one side since they are not essential to an understanding of Keynes's departure from orthodoxy (for a similar opinion see Garegnani, 1976, p. 40, *et seq.*).

C. REMNANTS OF ORTHODOXY

The novelty of Keynes's theory of output and employment based on the principle of effective demand, an essentially long-period theory, contrasts strikingly with two other prominent elements of the *General Theory*; Keynes's explanation of the determination of the level of investment and his theory of the rate of interest. For it is the case with both the marginal efficiency of capital theory of investment and the liquidity-preference theory of interest that they are neither especially new nor at all robust if applied to questions raised by long-period analysis. Indeed, it will be argued that the presence of these remnants of the orthodox position not only raises problems of consistency if we follow Keynes's lead and apply his theory of output and employment to long-period problems, but also provides another part of the explanation for the prevalence of the 'analysis of deviations' interpretation of the *General Theory* and the re-assertion of the orthodox marginalist position on long-period theory that this entails. Furthermore, it will become apparent that the aforementioned inconsistency is reflected by Keynes's failure to be completely convincing in subsequent debates with his critics over the significance of the *General Theory* itself.

But before proceeding any further there is an important characteristic of the structure of the *General Theory* that should be mentioned at the outset. It concerns the relationship between the theory of output (and employment) and the theories of investment and the rate of interest respectively. Unlike the orthodox marginalist position where one set of forces (demand and supply) serves for the study of output, employment, the rate of interest and the level of investment, in the *General Theory* the study of the forces determining output and employment requires that the level of investment and the rate of interest be determined exogenously (cf. e.g. Pasinetti, 1974, p. 47). However, it will be appreciated that in order to preserve this structure it is necessary that once an explanation of the forces governing output and employment has been given, the determinants of the level of investment, say, must not be set out in a form from which follow conclusions that are inconsistent with the conclusions of that other theory. In fact, it is this very problem that underlies the inconsistency between Keynes's theory of output and employment and the particular form he adopted for the theory of investment.

The marginal efficiency of capital schedule is one major strand of orthodox thinking incorporated in the *General Theory*:

> the schedule of the marginal efficiency of capital tells us . . . the output of new investment . . . [at any] given rate of interest (*J.M.K.*, vol. VII, p. 184).

On Keynes's definition, this 'investment demand schedule' (p. 136) is interest-elastic in the sense that the demand for new investment will vary inversely with the rate of interest★ (other things being equal). This, it will be recalled (Chapter IV, Section B), is precisely the way in which marginalist economic theory conceived of the relationship between the rate of interest and the demand for capital *as a flow* (investment). Indeed, Keynes had outlined the essentials of the marginal efficiency of capital in the *Treatise on Money* (*J.M.K.*, vol. V, p. 139), his earlier contribution to that very orthodoxy. But this relationship played a crucial role in the orthodox position. It was the expression of the orthodox explanation of distribution based on the notion of capital as a 'factor of production' employable in decreasing/increasing proportions to other 'factors' as the rate of interest (profit) increased/decreased. As already noted, this explanation provided the premises upon which orthodox marginalist theory based its assertion that there was a long-run tendency towards the full-employment of all 'factors of production' (cf. Garegnani, 1978–9, pt. I, pp. 348–9). To find it in the *General Theory*, where the principle of effective demand when applied to long-period analysis denies this tendency with regard to the employment of labour, raises a paradox with far-reaching consequences.

Even leaving aside for the present the fundamental problem that this relationship between the rate of interest and the demand for investment

---

★ The interest-elasticity of the marginal efficiency of capital is implied by Keynes: "there are forces causing the rate of investment to rise or fall . . . [with] the rate of interest" (*J.M.K.*, vol. VII, p. 165).

encounters once reswitching and reverse capital-deepening are admitted, a difficulty arises (because it is now necessary to supply a reason why the rate of interest will not 'gravitate' to a level that ensures full employment) for which the only solution is to have recourse to some assumption guaranteeing the 'rigidity' or 'inflexibility' of the rate of interest or to assert the inelasticity of the investment demand schedule. Either route would limit the problem of unemployment to short-period conditions. It is for this reason that there is a serious problem of consistency between the weight Keynes so obviously wished to place upon his theory of output and employment (which that theory is quite capable of bearing) and the presence of the marginal efficiency of capital theory of investment in the *General Theory* (see Garegnani, 1978–9, pt. II, pp. 77–79, for a similar argument). Furthermore, its presence provides another rationale (albeit ultimately mistaken) for those interpretations of the *General Theory* already mentioned that seek to deny the validity of Keynes's theory in long-period analysis and to re-assert the orthodox position in their general descriptions of the 'centre of gravity' of the system.

Since, as Keynes tells us, there is no "material difference . . . between my schedule of the marginal efficiency of capital or investment demand-schedule and the demand curve for capital contemplated by . . . [marginalist*] writers" (*J.M.K.*, vol. VII, p. 178) in order to eliminate the possibility of this rate adjusting to that which ensures a full employment level of investment Keynes is forced to take refuge in the 'short-period' by following the first route mentioned above. The rate of interest will be 'fixed' in the money market; "it is the 'price' which equilibrates the desire to hold wealth in the form of cash with the available quantity of cash" (p. 167). It is at this point in the argument that the second remnant of the orthodox position enters the picture— the liquidity-preference theory of the rate of interest.

Many commentators have noted the similarity between Keynes's liquidity-preference theory and the orthodox theory of the market rate of interest (cf. e.g. Marget, 1966, vol. II, p. 467; Johnson, 1951–1952 and Eshag, 1963, pp. 62–68). The idea that the demand for money arose

---

* In fact Keynes uses his term 'classical' in this passage and continues with the words "quoted above". He had just referred to Marshall, Cassel, Carver and Taussig—all marginalists (pp. 175–176).

from transactions and precautionary motives has a long history in
monetary theory (cf. e.g. Marshall, 1923, p. 45 and p. 227–228 and
Lavington, 1921, p. 30) and although the speculative motive was less
explicitly developed in this context, the *General Theory* can hardly be
said to be innovatory on this count. In so far as the essence of the
speculative motive involves connecting the demand for money with the
demand for securities it is certainly to be found in an undeveloped form
in Marshall's *Money, Credit and Commerce* in the following passage:

> everyone balances . . . the benefits, which he would get by enlarging his
> stock of currency in the hand, against those which he would get by
> investing some of it either in a commodity . . . or in some stock exchange
> security, which would yield him a money income (Marshall, 1923, pp.
> 38–39).★

Moreover, Keynes himself had discussed this motive in detail (without
naming it) when considering the effects of 'bull' and 'bear' behaviour on
the stock market in the *Treatise on Money* (*J.M.K.*, vol. V, pp.
256–257; Keynes concedes the similarity, vol. VII, p. 173).

It is true that the speculative motive takes over in the *General Theory*
in the sense that Keynes maintains that the demand for money may be
split-up and expressed by the equation, $M = M_1 + M_2 = L_1(Y) + L_2(r)$
(*J.M.K.*, vol. VII, p. 199), where M_2 corresponds to the speculative
demand for money and M_1 corresponds to the precautionary and
transactions demands taken together. In conjunction with the supply of
money (cf. *J.M.K.*, vol. VII, p. 205), the rate of interest is thus
determined by the function $M_2(r)$, "[and] what matters is not the
absolute level of r but the degree of its divergence from what is
considered a fairly safe level of r" (*J.M.K.*, vol. VII, p. 201). It is worth
emphasising that although $M2(r)$ can be regarded as a stable and
well-behaved function without too much difficulty, this position carries
with it a weakness that was noticed early-on by Hicks:

> to say that the rate of interest . . . is determined by nothing else but
> uncertainty of future interest rates is to leave interest hanging by its own
> boot-straps (Hicks, 1946, p. 164).

If the rate of interest is determined by reference to views about its

---

★ Further references to the literature may be found in Eshag (1963, p. 19, nn. 72–77).
The reader might also refer to Marshall's discussion of the 'bull' and 'bear' positions on
the Stock Exchange (1923, pp. 258–259).

'safe' or what might better be called its 'normal' level, then the application of liquidity-preference in long-period analysis is highly questionable, for liquidity-preference does not explain just what needs to be explained there—that 'normal' rate itself. Indeed, by running in short-period terms the presence of liquidity-preference theory has provided some writers with a basis for re-asserting the orthodox position on the forces ultimately determining the 'normal' rate of interest. Dennis Robertson is a good example:

> [according to Keynes] the rate of interest is what it is because it is expected to become other than it is; if it is not expected to become other than it is, there is nothing left to tell us why it is what it is. The organ which secretes it has been amputated, and yet it somehow still exists—a grin without a cat. . . . If we ask what ultimately governs the judgements of wealth-owners as to why the rate of interest should be different in the future from what it is today, we are surely led straight back to the fundamental phenomena of Productivity and Thrift (Robertson, 1966, pp. 174–175; see also, 1952, p. 114 and 1963, p. 308).

Nor do those writers who expressly set out to defend Keynes against this sort of interpretation provide any clear and consistent solution. Joan Robinson, for example, seems to argue that the question about what determines the 'normal' rate is simply irrelevant (Robinson, 1951–79, vol. III, pp. 134–135) while Harrod, who argued (exactly as John Robinson did):

> are not the critics going a little far? Did Keynes . . . say that liquidity-preference was the sole . . . reason why there ever had been or ever could be interest? Or did he not rather merely say that liquidity-preference was the sole determinant of the level of the interest rate? (Harrod, 1948, p. 67),

concluded in a very 'Robertsonian' fashion that Keynes's theory of the 'market rate' (Harrod, 1948, p. 70) did not compel us to "pay no regard whatever to . . . productivity and thrift" (p. 67) as the 'origin' of the rate of interest.*

---

* Another interpretation was offered by Kaldor (1939) who held that the 'bootstraps' problem could be eliminated by arguing, unlike Keynes, that the long-rate was determined by expectations about the future course of the short-rate. But Kaldor's account does not appear to provide a basis for an adequate general theory of the rate of interest where the ultimate 'governing forces', and hence causality, runs from long-period to short-period theory. Indeed, Kaldor's position is the reverse of what is needed (see the criticisms by Robertson, 1952, p. 114 and in a slightly different context, those by Kahn, 1954).

However, it would be a mistake to conclude from this that liquidity-preference theory cannot be combined with an explanation of the 'normal' level of the rate of interest, suitable for a long-period analysis of interest, without re-asserting the orthodox marginalist position on this subject. In fact, just such an alternative would appear to be entailed in remarks made by Keynes himself: "the rate of interest is a highly conventional, rather than highly psychological, phenomenon . . . [and] the level established by convention . . . [may be influenced by] a modest measure of persistence and consistency of purpose by the monetary authority" (*J.M.K.*, vol. VII, pp. 203–204). The potential significance of developing such an approach has been noted by Garegnani (1978–1979, pt. II, p. 73 n.2 and pp. 80–81; and *idem*, 1979, pp. 185–186); it will be returned to in Section E of this chapter.

D.   KEYNES AND MARGINALIST ECONOMIC THEORY

The arguments advanced in Sections A and B of this chapter make it apparent that Keynes's theory of output and employment represents a coherent alternative to the orthodox marginalist explanation of distribution that was conducted in terms of the demand for and supply of 'factors of production'. In particular, Keynes's explanation of the process through which decisions to save are adjusted to decisions to invest (and thus his characterisation of the persistent forces determining the levels of output and employment) contrasts sharply with the older marginalist idea that this process should be considered in terms of variations in the rate of interest and therefore, ultimately, in terms of the notion of capital as a 'factor of production' employable in decreasing or increasing proportions to other 'factors' as the rate of interest (profit) rises or falls.

The significance of Keynes's application of the principle of effective demand to the determination of the normal levels of output and employment is further highlighted by noting that Keynes thereby separates himself from the orthodox marginalist theory of distribution on its two main fronts; the theory of capital and the theory of employment. There is no place in Keynes's theory for the notion of the simultaneous determination of 'factor prices' (the real wage-rate and the rate of profit) and levels of utilisation (full employment and full capacity) by the forces of demand and supply; the very notion that lay at the heart of the dominant theory of value and distribution faced by Keynes in the mid-1930s. It is only necessary to recall the whole range of ideas that were shown in Chapter IV to be associated with orthodox marginalist theory (foremost of which were 'Say's Law' and the Quantity Theory of Money) to appreciate that these, too, play no part in Keynes's analysis.

An interpretation of Keynes that begins by recognising these facts (as well as leaving to one side the orthodox theory of investment adopted by Keynes in the form of the marginal efficiency of capital schedule for the reasons that were explained in the previous section of this chapter), leads to radically different conclusions as to the significance of Keynes's contribution than those which have surfaced in mainstream circles since the publication of the *General Theory*. In the first place, from such a foundation it would not be possible to claim that the *General Theory* presented an 'analysis of deviations' that was similar in form, though different in detail,* to those of Wicksell and the other writers whose work was examined in Chapter V above (where the orthodox marginalist theory as applied to long-period questions remains unchallenged). The fundamental inadequacy of this sort of interpretation is that it fails to recognise that the long-period theory of output and employment developed in the *General Theory* is not compatible with the orthodox marginalist position on long-period questions.

In the second place, because an interpretation running along the lines suggested in this study would view Keynes's departure from orthodoxy as arising *at the level of theory* (i.e. in opposition to the long-period marginalist theory of distribution), there would then be no grounds upon which to support the currently popular interpretation of Keynes that is couched in terms of the method of 'intertemporal equilibrium'. A consideration of the basis for this change in method and of the difficulties it encounters when confronted with the present interpretation of Keynes will be deferred to Chapters VIII and IX below.

---

* Of course, some writers who interpret the *General Theory* in this way find these 'details' highly interesting (witness Leijonhufvud's deviation amplifying 'income constrained' process), while others find them pedestrian (inflexible money wages, for example).

E.   KEYNES AND CLASSICAL ECONOMIC THEORY

When Keynes turns his attention to the old Classical economists, he directs his arguments towards two targets; 'Say's Law' (*J.M.K.*, vol. VII, p. 18, p. 32 and pp. 368–369) and the theory of interest (pp. 190–192). In view of what has already been said about Keynes's inappropriate interpretation of 'Say's Law' in Classical economic theory (see Chapter IV, Section C above) it does not seem necessary to dwell any longer on this aspect of Keynes's attempts to separate himself not only from the orthodox marginalist position but also from Ricardo and the other Classical writers. However, Keynes's attack on Ricardo's idea that "the rate of interest [is] ultimately and permanently governed by the rate of profit" (Ricardo, 1951–1973, vol. I, p. 297) is more significant and must, therefore, be examined in some detail.

In order to underline his differences with Ricardo on this point, Keynes chooses to contrast his position with the following passage from Ricardo's *Principles*:

> the interest for money . . . is not regulated by the rate at which the Bank will lend . . . but by the rate of profits which can be made by the employment of capital (Ricardo, 1951–1973, vol. I, p. 363).*

Keynes disputes this, arguing not only that the short-term rate of interest is a purely monetary phenomenon (determined by liquidity-preference) but also that the average long-period rate of interest, being a 'highly conventional phenomenon', is subject to influence by the action of the monetary authority so that even in long-period analysis:

> to every banking policy there corresponds . . . a number of positions of long-period equilibrium corresponding to different conceivable interest policies on the part of the monetary authority (*J.M.K.*, vol. VII, p. 191).

At first sight, this altered connection between the rate of interest and the normal rate of profit in long-period analysis appears to constitute a significant barrier to the incorporation of this aspect of Keynes's theoretical apparatus into the corpus of Classical economic theory.†

---

* Keynes slightly misquotes this passage (though without damaging Ricardo's meaning) on p. 190 of the *General Theory* (*J.M.K.*, vol. VII).

† Garegnani has suggested that there might be few problems with such an integration (1978–1979, pt. II, p. 81 and 1979, pp. 185–186). Joan Robinson, on the other hand, thinks that Garegnani's "suggestion that [the normal rate of profit on capital] . . . could be determined by monetary policy . . . [is] excessively fanciful" (Robinson, 1979, p. 180).

However, while it would be incorrect to think that the issues raised by this altered causal connection are not complicated, it is possible to show how some of these difficulties can be overcome and to show, thereby, that the incompatibility suggested by Keynes is more apparent than real.*

To begin with, consider the basis upon which Ricardo grounded his opinion:

> To suppose that any increased issues of the Bank can have the effect of permanently lowering the rate of interest, and satisfying the demands of all borrowers, so that there will be none to apply for new loans . . . is to attribute a power to the circulating medium which it can never possess. By creating paper money, and lending it three or two per cent. under the present market rate of interest, the Bank would reduce profits on trade in the same proportion . . . . To what absurdities would not such a theory lead us! Profits can only be lowered by a competition of capitals not consisting of circulating medium. As the increase of Bank-notes does not add to this species of capital . . . it cannot add to our profits nor lower interest (Ricardo, 1951–1973, vol. III, p. 92).

This, of course, is the 'early' Ricardo from his essay on the *High Price of Bullion* (1810), but the essentials of all his subsequent arguments are contained in this passage (differences of detail will be noted as we proceed). On the one hand, there is the idea that an increase in the quantity of money has no permanent effect on the rate of interest because this rate is ultimately (i.e. in long-period analysis) regulated by the rate of profit on capital.† On the other hand, there is the proposition that the rate of profit is determined by the 'competition of capitals'.‡ From this proposition derives the corollary that only those 'permanent

---

* Garegnani's idea (p. 98, n.† above) therefore appears to be quite sound.

† Ricardo maintains this idea in the *Principles*: "the rate of interest, though ultimately and permanently governed by the rate of profit, is however subject to temporary variations from other causes . . . [such as] fluctuation[s] in the quantity of money" (Ricardo, 1951–1973, vol. I, p. 297; see also p. 300 and p. 363). It is worth noting that this is a long-period doctrine. Some of Ricardo's less able followers who took up the 'currency principle' position in the debates over the Bank Act of 1844 seem to have applied it in a confusing and contradictory sense to short-period questions (see Marx's penetrating criticisms of these advocates in *Capital*, 1968, vol. III, p. 417 *et seq.*).

‡ Ricardo here adopts Adam Smith's argument (see Chapter IV, note *, p. 49 above). By the time of the *Essay on Profits*, and subsequently of the *Principles*, this idea had been replaced with the more correct idea that 'profits depend on high or low wages' (cf. e.g. Ricardo, 1951–1973, vol. I, p. 110; recall the discussion of Ricardo's own, subsequent, criticism of Smith's view in Chapter IV, Section C above).

causes' that lower the rate of profit can lead to a *permanent* lowering of the rate of interest (since the latter depends on the former).

If Adam Smith's doctrine that the rate of profit is determined by the 'competition of capitals' is replaced by the more formally correct theory of distribution presented by Ricardo in the *Principles*, it is easy to see the basis for these propositions. Once the wage is regarded as being determined at subsistence level and hence given, the rate of profit is determined together with natural prices so that 'profits depend on high or low wages'. (The importance of this last proposition about income distribution is not so much to be found in the direction of causality it envisages, but rather in the unique inverse relation between the wage and the rate of profit thereby expressed. A fact which is to be seen at its clearest in the corn-economy model.) If the rate of profit is determined in this way, there is no room for any permanent influence of the average long-period rate of interest on the rate of profit. Ricardo's propositions follow as a corollary of his explanation of distribution in terms of a given wage.

However, in view of the separability between the Classical theory of value and the explanation of distribution there is no necessary reason for retaining Ricardo's particular explanation of the determination of the wage-rate. Indeed, as Sraffa has since noted, once wages are allowed to share in the surplus the rate of profit may be treated as the independent variable (Sraffa, 1960, p. 33). There is then no objection in principle to Keynes's idea that the rate of profit is determined under the permanent influence of the monetary authorities and the effect of their policies on the long-period rate of interest (provided only that the unique relation between the wage and the general rate of profit is not violated; on this point, see Garegnani, 1978–1979, pt. II, p. 77, n.2).

Of course, it is at this very point that Sraffa's remark in *Production of Commodities* about the possibility that the determination of the rate of profit might be found in the money rate of interest (1960, p. 33), which is usually regarded as being a casual or even meaningless one (cf. e.g. Dobb, 1973, pp. 370–371 and Nuti, 1970, pp. 226–227), coincides exactly with this approach. Moreover, it is clear that the basic structure of the Classical theory would not be altered by the incorporation of such a mechanism. It goes without saying, of course, that even if the rate of profit is determined in this way, the surplus character of it (which is basic to Classical Economics) remains intact.

Finally, although it may be said that the early Classical Economists had not discovered the principle of effective demand (indeed, they had no real theory of output at all), it is nevertheless the case that there is no full-employment condition associated with their economic theory. Thus the possibility of persistent deficiencies of effective demand (that is, investment and savings being equalised at low levels of income), is capable of being inserted directly into the Classical theoretical apparatus. In short, this theoretical compatibility arises because Keynes's principle of effective demand provides the theory of output and employment that is missing from the work of the old Classical writers. And this is possible because long-period unemployment which is the essence of Keynes's theory is not pre-empted by the explanation of value and distribution offered by the Classical Economists* as it is in long-period marginalist theory (see also Garegnani, 1978–1979).

---

* It may be noted that Pasinetti has highlighted the compatibility between Keynes and the Classical economists: "the characteristic consequence of this . . . is the emergence in Keynes, as in Ricardo, of a system of equations of the 'causal type', or, as we may say, the 'decomposable type', as opposed to a completely independent system of simultaneous equations" (Pasinetti, 1974, p. 44). This argument would seem to accord with what has been said in this study, since Pasinetti would not appear to be referring simply to a mathematical distinction but rather to the same fundamental distinction between Classical economics, where the study of value is separated from the study of distribution and the study of output, and marginalist economics, where such a separation does not exist.

VII. THE THEORY OF CAPITAL AND THE THEORY OF EMPLOYMENT: THE NEGATIVE PART OF THE *GENERAL THEORY*

"Much of the modern controversy about capital is just the old controversy in a new guise. If the modern controversy is to be settled, its relation to the old is one of the things that will have to be understood" (Hicks, 1973b, p. 190).

Many modern reconstructions of Keynes's ideas take the form of the incorporation, in one way or another, of uncertainty into neo-classical general equilibrium models (accompanied by a variety of consequential behavioural hypotheses). These developments derive their credibility as 'Keynesian' analyses from conventional interpretations of the *General Theory* which assign a dual role to Keynes's emphasis on expectations and uncertainty. On the one hand Keynes's positive contribution is seen to consist of the formulation of a theory of the operation of a market economy in the face of uncertainty. On the other hand his *critique* of the various dimensions of what he called 'classical' theory is seen to consist of an attack on its alleged neglect of the influence of expectations and uncertainty. It follows, as a corollary of this second point, that if 'classical' theory were to be reconstructed by incorporating the effects of expectations and uncertainty then the reconstruction would represent (in some sense) an adequate, more general, 'classical' theory, which circumvents Keynes's criticisms.

Now, it has already been argued that the full significance of Keynes's positive contribution can be appreciated without appealing to the disappointment of expectations; a factor which deprives many contemporary reconstructions of part of their rationale. The purpose of this chapter is to consider the other aspect of these reconstructions: to consider, that is, whether Keynes's *critique* of the 'classical' theory must be reconstructed from the single premise that the orthodox theory was guilty of neglecting the implications of uncertainty. This view finds justification in the ambiguity of the critique of the 'classical' theory of interest launched in Book Four of the *General Theory*. It is there that Keynes includes the liquidity-preference theory of the rate of interest (based upon individuals' anticipations of an uncertain future) as part of the attack on the orthodox doctrine. However, it will be argued here that, at least in so far as liquidity-preference is concerned, Keynes did not himself regard that theory as an indispensable part of his criticism of the 'classical' theory of interest. What is more, there are places in which Keynes's remarks suggest a concern with problems of the orthodox theory of capital and interest that arise even in the absence of uncertainty. These considerations are all the more important given that the liquidity-preference theory on its own is unable to provide the internal critique of the 'classical' theory for which Keynes was searching.

While it has been argued that the principle of effective demand may be regarded as an alternative long-period theory of output and employment to that provided by the orthodox marginalist explanation of distribution and value, this positive alternative cannot itself be used as the basis for a critique of the internal logic of the orthodox position. The simplest way to grasp the distinction between the 'positive' and 'negative' aspects that characterise this particular case is to consider the competing theories themselves. The orthodox marginalist position holds that planned investment is adjusted to saving through variations in the rate of interest (profit). Keynes, on the other hand, maintains that saving is adjusted to planned investment through variations in the level of income. Now, in a critique of the orthodox position it is necessary to show *why* the postulated variation in the rate of interest (profit) *does not* have a tendency to produce the effects ascribed to it, given the premises from which these tendencies are deduced. But it is clear that Keynes's alternative theory does not address this question; it simply asserts that something else happens. It is for this reason that Keynes's positive theory does not constitute the basis for a critique of the internal logic of the orthodox position. Of course, the distinction between 'positive' and 'negative' aspects is not meant to be a rigid one; it is just a short-hand way of capturing this characteristic of Keynes's contribution.

A. THE INFLEXIBILITY OF MONEY-WAGES

Nowhere are the "habitual modes of thought and expression" that Keynes urged readers of the *General Theory* to abandon (*J.M.K.*, vol. VII, p. viii) more apparent than in opinions about the relation between money-wages and unemployment. It seems still to be widely believed that while there is, or might be, a *tendency* for *laissez-faire* capitalism to produce full employment, this mechanism fails to operate because it is *obstructed* by the presence of money-wage rigidity. Indeed, it is often argued that such an idea plays a central role in Keynes's own arguments in the *General Theory*.[*] Commencing with Hicks's second review of the *General Theory* in *Econometrica* for April 1937, this view has surfaced regularly in literature on Keynesian economics (see, for example, Modigliani, 1944, pp. 87–88, and Haberler, 1958, p. 242). There are, however, two problems with this view. First, no assumption of money-wage rigidity (or downward inflexibility) was used by Keynes in the *General Theory*, either as part of his own theory of output and employment or as part of his attack on the theoretical foundations of the orthodox position. Secondly, such notions are in any case perfectly compatible with orthodox marginalist theory, in the sense that the presence of certain frictions or rigidities does not overturn the general validity of that theory.

The error in attributing to Keynes an assumption about money-wage rigidity is easily revealed; for at no point in the whole of the *General Theory* does Keynes himself allow the validity of his theory of output and employment (based on the principle of effective demand) to turn upon any such assumption. In fact, Keynes stressed this point in the opening paragraphs of a preliminary summary of his basic contribution:

> In this summary we shall assume that the money wage . . . [is] constant.
> But this simplification, with which we shall dispense later, is introduced

---

[*] It should not be forgotten that this particular idea is just one species of a much larger genus of interpretations of Keynes's contribution that view it as holding that while orthodox marginalist theory states the *long-run* tendencies *correctly*, in the short-run certain frictions or rigidities (many are cited) prevent these underlying forces from fully asserting themselves (see, for example, Schumpeter, 1954, p. 624; Leijonhufvud, 1969, p. 22, n.1; Patinkin, 1976, pp. 114–115). In this framework, the notion that the economic system may become 'stuck', so to speak, in a *short period* position is all that Keynes's contribution amounts to.

solely to facilitate the exposition. *The essential character of the argument is precisely the same whether or not money wages . . . are liable to change* (*J.M.K.*, vol. VII, p. 27, italics added).

In Chapter 19 of the *General Theory* (and its appendix) Keynes went on to explore the implications for his own argument when this 'simplification' is relaxed (lamenting the disadvantage of having to postpone the discussion for so long; *J.M.K.*, vol. VII, p. 257). This argument, of course, renders visible the fact that an inflexibility of money-wages is not a necessary hypothesis in Keynes's theory which establishes the possibility of persistent unemployment solely through the principle of effective demand. The argument also leads up to Keynes's attack on the orthodox neo-classical position on money-wage flexibility. This attack merits careful consideration.

Keynes begins by considering, in terms of his own theory, the effects of a reduction in money-wages upon the level of employment, *ceteris paribus* (the 'other things' being kept 'equal' are the marginal propensity to consume, the marginal efficiency of capital schedule, and the rate of interest). In this framework, Keynes is able to conclude that a reduction in money-wages does not lead to an increase in employment (vol. VII, pp. 260–261). The *cet. par.* conditions are then relaxed one-at-a-time in true Marshallian style; and Keynes examines whether a decrease in money-wages might increase employment either by, (i) increasing the marginal propensity to consume, or (ii) increasing the marginal efficiency of capital,* or (iii) causing the rate of interest to fall. As far as the effects on the marginal propensity to consume are concerned, Keynes concludes that the redistribution of income entailed by a reduction in money-wages is likely to have a net effect that "is adverse [rather] than favourable" (p. 262) on the level of employ-

---

* Keynes conducts this analysis under the assumption of a closed economy. (For the effects of a reduction in money-wages in an open economy, see *J.M.K.*, vol. VII, pp. 262–263.) Of course, as a means of highlighting his differences with the traditional neo-classical position, such an assumption is not objectionable, for as Keynes correctly observed very early on in the *General Theory*, the conclusions of that theory "are supposed to be equally applicable to a closed as to an open system, and *are not dependent* on the characteristics of an open system or on the effects of a reduction of money-wages in a single country on its foreign trade, which lie, of course, entirely outside the field of this discussion" (vol. VII, p. 11, italics added).

ment.* Likewise, the effect on the marginal efficiency of capital is likely to be "unfavourable . . . [unless] money-wages are believed to have touched bottom, so that further changes are expected to be in the upward direction" (p. 265). From this Keynes is led to conclude that:

> It is . . . on the effect of a falling wage . . . on [the rate of interest] that those who believe in the self-adjusting quality of the economic system must rest the weight of their argument (p. 266).

Keynes had reached exactly the same conclusion in the appendix to Chapter 19, where he attempted to dissect Pigou's version of orthodox theory:

> [Pigou] assume[s] that the rate of interest always adjusts itself . . . in such a way as to preserve full employment. Without this assumption, Pigou's analysis breaks down (p. 275).†

From the content of this analysis by Keynes, two important points emerge. The first is that an inflexibility or rigidity in money-wages does not form the basis of Keynes's attack on orthodox theory. The second is that these arguments indicate that Keynes's critique of the orthodox position must be sought in precisely that area where the principle of effective demand departs so fundamentally from it—the traditional idea that planned savings and planned investment are brought into equilib-

---

* Whether Keynes did or did not ignore the so-called 'Pigou effect' in his discussion about the effects of a decline in money-wages on the marginal propensity to consume is not especially important. For, even if it exists, the 'Pigou-effect' does not re-establish a full-employment equilibrium between saving and investment in the traditional marginalist way (by variations in the rate of interest). Rather, as money-wages fall, the net value of real money balances thereby increasing, the 'Pigou-effect' operates by so *decreasing* the propensity to save of wealth-holders as to increase income and establish a new equilibrium between saving and investment in a very Keynesian way (cf. Haberler, 1958, pp. 169–170).

† Since this idea (that planned savings and planned investment are brought into equilibrium by changes in the rate of interest) was at the heart of the traditional neo-classical theory of employment, it is easy to understand why Keynes was nonplussed by Pigou's article in the *Economic Journal* for September 1937 (Pigou, 1937) which not only denied that savings were a function of income (*J.M.K.*, vol. VII, p. 264), but also overlooked the fact that even according to the traditional theory the effect of a reduction in money-wages on employment acts through the relationship between the rate of interest and planned investment (saving). (See Keynes's letters to Kahn (29 December, 1937) and Pigou (3 January, 1938), as reprinted in *J.M.K.*, vol. XIV, pp. 266 and 267, which record his astonishment; he suggests, in fact, that Pigou should (re-)read Chapter 19 (and appendix) of the *General Theory*.)

rium by variations in the rate of interest (on this point, see the discussion in Milgate (1977 and 1983b)).

Readers of the *General Theory* will be aware that in the very early parts of that book Keynes had stated that one of the reasons (he deemed it to be "theoretically fundamental", *J.M.K.*, vol. VII, p. 8) why a reduction in money-wages might not have the orthodox effect of increasing employment was that such a reduction (even an all round one) did not necessarily imply a reduction in *real* wages (pp. 8–9, 11 and 13). However, even though Keynes apparently accepted the traditional idea of an inverse relation between the amount of labour forthcoming and the real wage (but see *J.M.K.*, vol. XIV, pp. 34–45, for a qualification), it would be an error of interpretation to conclude from this that Keynes's theory of employment stands or falls on an assumption about real wage rigidity (cf. Sweezy, 1946, pp. 115–116). For Keynes considers a case where the real wage does vary, and yet does not reach the orthodox conclusion that this would promote a return to full employment. The source of his opposition to traditional theory has therefore to be traced to the grounds upon which he rejects this idea. In the case Keynes examines, the flexibility of real wages arises in the face of reductions in money-wages and prices, the quantity of money being held constant (*J.M.K.*, vol. VII, pp. 266–267). As Keynes correctly observes, for this situation to bring about full employment, marginalist theory requires that the rate of interest should fall so as to call forth an increased amount of investment until, once again it is equal to full employment savings (see, for example, Pigou, 1944, p. 16). It is this latter aspect of the argument to which Keynes objects, claiming instead that

> the same reasons . . . which limit the efficacy of increases in the quantity of money as a means of increasing investment . . . apply mutatis mutandis to wage reductions. Just as a moderate increase in the quantity of money may exert an inadequate influence over the long-term rate of interest, whilst an immoderate increase may offset its other advantages by its disturbing effect on confidence; so a moderate reduction in money wages may prove inadequate, whilst an immoderate reduction might shatter confidence even if it were practicable (*J.M.K.*, vol. VII, pp. 266–267).

Thus we are led, again, back to the point at which Keynes asserted his opposition to traditional neo-'classical' theory in Chapter 14 of the *General Theory*—the theory of interest.

The above considerations are sufficient to dispel any notion that a postulate of money-wage rigidity or inflexibility characterises Keynes's theory. It remains therefore, to show why a postulate of money-wage rigidity does not, in any case, amount to a theoretical challenge to the orthodox position. Fortunately on this point we can be brief, for Hicks had shown this as far back as 1937. His remarks are worth quoting again:

> [the downward inflexibility of money wages] is not a matter on which there can be any theoretical *contradiction*; it is the kind of change in the exposition of a theory which we ought to be making, all the time, in response to changing facts (Hicks, 1937, p. 147, italics in original).*

Indeed, Keynes knew this only too well, and saw this position as that which he had to refute:†

> "Classical Theory . . . rest[s] the supposedly self-adjusting character of the economic system on an assumed fluidity of money-wages; *and, when there is rigidity . . . lay[s] on this rigidity the blame for maladjustment*" (*J.M.K.*, vol. VII, p. 257, italics added).

It would have been quite extraordinary if Keynes had based his own theory on the very proposition that he intended to criticise. Thus, the notion of inflexible money-wages, far from being something peculiarly Keynesian, is firmly neo-'classical'.

Writers who espouse the 'money-wage rigidity' interpretation of the *General Theory* are following in the footsteps of a long line of orthodox misinterpretations of Keynes, and are unfortunately led to confine the significance of Keynes's contribution to a consideration of that class of short-run circumstances where certain frictions or rigidities prevent, in the first instance, the systematic forces outlined by the traditional neo-classical theory from producing a result that they ultimately have a

---

* It is interesting to note that in a later paper Hicks (1967) was to abandon the money-wage rigidity interpretation in favour of a rigidity in the rate of interest.

† At one point, Keynes argued: "the classical school [agree that] . . . the demand for labour at the existing money wage may be satisfied before everyone willing to work at this wage is employed, but this situation is due to an open or tacit agreement amongst workers not to work for less . . . such unemployment . . . [is] due to the effects of collective bargaining etc." (*J.M.K.*, vol. VII, pp. 7–8). Note the equivalence between what Keynes sees here as being the traditional marginalist theory of unemployment, and what the money-wage rigidity school believe to be 'Keynesian'. In another case: "a classical economist may sympathise with labour in refusing to accept a cut in its money-wage . . . scientific integrity forces him to declare that this refusal is, nevertheless, at the bottom of the trouble" (p. 16; see also *J.M.K.*, vol. XIV, pp. 26 and 43). On this point see also Milgate and Eatwell (1983).

tendency to produce—full employment. Such interpretations render the *General Theory* and the pre-Keynesian orthodoxy perfectly complementary—they stand in relation to each other in the same way as a 'special' case (Keynes) stands in relation to the 'general' case (neo-'classical' theory). In fact, the only thing that this modified version of the orthodox position has in common with Keynes is that it has been used to support measures to increase employment *via* an expansion of aggregate effective demand. But from a theoretical point of view, even this policy conclusion has little to recommend it—for as long as the belief persists that the rate of interest is free to vary, and/or that the level of investment responds in the opposite direction to such changes (so that the imbalance between planned savings and planned investment, which is a characteristic of the kind of neo-'classical' unemployment being discussed here, can be removed), then an equally feasible short-run policy for an economy where money-wages were inflexible downwards would be an increase in the available quantity of money engineered by the monetary authorities (as was suggested, years ago, by Modigliani, 1944, p. 225; see also, Hicks, 1937, p. 130).

Modern monetarists would, of course, reject *both* approaches (some might even argue that the former, in so far as the level of activity was expanded through an increase in central government net indebtedness to the banking system, amounts to the same thing as the latter—but see Friedman, 1980, for the necessary qualifications). However, it is crucial to realise that the grounds for such a rejection are *not* that money and real forces cannot interact in the way described by the 'imperfectionists' *in the short-run*, but rather that the only *permanent* effects of such temporary palliatives will be either an increase in the general level of prices or an encroachment by the government on the 'supply-side' of the economy (*either* because the monetary authority's financing activities raise the rate of interest above that level which is consistent with optimal holdings of capital assets and full employment—a level which, according to marginalist theory, an unimpeded capital market would *tend* to produce; *or* by preventing a proportion of full employment savings from being channeled into private investment). Since the 'imperfectionists' share the *same* theoretical framework, the most they can do to oppose this position is muster *practical* objections. Whatever form these objections may take (and recall that money-wage rigidity is not in this case a sufficient objection), they *do not* extend to the *theoretical* foundations of the monetarist position (see, for example,

Tobin, 1980; Solow, 1980; Modigliani, 1977 for the wide variety of such practical objections one might advance—note also that Barker, 1980, p. 321, n.†, is thus mistaken in regarding these as "cogent theoretical critiques").

This conclusion can be put in a slightly different way. One often hears modern authors speaking in terms of 'automatic forces' that 'tend' to return the economy to full employment implying, as in all modified versions of orthodox theory, that such forces actually characterise, in the final analysis, the basic workings of a market economy.* Of course, it is well known that in orthodox neo-classical theory these 'automatic forces' are supposed to be those of demand and supply. Now, if Keynes's contribution is to be viewed as providing a theoretical system different in character and content from marginalist theory, it can be viewed neither as arguing that these traditional 'automatic forces' (demand-and-supply), although present, are weakly felt, nor as denying altogether the presence of any 'automatic forces' at all. Instead, it must be that whatever automatic forces are present, *they are not those outlined by traditional theory*. Thus the free-play of the market mechanism (though subject to innumerable disturbances and cross-currents), far from *tending* to produce full employment, may well *tend* to produce unemployment. This is exactly what Keynes himself claimed to have shown:

> [the system] oscillate[s] . . . round an intermediate position appreciably below full employment . . . this mean position [is] determined by "natural" tendencies, namely by those tendencies which are likely to persist (*J.M.K.*, vol. VII, p. 254).

This is why Keynes insisted that "the weight of my criticism is directed against the *theoretical* foundations" (vol. VII, p. 339, italics in original) of the traditional neo-'classical' position (see also *J.M.K.*, vol. VII, p. 175; vol. XIV, p. 110 and p. 212, for the target of that criticism). It was certainly *not* Keynes's contention in the *General Theory* that persistent

---

* Having once accepted this idea, the rationale for employment policies based upon the manipulation of effective demand loses its force when one moves beyond strictly *short-period* problems. Some money-wage rigidity 'Keynesians' almost stumble upon this fact: for example, "Keynesian . . . models [envisage] . . . a central role for stabilization or demand management to maintain full employment, certainly in the short-run, and possibly in the long-run as well" (Barker, 1980, p. 322).

unemployment was to be explained by a rigidity or downward inflexibility of money-wages. On the contrary, this idea was seen by Keynes as being part and parcel of the orthodox neo-classical doctrine to which he was so radically opposed. On this analytical point, Keynes was perfectly correct.

The orthodox character of the argument that seeks to explain unemployment through money-wage rigidity is well illustrated by the case of Marshall. In the *Principles* Marshall had discussed many kinds of frictions and rigidities that could temporarily prevent the system from settling down at full employment; and one of these was exactly the money-wage rigidity case that is incorrectly ascribed to Keynes. According to Marshall, whenever trade unions refuse to accept a diminution of money-wages, then "the more such a policy is persisted in . . . the less is the aggregate employment . . . throughout the country" (Marshall, 1920, pp. 709–710). It goes without saying of course, that Marshall realised that such 'temporary irregularities' could extend over considerable periods of calender time without damaging in the slightest way the theoretical foundations of the argument from which the traditional doctrine that there exists a natural tendency towards the full employment of labour was derived (see, for example, Marshall and Marshall, 1879, p. 131).

B.   KEYNES ON THE 'CLASSICAL' THEORY OF INTEREST: I

Unfortunately, Keynes's position with respect to the criticism of the 'classical' theory of interest has been progressively obscured by conventional interpretations. There is, for example, a large group of writers who agree that the fourteenth chapter of the *General Theory* ('The classical theory of the rate of interest') (*J.M.K.*, vol. VII) is the platform upon which to build an interpretation of Keynes's criticisms of the 'classics', and that Keynes's critique should be sought in the theory of liquidity-preference. This places liquidity-preference theory squarely in the *negative* or *critical* part of the *General Theory* (as distinguished from the positive or constructive part).★ Against this

---

★ This separation was maintained by Keynes and will be amplified in Section C below.

view, however, may be set Keynes's subsequent arguments in his 'Alternative theories of the rate of interest' (*J.M.K.*, vol. XIV), which clearly assign the theory of liquidity-preference to the *positive* part alone. There, Keynes poses once more the question which originally led him to liquidity-preference theory:

> *If* the rate of interest is not determined by saving and investment in the same way in which price is determined by supply and demand, *how* is it determined? (*J.M.K.*, vol. XIV, p. 212, italics added).

He goes on to state that it was in the course of providing the 'how' that he 'hit on . . . the true explanation'—the theory of liquidity-preference. This constructive task is quite distinct from the critical task of substantiating the conjectural 'if'.

Contemporary confusion is due in part to the fact that, in Chapter 14, liquidity-preference theory is mixed in with the anti-'classical' arguments. But with the recent publication of the variorum drafts of the *General Theory* and the related Keynes–Harrod correspondence (*J.M.K.*, vol. XIII and vol. XIV), it is possible to view this chapter and its contents in a new perspective. This evidence suggests an interpretation that has a much closer affinity with Keynes's subsequent statements and casts doubt upon conventional interpretations of Keynes's attack.

The interpretations which fall into this latter class encompass a wide variety of models. Included are all those that might be called the 'special case' interpretations of the *General Theory*, which begin by assigning to liquidity-preference theory the role of critique of the 'classical' theory of interest (as, for example, in Hicks's claim that 'it is the liquidity-preference doctrine which is vital', Hicks, 1937, p. 133) and end by concluding that this criticism does not make much impact on the 'classical' theory of interest, either because it only makes a difference 'to a number of short-cut conclusions' (Harrod, 1937, p. 238), or because the question of which the *n* equations is dropped from the determination of general equilibrium prices (the demand-and-supply for 'loans' or the demand-and-supply for money) is 'purely a question of convenience' (Hicks, 1936, p. 246). Included too is a very different variety of interpretation, which derives from Hicks's review of the *General Theory* (Hicks, 1936). This interpretation is based on what Hicks calls the 'method of expectations'; here the negative part of the *General Theory* is held to consist of the argument that 'classical' theory had ignored the fact that the forces of demand-and-supply might be kept at bay by uncertainty and expectations.* Liquidity-preference theory, in which anticipations are vital, is thus associated with the critique.

The one significant group of writers who may be excluded from these classes of interpretations are Keynes's immediate followers in Cambridge, who seem never to have inserted liquidity-preference theory into the negative or critical part of their subsequent descriptions and developments of the *General Theory* (see Joan Robinson, 1951–79, vol. II, p. 148, and 1973, p. xii, p. xiv and Chapter 8 *passim*; Kahn, 1954; Pasinetti, 1974, p. 48).

With the aid of the evidence provided in the thirteenth and fourteenth volumes of Keynes's *Collected Writings*, it is argued below that there is a clear implication that the theory of liquidity-preference plays a rather different part in the *General Theory* than that which has been assigned to it. To substantiate this claim, the evidence will be presented in the following way. In the following section the draft version of Chapter 14 is examined to show both how it was intended to fit into the scheme of the *General Theory* and what criticisms of the 'classical' theory of interest were then offered. Then Harrod's reaction to the draft is considered. Harrod's reaction will be shown to have been a decisive factor in moulding the final version of the chapter when attention is focussed on the published version, in order to highlight what might be called its 'hybrid' nature.

C. KEYNES ON THE 'CLASSICAL' THEORY OF INTEREST: II

The successive tables of contents which Keynes began to propose for the *General Theory* in 1933† indicate that his vision was of a book that

---

* The 'remedy', according to Professor Hicks, is to being 'people's anticipations of the future' into the determination of a temporary equilibrium (Hicks, 1936, p. 240). But Professor Hicks expressed doubts on the theoretical viability of this approach (Hicks, 1936, p. 241). Moreover, there are other, broader, reasons why this interpretation of Keynes should be treated with caution (see Garegnani (1976) and Chapter VIII below for a further discussion).

† The first surviving table of contents dates from December 1933 (see *J.M.K.*, editorial comment, vol. XIII, p. 421).

would be divided into two *mutually exclusive* parts. There was to be a positive part, consisting of the work on the relationship between saving and investment, the principle of effective demand and the multiplier analysis. And there was to be a negative part which would be concerned with the flaws in 'classical' theory.* Into this schema, which crystallised in the draft of the *General Theory* that Keynes circulated privately in June 1935, liquidity-preference theory fitted unambiguously into the *positive* part and Chapter 14, numbered as Chapter 15 in the draft (see *J.M.K.*, vol. XIII, p. 526), fitted unambiguously into the *negative* part.† This separation is clear from the stylised way in which Keynes chose to structure his argument in the relevant chapters of the draft version. (In referring to the draft we shall adopt the convention of citing its chapters according to their number in the final text, attaching in square brackets their number in the table of contents of the privately circulated version.)

Chapter 13 [14], under the title 'The general theory of the rate of interest', opens as follows:

> To complete our theory . . . we need to know what determines the rate of interest. In Chapter 14 [15] and its Appendix [16] we shall consider the answers to this question which have been given hitherto . . . What, then, is our own answer to this question? (*J.M.K.*, vol. VII, pp. 165–166).‡

This programme embodies the separation between the positive and negative parts. Already, therefore, one encounters a discrepancy between, on the one hand, the place of liquidity-preference theory in the proposed plan of this part of the *General Theory*, and, on the other, its place as portrayed in the type of interpretation mentioned earlier. Indeed in the draft version of the 'critical' Chapter 14 [15], liquidity-preference theory is not mentioned at all.

Although Keynes claimed in both draft and final text to have found it

---

* In the correspondence on the drafts Keynes uses this characterisation of his work explicitly. He writes, for instance, of his 'criticism of the classical theory of the rate of interest *as distinguished from* my own theory' (*J.M.K.*, vol. XIII, p. 538, italics added), and elsewhere that 'I am still of the opinion that if my constructive sections are correct, my critical sections are more than justified' (*J.M.K.*, vol. XIII, pp. 547–548).

† This would seem to be further supported by Keynes's references to himself as 'the critic' in the draft of the chapter (see, for example, *J.M.K.*, vol. XIV, p. 477).

‡ This part of the passage remained unchanged from draft to final text (cf. *J.M.K.*, vol. XIV, pp. 470–471).

difficult to reconstruct the 'classical' theory of interest (see *J.M.K.*, vol. VII, p. 175), it seems fairly clear that he saw it as a theory which embraced the following postulates. First, that the real rate of profit regulates the money rate of interest. Second, that variations in the rate of interest ensure the equilibrium of the demand and supply for capital (investment and savings). For Chapter 14 [15] Keynes reserved the task (the negative task) of demonstrating why 'the notion that the rate of interest is the balancing factor which brings the demand for saving in the shape of new investment forthcoming at that rate of interest into equality with the supply of saving . . . makes no sense' (*J.M.K.*, vol. XIV, p. 471).*

Some useful additional clues about the intended target of Keynes's attack are provided by the passage from Marshall's *Principles* which Keynes chose to represent the 'classical' argument.

> Interest, being the price paid for the use of capital in any market, tends towards an equilibrium level such that the aggregate demand for capital in that market, at that rate of interest, is equal to the aggregate stock forthcoming at that rate (Marshall, 1961, p. 534; quoted in *J.M.K.*, vol. VII, pp. 175–176).

This is a statement about long-period 'normal' interest. Indeed, Marshall indicates as much in the marginal summary which accompanies the passage (Marshall, 1961, p. 534).† The demands and supplies are for 'saving in general' or 'capital in its free form' or 'real capital' (Marshall, 1961, p. 533) and are expressed as quantities forthcoming

---

* This is at the beginning of Chapter 13 [14], where Keynes sets out his ground-plan for what is to follow. The same words appear in a slightly altered paragraph in the final text (*J.M.K.*, vol. VII, p. 165). Keynes reiterates that this is, in fact, the proposition he intends to consider in Chapter 14 [15] at the opening of that chapter, when he attempts to spell out what 'classical' theory had maintained (cf. *J.M.K.*, vol. VII, p. 175). The final text differs little from the draft here (the changes are listed in *J.M.K.*, vol. XIV, p. 474).

† 'The rate of interest is determined *in the long run* by the two sets of forces of supply and demand respectively' (italics added). It is perhaps worth noting here that this was the theory of long-period interest (i.e. of the 'natural rate') to which Keynes had subscribed in the *Treatise* (see, for example, *J.M.K.*, vol. V, pp. 139, 142, 166, and 170–171). Furthermore, although Keynes does not state explicitly that Chapter 14 [15] of the *General Theory* was an intended critique of his *Treatise* views, his reference to the theory 'upon which we have all been brought up' (*J.M.K.*, vol. VII, p. 175) lead one naturally back to the *Treatise* (see below, Chapter XI, Section B).

per unit of time.* Although there is a moment in the draft of Chapter 14 [15] when Keynes begins to tackle a rather different idea (that interest proper is a monetary phenomenon, not a real phenomenon),† in the main his criticisms are directed against the foregoing aspects of the 'classical' theory of interest.

In the draft chapter there are three main lines of attack (though, as will become apparent, the first two may be conveniently reduced to one). The first, which appears only in the draft, is expressed as follows:

> The analogy with the demand and supply for a commodity at a given price is a false analogy. For whereas it is perfectly easy to name a price at which the supply and the demand for a commodity would be unequal, it is impossible to name a rate of interest at which the amount of saving and the amount of investment could be unequal (*J.M.K.*, vol. XIV, p. 476).

The second, which appears in both draft and final text, is that:

> The traditional analysis is faulty because it has failed to isolate correctly the independent variables of the system. Saving and investment are the determinates of the system, not the determinants (*J.M.K.*, vol. VII, p. 183).

These criticisms derived from a common position. They both stem from the belief that if the *positive* parts of the *General Theory* are valid (in this case the principle of effective demand) the other theories must, therefore, be invalid.‡

The third line of attack is of a rather different nature, in that it is levelled against the internal logic of the 'classical' position. As far as the marginal productivity theory of interest was concerned, Keynes argued that

> an attempt to derive the rate of interest from the marginal efficiency [productivity§] of capital involves a logical error (*J.M.K.*, vol. XIV, p. 477),¶

---

* Thus the 'classical' association between the 'demand-and-supply of capital' and 'investment and saving' (see Knight, 1915, pp. 301–302 and Eshag, 1963, p. 47).
† Keynes relegates this argument to the appendix in the final text (*J.M.K.*, vol. VII, p. 186, n.1).
‡ Recall Keynes's own statement of this point in the letter to Harrod quoted above (n.*, p. 114).
§ Keynes insisted upon this association (cf. *J.M.K.*, vol. VII, p. 137).
¶ A differently worded statement of the same point appears in the final text (*J.M.K.*, vol. VII, p. 184).

and this error arises because

> the 'marginal efficiency [productivity] of capital' partly depends on the scale of current investment, and we must already know the rate of interest before we can calculate what this scale will be ($\mathcal{J}.M.K.$, vol. VII, p. 184).*

Although this argument touches on the treatment of capital in 'classical' theory, the degree to which Keynes meant to emphasise the problems associated with this treatment is difficult to judge.† He does, however, extend his critique to the demand-and-supply approach of Marshall and of Walras, and once again the treatment of capital is called into question. Three uncharacteristically long footnotes attached to the discussion at this point in the draft concern (either wholly or partly) questions in the theory of capital (cf. $\mathcal{J}.M.K.$, VII, p. 176, nn. 2 and 3; vol. XIV, pp. 474-475). But Keynes never really specifies *why* the internal consistency of the 'classical' position turns on its treatment of capital—instead, after suggesting this possibility, he switches to other lines of attack ($\mathcal{J}.M.K.$, vol. XIV, pp. 474-475).

Two points emerge from the criticisms contained in the draft of Chapter 14 [15]. The first is that *liquidity-preference theory is nowhere mentioned in the draft of the chapter* and the second is that *the only criticisms directed at the internal logic of the 'classical' theory show a concern for issues which would today be identified with problems in the theory of*

---

* The passage appears in the draft and the final text.

† At one point in Chapter 11 [12] Keynes does focus directly on these problems. He speaks there of the ambiguity as to 'whether we are concerned with . . . one more *physical* unit of capital, or with . . . one more value unit of capital' ($\mathcal{J}.M.K.$, vol. VII, p. 138, italics added). Keynes argues that the problem of the *physical* measure involves difficulties which are both 'insoluble and unnecessary'. The reasons for its insolubility are presumably the same as those which preclude the possibility of measuring aggregate output in physical terms, which Keynes had set out in Chapter 4 ($\mathcal{J}.M.K.$, vol. VII, p. 38).

However, the reason which Keynes advances for the dependence of the *value* measure on the rate of interest misses the point of the problem of orthodox capital theory. Keynes argues that the problem is that the 'classics' had ignored the increment of value 'expected to obtain *over the whole life* of the additional capital asset; i.e. the distinction between Q_1 and the complete series $Q_1, Q_2 \ldots Q_r$' ($\mathcal{J}.M.K.$, vol. VII, p. 138). They had instead concentrated their attention only on Q_1. 'Yet this cannot be legitimate except in a static theory, for which all the Q's are equal. The ordinary theory of distribution . . . is only valid in a stationary state' ($\mathcal{J}.M.K.$, vol. VII, p. 139). But it is clear that this has nothing to do with the problems of traditional capital theory—for these apply (with the exception of one-commodity worlds) even to those versions of traditional theory built within a framework of static assumptions.

capital. The significance of these two points for any attempt to reconstruct Keynes's critique of the 'classical' theory of interest will become evident in the following section after the extent of Harrod's influence on this part of the *General Theory* has been examined.

The Keynes–Harrod correspondence on the draft version of this chapter (*J.M.K.*, vol. XIII, pp. 526–565) indicates that Harrod was highly critical of its content. His criticisms fall broadly into two categories. At one level Harrod questions Keynes's tactics in his rôle as critic of the 'classical' theory of interest, and on another level he challenges Keynes's anti-'classical' arguments on points of substance.

In his biography of Keynes Harrod remarks that he had objected to the chapter as it stood in draft, because he felt that it was 'pushing criticism too far', that it would 'make too much dust' and hence give rise to 'irrelevant controversies' (Harrod, 1972b, p. 534). But it is only now, with the publication of both sides of this correspondence, that it is possible to see the full extent of the impact of Harrod's argument. On the tactical level, Harrod's disquiet over Keynes's attack on the 'classical' position is manifest again and again.

He wrote, for instance, that 'in your [Keynes's] critical part I think you have fallen into what I can only characterize as a confusion . . . I feel it has made you quite unnecessarily critical of Marshall and others' (*J.M.K.*, vol. XIII, p. 530). And later, in another letter, that 'the effectiveness of your work . . . is diminished if you try to eradicate very deep-rooted habits of thought *unnecessarily*. One of these is the supply and demand analysis' (*J.M.K.*, vol. XIII, p. 533, italics in original). In another letter Harrod refers to Keynes's criticism of the 'classics' on this point as 'guerilla skirmishing' (*J.M.K.*, vol. XIII, p. 534), and in still another Harrod claims that such criticism 'is not essential for your purpose' (*J.M.K.*, vol. XIII, p. 546).*

All manner of argument was used to try to dissuade Keynes from engaging in what Harrod saw as 'fussy, irrelevant, dubious, hair-splitting and hair-raising' (*J.M.K.*, vol. XIII, p. 556) criticism of the 'classical' theory of interest. One variety of argument re-appeared frequently; it was that if Keynes desired to have his positive part

---

* See also the letter from Harrod, 6 August 1935 (*J.M.K.*, vol. XIII, p. 537), where the same point is made.

accepted he would do well not to make his critical part too harsh. For example, Harrod argued as follows:

> Suppose your reasons in the constructive and critical parts were equally good, you would have a far greater chance of carrying conviction in the former because your adversaries had not had years of thought in which to prepare an answer (*J.M.K.*, vol. XIII, p. 536).

Harrod also argued that Keynes was doing a serious injustice to the younger generation in attacking the demand-and-supply theory of the rate of interest—'doing great violence to their fundamental groundwork of thought' (*J.M.K.*, vol. XIII, p. 533). Yet another argument was that Keynes would not be able to substantiate his arguments against, for instance, Marshall, 'on the basis of short passages torn from their context' (*J.M.K.*, vol. XIII, p. 546).

By these polemics Keynes remained profoundly unimpressed,* but on the points of substance made by Harrod he tried to come to some accommodation.† There were, in the final analysis, only two substantive points. They were directed against the first and third lines of attack which had been adopted by Keynes in the draft of Chapter 14 [15]. Against the first line of attack Harrod argued:

> This doctrine [demand-and-supply] makes perfectly good sense, but is open to the charge of being incorrect. I find no sense in saying that this doctrine makes no sense *because* in this case supply is always and necessarily equal to demand (*J.M.K.*, vol. XIII, p. 530, italics in original).‡

And further, that

> the notion that price is determined by supply and demand always rests on a *cet. par.* assumption . . . What you seem to me to have shown is that there are changes in other things which are so relevant and of such overpowering importance, that the old s. and d. analysis had better be put away (*J.M.K.*, vol. XIII, p. 531).

---

* Keynes replied to Harrod that his purpose in writing the *General Theory* was 'not in order to get read . . . [but] in order to get understood' (*J.M.K.*, vol. XIII, p. 548) and that what was at stake in their dispute was a 'big question of substance, not of manners or controversial fairness' (*J.M.K.*, vol. XIII, p. 547).

† This was no doubt due to the clarity of Harrod's précis of the positive structure of the *General Theory* (*J.M.K.*, vol. XIII, p. 553; see also Keynes's reply, p. 557).

‡ To this Harrod adds a tactical point: 'in order to give you pause for thought, I should like to add that this was the most criticised part of your address in Oxford . . . Frankly it convinced no one' (*J.M.K.*, vol. XIII, p. 531).

Harrod's argument here is clear; the existence of competing theories is not sufficient to demonstrate that one of the alternatives is logically unsound.

On Keynes's suggestion of a lack of internal consistency in the 'classical' theory itself, Harrod mixed tactical arguments with his substantive point. He wrote:

> to convict the classical economists of confusion or circularity within the limitations of their own premises . . . is not essential for your purpose. And if not essential I should have thought it had much better be left out. . . . Such a criticism is bound to seem unfair and I believe it is unfair (*J.M.K.*, vol. XIII, p. 546, italics omitted).

In retrospect, this belief is revealed to be unfounded. Keynes had attempted to portray the internal problems of the 'classical' theory of interest as part of the more general problem of orthodox capital theory, and, remarkably, recent work in this field has revealed these problems to be of a far more serious and fundamental character than Keynes (or Harrod) then realised.

Nevertheless, Harrod was led to conclude that it was both possible and desirable to provide a 'reconciliation' of the two theories (cf. Harrod, 1972b, p. 534).

> I feel that the only way I could possibly be of any assistance is not in the elaboration of your own view, but in endeavouring to restrain you in your criticisms (*J.M.K.*, vol. XIII, p. 536). *

In this role, judging from the change in emphasis Chapter 14 [15] underwent before it reached the printer, Harrod seems to have succeeded only in clouding the issues.

Almost 60% of the published text of Chapter 14 had not appeared in the draft version. The added section runs from p. 177, line 32, to p. 183, line 28, in the final text of the *General Theory*.

Harrod's letter of 30 August 1935 contains the following attempted reconciliation of the 'classical' theory of interest with Keynes's theory:

> generally when you draw a supply curve $x = f(y)$, it is assumed that you are treating x as a function of a single variable, price, and other things including income were equal. That is the classical supply curve. To relate the classical supply curve to yours, you would have to draw a family of

---

* The same idea is echoed in Harrod (1972b), p. 534.

classical supply curves corresponding to different levels of income and to show that the value of each corresponding to a given rate of interest was identical with that of the demand curve ($\mathcal{J}.M.K.$, vol. XIII, p. 555).

To this passage of the letter Harrod appends the following note:

> Let y_1, y_2 etc. be rates of interest and Y_1, Y_2, etc. incomes corresponding to them (Y_1 being derived from y_1 via marginal efficiency cap. and the multiplier). For each value of Y draw classical supply curves, of which each curve shows the amount of saving corresponding to various values of y at a given level of Y. Then according to you it will be found that the value of y at which the curve appropriate to income Y_r intersects the demand curve is in fact y_r, where Y_r represents any given rate of interest whatever ($\mathcal{J}.M.K.$, vol. XIII, pp. 556–557, italics omitted).

This construct was adopted by Keynes (as a 'very useful . . . help to exposition') in his reply to Harrod of 10 September 1935 ($\mathcal{J}.M.K.$, vol. XIII, p. 557), and it appears on p. 180 of Chapter 14 of the final text of the *General Theory*, where it forms the basis of the six pages of argument that Keynes added during revision.

Not surprisingly, a rather new and different thread is thereby woven into the anti-'classical' arguments of the draft. It is this thread which is in large measure the source of the confusion described in Section B above.

Gone completely is Keynes's criticism based on the first line of attack which was set out above.* More significantly, the criticisms concerning the internal logic of the 'classical' position are considerably watered-down. In particular, those which touched on 'capital theory' are much reduced (cf. $\mathcal{J}.M.K.$, vol. XIV, pp. 476–478 for the changes). Moreover, the adoption of Harrod's reconciliation makes way for the belief that if the level of income were given then the 'classical' theory of interest would be sound. But more important still is the fact that liquidity-preference theory is now mentioned explicitly in the negative or critical part of the *General Theory* ($\mathcal{J}.M.K.$, vol. VII, pp. 180 and 181).

The combined effect of these changes opened the door for the variety of interpretations summarised in Section B above. But it has been shown that these interpretations are at odds with the draft of this part of

---

* The previously cited statement of the first line of attack is replaced by Keynes's version of Harrod's reconciliation.

the *General Theory*. They imply that Keynes introduced liquidity-preference theory to show, in some sense, where the traditional theory had gone wrong, whereas, on the contrary, Keynes introduced it to explain the rate of interest. Why the 'classical' theory was false was, for Keynes, an entirely separate question.

D.   RECONSTRUCTING A CRITIQUE

Upon which version, then, should attempts to reconstruct Keynes's critique of the 'classical' theory of interest be based? The evidence seems weighted against an unqualified acceptance of the final text of Chapter 14 for the following reasons.

Firstly, although revision wrought important changes in the final content of Chapter 14, it was accompanied by no parallel alteration in the ground-plan which Keynes had set out in the preceding chapter, which assigned liquidity-preference theory to the positive rather than the negative part of the work. All the passages cited in Section C which established this fact appear in the final text. Furthermore, there is no evidence that Keynes had changed his mind about them.

Secondly, even after the publication of the *General Theory*, Keynes again emphasised that liquidity-preference theory was designed as an alternative theory of the rate of interest and that it therefore fell into the positive part of his work. Moreover, a lack of zealous attachment to this theory (see *J.M.K.*, vol. XIV, pp. 111, 213, 215) indicates that it was not Keynes's conviction that if liquidity-preference theory was wrong, then the 'classical' theory would be right.

Finally, it does not seem that Keynes deflated his one line of attack directed towards the internal logic of the 'classical' theory because he thought it to be unfair, but rather, as Harrod put it, because it was bound to seem unfair.

It may be concluded that, although Keynes was clearly convinced of the necessity of complementing his positive contribution with a logical critique of the 'classical' theory, and that he believed that the logical flaws were to be found in the 'classical' theory of capital and interest, the limited scope of his undeveloped criticisms led him to accommodate Harrod's reconciliation so that he might not 'seem unfair'. However, recent debates in the theory of capital have shown Keynes's initial intuition to be well founded. The deficiencies of the marginalist theory of employment are synonymous with the logical deficiencies of the marginalist theory of capital. These problems are quite different from the difficulties encountered when attempting to deal with expectations and uncertainty. Indeed, these forces can be incorporated within the orthodox framework, though not without some difficulty and circumlocution.

In adopting Harrod's reconciliation Keynes sacrificed his negative argument on the altar of the immediate success of the positive theory. This has had the unfortunate consequence of lending support to interpretations of the *General Theory* which distort both the positive and negative parts of Keynes's contribution to the theory of interest.

E.   CAPITAL AND EMPLOYMENT

It is worth noting at this point that the above discussion only serves to highlight a certain ambiguity which was present in Keynes's own position on the whole of the question of the orthodox marginalist theory of the equilibrium of saving and investment (i.e. of its theory of capital and interest). For, on the one hand, Keynes was clearly aware of the need to provide a critique of that theory with which he could complement his own positive contribution (this was, in fact, the stated aim of Chapter 14), but on the other hand, he was at times prepared to rest his case on the positive theory alone. This can only be explained if one is prepared to accept that the pressing practical problem of the relief of mass unemployment made it imperative for him to get the positive theory across, and that, in addition, Keynes did not at that time possess the weaponry with which to dismantle the internal logic of the neo-classical position. For this, we have to be prepared to go beyond the *General Theory* in order to develop any reconstruction of the critique. But in taking such a step care must be taken not to do violence to the hints Keynes gives us.

The theoretical departure of the *General Theory* seems, therefore, to have been to provide a correct theory of employment while, at the same time, implying that the orthodox theory of capital and interest needed re-assessing. A clearer hint about the connections between the orthodox theories of capital and employment could not be given.

If it is accepted that the point of departure of Keynes's *General Theory* from the prevailing orthodoxy is to be found at the level of *theory* and not at the level of *method*, then it is essential to enquire into the manner in which the *General Theory* achieved this theoretical departure. Almost at once, however, an apparent paradox arises. It arises because it would seem that this theoretical departure should be sought in the theory of capital, whereas it is more usual to seek it in the theory of employment. Nevertheless, this paradox vanishes when it is realised that the marginalist theory of capital is *one and the same thing* as its theory of employment. In discovering the correct theory of employment Keynes *contradicts* what the later controversies in the theory of capital *negate*. There is, therefore, a confluence of these two otherwise apparently separate streams of criticism of neo-'classical' theory. It is here, of course, that there is a strong 'potential' compatibility between Keynes's theory and the theory of the old Classical Economists. This arises because the foremost characteristic of Classical Economic theory is that it allows for the provision of separable theories of value and output. It is in this light that it can be said that one of the major theoretical implications of the *General Theory* is that the unification of all questions in economic theory under the umbrella of 'demand-and supply' (based on individual utility maximising and profit maximising behaviour) is seriously to be questioned.

VIII. THE METHOD OF 'INTERTEMPORAL EQUILIBRIUM'

After more than two decades during which the formal model derived from the *General Theory* remained substantially unchanged, a number of research workers have recently undertaken a reconsideration that . . . should now lead us to a better understanding of the unemployment phenomenon. (Malinvaud, 1977, p. vii).

If one accepts what has been said in the previous two chapters about the positive theoretical content and the critical thrust of the *General Theory*, then the contemporary reconsideration of Keynes's contribution along the lines suggested by Malinvaud in the above passage has not been that which might have been expected. Indeed, rather than concentrating on the theoretical implications of the principle of effective demand, which has already been shown to involve a *theoretical* departure from the orthodox marginalist explanation of value and distribution rather than an assault upon the traditional long-period *method*, the reaction to Keynes that dominates the mainstream of contemporary economic analysis is confined to the elaboration of the very same demand-and-supply theory with a change in one important respect. In place of the traditional long-period method, modern economics has substituted the method of 'intertemporal equilibrium'—this being the development to which Malinvaud refers.

A. THE TREND IN MODERN 'KEYNESIAN' ECONOMICS

The really interesting question now to be asked is, of course, why theoretical economics in the period (down to the present day) after the

General Theory has taken this path. On one level, part of the answer is to be found in the elevation of the concepts of uncertainty and expectations to the centre of the stage in the Keynesian system.* This prompted the focus of demand-and-supply theory upon the maximising behaviour of individual consumers and producers to be shifted from what Hicks called the 'static' case to the 'dynamic' case—and by the 'static' case Hicks meant the traditional long-period method, by the 'dynamic' case, he meant the method of intertemporal equilibrium (see e.g. Hicks, 1946, p. 115, *et seq.*).

However, since the question of uncertainty and expectations will form the subject matter of the next chapter, it would not seem useful to dwell upon it at any length here; save to say that the interpretation of its role in economic theory as being incompatible with any conceptual framework other than intertemporal equilibrium, enforces (among other things) an interpretation of the history of economics that would stress the absence of any potentially viable treatment of uncertainty in the entire pre-Keynesian period, as well as implying that the traditional method contains some flaw which precludes it from discussing uncertainty and expectations. It remains to be seen whether such a position bears closer scrutiny. More will be said on this subject in the next chapter. Another part of the explanation for the path that interpretations of the *General Theory* have taken is connected with the difficulties encountered by the orthodox marginalist theory of capital, the number and seriousness of which took a dramatic upswing in the 1960s. The remainder of this chapter will consider the method of intertemporal equilibrium, in an attempt to come to some conclusions about the emergence of this notion.

---

* "Uncertainty was the new strand placed gleamingly in the skein of economic ideas in the 1930's", writes Shackle (Shackle, 1967, p. 6). Furthermore, Garegnani has commented that "after Keynes, this alluring picture of a tidy interplay between demand and supply in the labour- and capital-markets would . . . be qualified as applying 'in the absence of risk and uncertainty'" (Garegnani, 1970a, p. 272), and elsewhere he has spoken of demand-and-supply being 'kept at bay' by 'uncertainty and expectations' (Garegnani, 1976, p. 42).

B.   THE METHOD OF 'INTERTEMPORAL EQUILIBRIUM'

A striking feature of contemporary economic theory is the widespread use of the notion of intertemporal equilibrium. This notion consists of analysing *short-period* positions of a market economy *in sequence over time*;* a procedure which is customarily regarded as being a 'formalisation' of the notion of equilibrium adopted by Walras (see, for example, Grandmont, 1977, p. 535). Many would also claim that it is nascent in the work of Böhm-Bawerk and Wicksell. In the modern literature on general equilibrium theory, though historical sketches are not especially common, the names of Malinvaud, Arrow and Debreu are associated with completing the task of formalisation—a task which had been begun by the leading writers of the Swedish School, and in England by Hicks (see Koopmans, 1957, p. 114, Dixit, 1977, p. 2 and Grandmont, 1977, p. 536). But in the entire period over which this 'formalisation' was undertaken, no fundamental changes in the notion of equilibrium are generally believed to have taken place.

In the present chapter it will be argued that this characterisation of the development and role of the notion of intertemporal equilibrium is mistaken. Significant *original* developments in fact took place in the 1920s and 1930s (not before), and that to the three names commonly mentioned from this period in this regard (Lindahl, Myrdal and Hicks) must be added the name of Hayek. His role in the origin of the notion of intertemporal equilibrium seems not to have been widely appreciated. Furthermore, it will be shown that the chief impetus towards the formulation of this new notion of equilibrium resided in a growing

---

* It is worth noting that the idea of 're-interpreting the commodity space', so that commodities are defined according to the time and place at which they become available, mirrors the sequential nature of modern equilibrium theory. For, since this re-definition is carried out on the basis of the data (about commodities, capital stock etc.), characterising the short-period position taken as the starting point (a choice which is quite arbitrary), the operation involves 'telescoping' the initial position into the future in the same manner in which a sequence of points is, given the rule defining the sequence, a projection of its first element.

The sequential character of this notion of equilibrium is the same whether or not one models to incorporate uncertainty. Thus, temporary equilibrium theory (however modified) is just one species of this larger genus. Hahn (1973, p. 16) has characterised this distinction in terms of 'essential' and 'non-essential' sequence economies.

realisation among these writers, simultaneously though not entirely independently, that if the demand-and-supply approach to the theory of capital and interest was to be retained, something would have to be done to free it from the bounds imposed by its need to deal in terms of a 'quantity' of capital. Finally, it will be argued that it is not possible to claim that this change has anything to do with what Keynes actually said in the *General Theory*.

As was shown in Chapter III above, the dominant characteristic in economic theory from Adam Smith down to Marshall—one which sets it apart from this notion of intertemporal equilibrium—was that all of the writers of this period assigned themselves the task of explaining the working of a market economy under circumstances which were variously referred to as natural, or long-period normal, conditions (see, Dobb, 1937, ch.2, Meek, 1965, p. 10 and Garegnani, 1976). These conditions were associated with a stock of capital which had been so 'adjusted' as to yield a *uniform* rate of return on its supply-price. It is therefore the *object* of these investigations which constitutes the element that links what are otherwise very different theoretical approaches to determining natural or normal prices and distinguishes them from the framework of intertemporal equilibrium. Because of this strong continuity relating to the object or the conceptual framework of theoretical economics during the nineteenth and early twentieth century, the shift to the notion of intertemporal equilibrium cannot be regarded, historically speaking, as a 'slightly new twist' in economic theory (cf. Dixit, 1977, p. 2).

Contrary to this argument, it has been suggested in the literature that the 'time-preference' approach to the theory of capital and interest, associated in particular with Irving Fisher, is a precursor of the notion of intertemporal equilibrium. However, the structure of Fisher's theory prevents it from ever coming fully and independently to this notion. For with intertemporal equilibrium it is the *formation* of prices within each period, and between periods, which determines the commodity-own-rates of interest, whereas in Fisher's approach a stationary price vector is arbitrarily fixed so that a unique internal rate of return follows. In short, it is because this approach lacks a theory of value that it was prevented from arriving at the notion of intertemporal equilibrium. Fisher did observe that as prices changed from period to period there would be as many own-rates of interest as there were commodities (Fisher, 1930, p. 42), but this much he had said before the turn of the century in his small tract *Appreciation and Interest* (p. 91), and he had still not seen the way to 'convert' it into intertemporal equilibrium by the time he came to produce *The Theory of Interest* in 1930. The same can be said of F. W. Fetter (1904, Chapter 17 and 1927, p. 75), who also saw that prices of the same good will be different in different periods. Like Fisher, he does not arrive at the notion of intertemporal equilibrium.

It is perhaps also worth mentioning at this point the questionable nature of a link that has sometimes been suggested between the analytic framework of intertemporal equilibrium and the work of Böhm-Bawerk and, more particularly, Wicksell. Such conjectures are generally based on a claim that both attempt to 'deal with time in an essential way'. But even leaving aside the fact that the object of these earlier writers differed markedly from that of the intertemporal equilibrium approach, it can readily be shown that 'time' enters each system in a different way and for different reasons.

If, as was the case with Wicksell and Böhm-Bawerk, the object of the analysis is to determine the general rate of profit in terms of demand and supply, it is necessary to have a market for 'capital' upon which quantity and price may be expressed independently. This gives rise to the familiar problem concerning the definition of the 'quantity' of capital as soon as the system consists of more than one commodity (recall Chapter IV, Section B above). It was in his attempt to resolve this problem that Wicksell, following Böhm-Bawerk, introduced 'time'. 'Time', in the form of the length of the period of production, was the measure of the 'quantity' of capital. It is with the express purpose of *avoiding* the need for such a measure that 'time' is introduced in the intertemporal equilibrium approach. These two treatments could not be more dissimilar.

C. THE ORIGIN OF THE NOTION OF 'INTERTEMPORAL EQUILIBRIUM'

Confronted with these facts, most Anglo-Saxon economists would probably agree that it was Hicks's *Value and Capital* which heralded the introduction of the notion of intertemporal equilibrium. Part III of that book opened as follows:

> I call Economic Statics those parts of economy theory where we do not trouble about dating; Economic Dynamics those parts where every quantity must be dated (Hicks, 1946, p. 115).

Hicks developed the same theme and argued:

> By using the 'week', we become able to treat a process of change as consisting of a *series of temporary equilibria*; this enables us to use equilibrium analysis in the dynamic field (1946, p. 127, italics added).

Finally, when Hicks turned to the theory of capital and interest, he arrived at the essential object of the intertemporal equilibrium approach:

> "We cannot . . . determine *the* rate of interest excepting in a system where there is only *one* rate of interest; in any other case we have to deal with a whole system of interest rates" (1946, p. 154, italics in original).

This much is clear and, in fact, well-known.

Less well-known (or, at least, less well publicised) is the fact that around this time Hicks was not the only one calling for economic analysis which ran along these new lines. In 1941 another expression of the notion of intertemporal equilibrium appeared that was every bit as clear as that contained in *Value and Capital*. The vehicle was Hayek's *Pure Theory of Capital*.* There, Hayek claimed that "there is a very significant sense . . . in which the concept of equilibrium can be of great use . . . [this is] . . . if it is made to include plans for action varying at *successive moments of time*" (Hayek, 1941, p. 22, italics added). He also argued that "this extension of the equilibrium concept provides the bridge from equilibrium analysis to explanation in terms of causal *sequences*" (1941, p. 23, italics added). Hayek referred to this notion as 'intertemporal equilibrium' (p. 22). There is no conceptual difference between it and the notion which characterises value theory today.

Hayek was also aware of the fundamental object of the intertemporal equilibrium approach. The following passage, embodying the shift in object and conceptual framework mentioned in Section B above, appeared in a footnote in the *Pure Theory of Capital*:

> "Much confusion has been caused . . . by the assumption sometimes made that . . . there would be some determinate *in natura* rate of interest.

---

* The 'intertemporal equilibrium' aspect in Hayek's work is briefly commented upon by Machlup (1977, p. 29). Hicks also, as will be shown later, often draws attention to this aspect of Hayek's work. One will not, however, find any mention of his name in the variety of 'historical sketches' cited in Section A of this chapter.

In fact there would not and could not be *one* rate of interest" (p. 35, n.1, italics added).*

In view of the fact that Hayek's part in the origin of this notion of equilibrium seems not to have received much attention, there may be a temptation to view its introduction in the *Pure Theory of Capital* either as a case of simultaneous discovery or, perhaps, as a restatement of a position that Hayek had taken from others. Such views are unfounded. In the first place, it is improbable that the discovery could have been made independently because Hicks and Hayek were in close contact for more than a decade at the L.S.E.† Secondly, Hicks has since claimed to be able to date his own 'personal revolution' as beginning with Hayek (Hicks, 1963, p. 307).

The year 1932 provides a useful point of reference for resolving these issues, as it saw both Hicks and Hayek produce relevant material. Hicks published his *Theory of Wages* while Hayek (1932) was in debate with Sraffa (1932a, b) over *Prices and Production* (1931). A comparison of these publications reveals that in the case of Hayek the notion of intertemporal equilibrium already appears to be present, whereas in the case of Hicks it is completely absent.

In the *Theory of Wages* Hicks merely re-expressed the traditional marginal productivity theory of distribution which attempted to determine a uniform rate of profit on the supply-price of capital. This was entirely within the traditional long-period framework. As Hicks himself observed, in this version of the theory of distribution "we are

---

* The same point is made later when he writes: "in so far as rates of interest . . . are concerned, there is . . . no reason why they should be the same in a non-stationary economic system" (p. 397). It should be added at this stage that the quality of the theoretical exercises differs markedly between the two books. But then *Value and Capital* was all about these exercises, Hayek's book, on the other hand, was concerned with "laying the foundations for the treatment of these problems [of capital], not to discuss them in any detail" (p. 354).

† In the books concerned the citation practice of each author is both interesting and curious. In *Value and Capital* Hayek's name does not appear, while in the *Pure Theory of Capital* Hicks's book appears in the bibliography (p. 444) but receives no citation in the text (unless it is to *Value and Capital* that the footnote on p. 400 of Hayek's text refers—and this is by no means obvious). However, Hayek wrote in his preface as follows: "in so far as the more recent contributions are concerned, I have listed those which have come to my knowledge in the bibliography. . . . Absence of further reference to any particular work must not be taken to mean that I have not profited from it in one way or another."

concerned . . . with the real demand for a general group of factors of the traditional kind 'labour' and 'capital'" (Hicks, 1963, p. 246). This approach, as we have already seen and as Hicks was later to indicate (1963, p. 308), contained no sign of the notion of intertemporal equilibrium.

Of Hayek, on the other hand, the same cannot be said. When Sraffa (1932a) had focussed attention on the implications of Hayek's analysis in *Prices and Production*—that of substituting the goal of explaining many commodity-own-rates of interest for the goal of explaining a uniform rate of profit (Sraffa, 1932a, p. 49, *et seq.*)—he correctly contrasted this with the traditional approach to the theory of capital which was undertaken within a long-period framework. But that it was not of this framework which Hayek was thinking is clear from his response:

> I think it would be truer to say . . . that there would be *no single rate* [of interest] . . ., but that there might . . . be as many 'natural' rates of interest as there are commodities *all* of which would be *equilibrium rates* (Hayek, 1932, p. 245, italics in original).

In fact, Hayek had mentioned the notion of intertemporal equilibrium in *Prices and Production* itself (pp. 29–30).* In his earlier *Monetary Theory and the Trade Cycle* (1929), when speaking of the necessity of establishing intertemporal prices as the basis of the theory of capital and interest, Hayek wrote that "in this field . . . the extension of equilibrium analysis to *successively occurring phenomena* . . . may prove fruitful" (Hayek, 1929, p. 230, italics added).

All of this, of course, establishes Hayek's primacy over Hicks in the origin of the notion of intertemporal equilibrium,† but it does not date

---

* Hayek writes: "the concept of relative prices includes the prices of goods of the same kind at different moments . . . as in the case of interspacial relationships" (p. 29). This is unmistakably the framework of intertemporal equilibrium (the latter term is used explicitly on p. 30).

† A claim which, as already mentioned, Hicks has never disputed. Hicks recollects: "I can date my own personal 'revolution' rather exactly to May or June 1933. . . . It began (rather oddly, as it turned out) with Hayek" (Hicks, 1963, p. 307). More recently, Hicks has elaborated on this. He recalls: "there were four years, 1931–5, when I myself was a member of [Hayek's] seminar in London; it has left a deep mark on my thinking. . . . At the end of the discussion in that seminar . . . we were, I believe, on the point of taking what now seems to me to be a decisive step. I was, at least, on the point of taking it myself. There is evidence for that, in my *Value and Capital*" (Hicks, 1973a, p. 190).

with accuracy its origin in Hayek's own work. Yet this is readily established.

In 1928 Hayek produced what can be regarded as a seminal paper in this field under the title "Das intertemporale Gleichgewichtssystem der Preise und die Bewegungen des Geldwertes." There he spoke of the necessity of considering the formation of prices in successive periods of time ["notwendig *sukzessiv* erfolgende(n) Preisbildungen" (p. 34)] and he contrasted this methodological approach to the theory of capital with what he saw as the older 'static' theory of the early neo-classical economists:

> Die Einsicht in die Notwendigkeit des Bestehens eines intertemporalen Preissystems ist nun mit der weitverbreiteten Vorstellung, dass die zeit-liche Konstanz der Preise eine Voraussetzung für einen ungestörten Wirtschaftsablauf bilde, nicht nur nicht verträglich, sondern steht zu ihr im schärfsten Gegensatz. (Hayek, 1928, p. 37).*

The idea of distinguishing between the prices of the same commodity at different points in time is introduced (Hayek speaks of "Preise(n) gleicher Güter in verschiedenen Zeitpunkten" (p. 33)†) and the now familiar analogy between intertemporal and interspacial theory is adopted: "Diese Verschiedenheit der Preise gleicher Güter in vers-chiedenen Zeitpunkten . . . wird dabei ebenso notwendige Vorausset-zung . . . sein, wie die durch die Transportkosten u. dgl. bedingten Verschiedenheiten der Preise eines Gutes an verschiedenen Orten" (p. 36).‡

In so far as the multiplicity of commodity-own-rates of interest is concerned the three sections of the paper devoted to intertemporal exchange clearly envisage that there will be different rates of intertem-

---

* "The examination of the necessity for the existence of an intertemporal price system is not only incompatible with the widespread assumption of the temporal constancy of prices, but strongly contradicts such an assumption" (see also p. 35). This contrast between earlier 'static' theory and intertemporal equilibrium is subject to the same caveats as apply to Hicks's similar distinction (see Chapter III above).

† See also p. 35 and pp. 40–41. Hayek also adopts the now conventional notation in this regard by subscripting each commodity according to the time at which it becomes available (hence x_1 and x_2 on p. 42).

‡ "This difference of the prices of the same goods at different points of time . . . will be thereby just as necessary an hypothesis . . . as that which, through the costs of transportation and the like, causes differences in the price of a good in different places . . ."

poral exchange for different commodities and that this should be adopted as the basis of the theory of capital and interest. The following passage manifestly embraces this principle:

> Dass bei Bestehen reinen Naturaltausches *der Tausch zwischen* in verschiedenen Zeitpunkten zur Verfügung stehenden *Gütern gleicher Art in der Regel nicht in Verhaltnis 1:1 erfolgen wird*, sondern je nach den Umständen in jedem beliebigen andern Verhältnis erfolgen kann und diese Tauschrelation genau denselben Gesetzen folgt wie sonst die Preisbildung zwischen verschiedenen Gütern, dürfte damit hinreichend klargestellt sein (p. 43, italics added).*

Although, as already noted, Hayek's role in this context has not been widely publicised it cannot be said that Hayek's contribution has exerted no influence at all upon the subsequent development of intertemporal equilibrium theory. For apart from Hicks,† there is evidence which suggests that Hayek may have exerted an influence on Malinvaud's early work. In Malinvaud (1953), among the extensive list of references appended (pp. 266–268), *Value and Capital* does not appear. Hayek's *Pure Theory of Capital*, on the other hand, is listed. Malinvaud does not specifically cite Hayek in the text of his paper as the originator of the notion of intertemporal equilibrium, yet it is hardly possible, in view of the precision with which Hayek had outlined the notion in the *Pure Theory of Capital*, that his influence on Malinvaud's thinking could have been negligible.‡

Turning next to the Swedish economists, there is far less to say with respect to the origin of the notion of intertemporal equilibrium. Much of what is important here has been widely known for a number of years. Debreu (1959, p. 35) cites Lindahl as having been the first to produce "a general mathematical study of an economy whose activity extends over

---

* "It should, then, be sufficiently clear (from the argument thus far) that exchange between different goods, which become available at different points of time but which are of the same sort, will not occur in a 1:1 relation; it is rather the case that such exchange can occur, according to the circumstances, in absolutely any other relationship. Furthermore this exchange relation follows exactly the same laws as those which govern price formation between different goods."

† With Hicks the connection is obvious (see n.†, p. 132 above, this chapter). However it will be shown below that Hayek provided at least vindication for Lindahl's work as well (see n.*, p. 135).

‡ Paradoxically, in a later paper (Malivaud, 1960–1961) Malinvaud was to drop this reference to Hayek and replace it with one to Hicks.

a finite number of elementary time intervals."* Lindahl's paper appeared in *Ekonomisk Tidskrift* in 1929, but not in English until 1939 (Lindahl, 1939, Pt. III).

Lindahl set up the intertemporal equilibrium problem as follows:

> If the supply of productive services, the demand for consumption goods and the technical coefficients relevant to the production of these goods are given for all periods—starting from a given point of departure . . . what are the prices and rates of interest at which goods will be produced and consumed in all these periods (Lindahl, 1929a, pp. 321–322).

No one would dispute Debreu's claim that Lindahl gave the first mathematical treatment of the intertemporal equilibrium system, nor would they dispute any claim Lindahl may have to primacy in the origin of the notion. For on this question the single year which separates Lindahl's paper from Hayek's paper of 1928 is of no consequence. On all of these points there is nothing of substance to add. However, it is interesting to note that in a slightly later paper (Lindahl, 1930, translated in Lindahl, 1939, Pt. II) Lindahl indicates his acquaintance with Hayek's 'Das intertemporale' (1939, Pt. II, p. 142, n.1). Lindahl cites Hayek at the end of the following passage: "if the theory is extended to dynamic conditions it must include the treatment not only of the relative prices in each period, but also the price relations between the different periods included in the dynamic process" (italics omitted). It cannot have been long after Lindahl's earlier paper that he became aware that Hayek had been moving along similar lines; the 1930 paper was, in fact, circulated in 1929 (see Lindahl, 1939, Pt. II, p. 9). Hayek, at least in the initial stages up to, say, the mid-1930s, makes no reference to Lindahl. By the *Pure Theory of Capital*, however, not only was Hayek aware of Lindahl's work, but he had reviewed its English translation (Hayek, 1940).

There are, however, some secondary matters upon which further comment would not seem out of place. These concern the connection between Wicksell's analysis of the 'cumulative process', Myrdal's *ex ante/ex post* method, and the notion of intertemporal equilibrium. In particular, it should be clear from what was said in Chapter V above that to distinguish between 'planned' and 'actual' demands and supplies is

---

* Hicks acknowledges that Lindahl had influenced *Value and Capital*, not, though, via any of his published writings (Hicks, 1963, p. 309, n.2).

not *necessarily* the same as arguing for a move to the notion of intertemporal equilibrium. The failure to 'realize' 'planned' results can be treated simply as a short-period *deviation* of the actual system from its long-period normal position. Indeed, this was the very manner in which Wicksell had viewed the analytical construction involved in the analysis of the cumulative process (see Wicksell, 1901, vol. II, pp. 145–146 and p. 159). Thus, in this approach the *ex ante/ex post* distinction is encompassed by the straightforward notion of a deviation between the market rate of interest and the 'natural' rate (in Wicksell's theory this is the rate of interest that at once ensures the balance between saving and investment and produces full employment).*

To arrive at the notion of intertemporal equilibrium, one has first to cut loose the short-period problem from its traditional long-period moorings (which amounts to a severing of the traditional conception of the connection between 'equilibrium' and 'disequilibrium') and then to install it into the centre of the picture. This, of course, is precisely the point at which the early work of Lindahl and Myrdal is so strikingly at variance with that of Wicksell. Having thus converted the traditional 'disequilibrium' position into intertemporal equilibrium one is then free to re-apply the distinction between 'planned' and 'actual' outcomes; but this time to a different case.

D.   REASONS FOR THE EMERGENCE OF THE NOTION OF 'INTERTEMPORAL EQUILIBRIUM'

If, therefore, we must conclude that the origin of the notion of intertemporal equilibrium cannot be traced back to the 1870s, it would be interesting to examine the reasons for the emergence of this new notion of equilibrium. Because here, as in the case of the question of dating its origin, there is an opinion gaining currency among theorists which, even in its most plausible form, represents only half of the story. This is the view that the change was inspired by the 'need' to bring economic theory into closer touch with 'reality' by introducing uncertainty and expectations.

---

* This, of course, was Keynes's approach in the *Treatise on Money* (see below, Chapter X).

While there is no doubt that this is how most of the writers in the vanguard of the change advertised their contributions (see e.g. Lindahl, 1939, p. 271, Myrdal, 1939, p. 32 and Hicks, 1936, p. 239), it is nonetheless the case that there was another element present. This derived not from any desire to get nearer 'reality', but from a desire to avoid a theoretical difficulty which had been encountered by earlier writers. This was the problem of defining the quantity of capital outside a one-commodity world. The existence of this problem for demand-and-supply explanations of the rate of profit was, of course, perceived almost as soon as the marginal 'revolution' was ushered in during the closing decades of the nineteenth century. Clark and Böhm-Bawerk had debated the merits of the 'average period of production' *versus* the 'amount of free capital' as the appropriate measure at the turn of the century, Irving Fisher produced a series of papers on the subject at about the same time, and Frank Knight raised the issue once again in the early 1930s. It would be true to say, I suspect, that all of these writers saw the problem as one which was, in principle, capable of resolution in its own terms. Indeed, most of these authors seem to have thought that they themselves had found the appropriate measure. Walras attempted to deal with heterogeneous capital goods measured in their own technical units only to find that this did not determine the unique rate of net income (interest) that he was after.*

But the group of writers whose work on the notion of intertemporal equilibrium is under consideration at present, took a rather different view. For they, unlike their predecessors, framed their response to the problem by evolving a new approach to economic analysis; an approach which they saw as avoiding the entire issue. They achieved this by abandoning the idea that the natural rate of interest should be the object of their investigations.

In arguing the case for this idea, Lindahl very nearly hit upon the reason why this problem was, in fact, insoluble within the traditional long-period frame of reference:

> Only under very special assumptions is it possible to conceive of a natural rate of interest determined purely by technical considerations, and thus

---

* Walras's object was clearly asserted (see above, p. 22). Wicksell had noticed Walras's problem very early on (see 1901, vol. 1, pp. 149 and 171) and much more recently Garegnani (1960) has amplified its significance.

independent of the price system. For this to be true it must be supposed that the productive process consists only in investing units of goods . . . of the *same type* as the final product (Lindahl, 1939, p. 247, italics added).★

To this passage Lindahl added a footnote (n.★, p. 247) indicating that an economy consisting of a single agricultural product would satisfy such a condition. After Sraffa (1960), it has become apparent that this is the only way that the problem can be resolved while maintaining the traditional object. It was as much for this reason as for that of incorporating uncertainty and expectations that Lindahl moved to the notion of intertemporal equilibrium. According to Lindahl, it was the existence of this problem of capital that rendered the concept of the natural rate of interest empty of any "clear and precise content" and therefore lacking in "scientific value" (1939, pp. 245–246; see also Myrdal, 1939, p. 50 for a parallel argument). It should be noted, however, that contrary to Lindahl's opinion this does not constitute a "*refutation* of Wicksell's basic *assumption*: the idea of a 'normal' rate of interest" (Steiger, 1976, p. 356, italics added) but rather it amounts to the abandonment of Wicksell's object. This is because the particular problem of capital to which Lindahl alludes is a problem of the theory (i.e. of the explanation of the object) not of the object.

A little later Hicks was to argue for the same programme of action on similar grounds:

> people used to be able to content themselves with the static apparatus, only because they were imperfectly aware of its limitations. Thus they would often introduce . . . a 'factor of production' capital and its 'price' interest (Hicks, 1946, p. 116, n.1).

From this passage it is obvious that Hicks saw the extent of the problem of capital less clearly than Lindahl. Because even in a theoretically perfect stationary-state within the traditional long-period framework, the problem of capital does not disappear (the idea of arbitrarily fixing the steady-state rate of growth need not be considered, as this course was not adopted by the practitioners of the traditional method). It is clear that these qualms about the problems associated with the 'quantity' of capital form a well-defined part of Hicks's reasons for adopting the notion of intertemporal equilibrium. In fact, in Hicks's

---

★ See also Lindahl's reference to the 'same real unit' of capital (p. 248).

case the impetus from the capital theory side was apparent in his reaction to Shove's critical review (1933) of the *Theory of Wages*, where one of the main points of contention was the problem of defining the 'quantity' of capital upon which the *Theory of Wages* model had relied (see Hicks, 1963, p. 268).

The same thread of dissatisfaction over the problems of the theory of capital in its traditional long-period setting was present in Hayek's work:

> the attempts to explain interest, by analogy with wages and rent, as the price of the services of some definitely given 'factor' of production, has nearly always led to a tendency to regard capital as a homogeneous substance the 'quantity' of which could be regarded as a 'datum', and which . . . could be substituted . . . for the fuller description of the concrete elements of which it consisted (Hayek, 1941, p. 5).

Moreover, it was Hayek's opinion that "it is more than doubtful whether the discussion of 'capital' in terms of some single magnitude, however defined, was fortunate" (p. 6). It was on these grounds that Hayek argued the need for a "complete recasting" (p. 4) of the theory of capital and made his own contribution by sponsoring the introduction of the notion of intertemporal equilibrium.

What distinguishes Hayek's view of the purpose that the notion of intertemporal equilibrium was to serve from that of his contemporaries is that he was at times prepared to admit the fundamental break with tradition that it involved (the 'complete recasting' as he called it). In the most celebrated of his contributions to the 1930s capital theory debates, he wrote the following:

> [Professor Knight] uses very similar arguments to those which Professor J. B. Clark employed against Böhm-Bawerk. However, I am not concerned . . . with a defense of the details of the views of the latter. In my opinion the oversimplified form in which he . . . tried to incorporate the time element into the theory of capital prevented him from cutting himself finally loose from the misleading concept of capital as a definite 'fund'. . . . But Professor Knight, instead of directing his attack against what is undoubtedly wrong . . . in the traditional statement of this theory and trying to put a more appropriate treatment of the time element in its place, seems to me to fall back on . . . the error . . . of forty years ago (Hayek, 1936, p. 200).

In this light it seems that it is also necessary to question the commonly held view that the subsequent debates between Knight and Hayek are simply replays of the controversy between Clark and Böhm-Bawerk (with Hayek taking the Austrian position). For Hayek's "more appropriate treatment of the time element" was not to use time to measure the quantity of capital but to use it in order to restate the object of theory of capital and interest in terms of the notion of intertemporal equilibrium.

E.   HISTORICAL RECONSTRUCTION

There are a number of inferences to be drawn from the foregoing discussion.

The first is on a rather general level. It concerns the viability of arguments advanced on seemingly theoretical grounds, but which purport to relate early economics to current theory. In particular, it should be clear from our discussion that to represent the development of economic theory from 1870 down to the present day as a process of 'successive generalization' is seriously to obscure the fundamental shift to the notion of intertemporal equilibrium. One often hears the claim that modern economic theory deals with 'more complex' cases (that is, 'general' as opposed to 'special' cases) than did the economics of the nineteenth, and early twentieth century (e.g. Dixit, 1977, p. 17, *et passim*). It would be more correct to say, however, that it deals with an entirely different question.

The second observation derives from this general point and relates to the significance of the reswitching controversies of the mid-1960s. Here again, a familiar claim based on the 'successive generalization' hypothesis is that these debates were restricted to a special class of 'aggregate models' whose logical deficiencies (as pointed out by Sraffa, 1960) in no way reached to the centre of the 'general' version. This, however, is not a view especially suited to producing an understanding of the significance of those debates. In as much as the debates have shown that it is impossible to offer a demand-and-supply explanation of the general rate of profit within the traditional long-period framework without resort to the assumption of a one-commodity world (because of the dependence of the supply-price of capital upon the rate of profit), they imply that if the traditional object of economic analysis is to be retained one has to look beyond the demand-and-supply explanations offered by marginalist economic theory. To alter the object, by adopting the notion of intertemporal equilibrium, and then to proclaim the 'irrelevance' of reswitching without making any concomitant statement about the altered object, is manifestly an inadequate way to make pronouncements about the significance or otherwise of any doctrine not connected with the new notion of equilibrium. Nor can it be said to resolve the original problem in its own frame of reference.

Finally, it is interesting to observe that since much of what goes under the heading of modern 'Keynesian' economics is conducted within the framework of intertemporal equilibrium (by using some form of temporary equilibrium theory) this work, too, has its origin with Lindahl, Myrdal, Hicks and Hayek. To establish that there is anything particularly 'Keynesian' in flavour about this approach, one would need to establish (among other things) that in the *General Theory* Keynes himself introduced the notion of intertemporal equilibrium. Evidence to substantiate such a claim, as is clear from the arguments of Chapters VI and VII, just does not exist.

F.   THE STATIONARY-STATE HYPOTHESIS REVISITED

The preceding discussion leads directly to a consideration of the implications of the use of the demand-and-supply theory within the framework of the method of intertemporal equilibrium. As a direct result of the application of this particular theory/method combination there has developed a tendency to equate, mistakenly, the conditions which are required under it to obtain a solution where all commodity own-rates of interest are equal with the conditions 'required' for the application of the traditional long-period method (cf. Bliss, 1975, *passim.*). But nothing has yet been said of the logical structure of the 'new' method. Much, here, hinges upon the different way in which short- and long-periods are perceived to relate to one another.

When the relationship between the conceptual framework of the traditional long-period method and the condition of stationarity was examined (Chapter III, Section D above), it was found that stationarity assumptions were not necessary. But a question was left open at the end of that same section, to which the discussion may now return. The question was: Why have Hicks and others been led to offer an interpretation of the relation between the long-period method and stationarity in terms of their equivalence? The answer lies in the very characteristic of the method of intertemporal equilibrium which was set out at the beginning of this section—that is, the manner in which long-period questions are thought to concern uniform commodity own-rates of interest regimes.

Because intertemporal equilibrium views a 'long-period equilibrium' of the system as being a *sequence in time* of short-period positions, this *sequence* itself must have properties which act in such a way as to equalise the different commodity own-rates of interest which are the object of the analysis. It is important to realise that this requirement is imposed because of the method adopted and not because of the theory proposed. The property which the sequence must satisfy is that its elements can differ, if at all, only by a constant factor of proportionality. This amounts to nothing more than a condition of stationarity (which, as the reader will recall, was defined in Chapter III as also encompassing steady proportionate growth).

It is this fact, more than any other, which accounts for Hicks's misinterpretation of the early marginalist authors. He has simply confused the conditions which his method (i.e. method of intertemporal equilibrium) requires to obtain an identity between own-rates of interest, with those which the traditional long-period method 'requires' for the discussion of a general rate of profit. Indeed, Hicks' *Value and Capital* illustrates this point clearly. One of the reasons given by Hicks for moving to the 'new' method was that the 'old' method was suited only to the study of a stationary economy. However, in changing the method in this way Hicks has not really resolved the stationarity question, rather he has side-stepped it. This is because the question of stationarity applies to the explanation given for the determination of equal commodity own-rates of interest under the method of intertemporal equilibrium—a situation which Hicks mistook to be analogous to the general rate of profit framework of the long-period method.

IX. UNCERTAINTY AND EXPECTATIONS

Once the missing element—anticipations—is added, equilibrium analysis can be used, not only in the remote stationary conditions to which many economists have found themselves driven back, but even in the real world in 'disequilibrium'.

This is the general method of [the *General Theory*] . . . from the standpoint of pure theory, the use of the *method of expectations* is perhaps the most revolutionary thing about this book (Hicks, 1936, p. 239, italics added).

In those interpretations of Keynes that rely on the method of intertemporal equilibrium and the related notion of temporary equilibrium, it has become traditional to regard uncertainty and expectations and their inclusion in economic theory as the most fundamental contribution of the *General Theory*. Indeed, this prevailing tradition has been the blanket under which the shift towards the modern method of intertemporal equilibrium has occurred. Therefore it was essential to secure a clear appreciation of the implications of this shift, as we did in the previous chapter, before proceeding to a consideration of the role of uncertainty and expectations in this process. It is now possible to return to this aspect of the movement away from the traditional long-period method. It will be appreciated that this issue raises some quite basic historical and analytical questions about the sources of this impetus, about its implications for the division of economic theory into 'statics' and 'dynamics', about the relationships that all of this bears to Keynes's work, and about its treatment of monetary questions. For the present, however, it will be sufficient to consider the contribution made by the 'method of expectations' towards the emergence of the intertemporal equilibrium method. The broader issues will be returned to in Chapters X and XI.

A. THE 'METHOD OF EXPECTATIONS'

It was in Hicks's review of the *General Theory* in the *Economic Journal* for June 1936 that the 'method of expectations' was first ascribed to Keynes. Hicks was subsequently to explore this method in detail in his *Value and Capital* (Hicks, 1946) and it is this latter version that has been woven into the fabric of modern 'Keynesianism' based on the notion of intertemporal equilibrium. However, before considering the extent to which Hicks may be said to have found the 'method of expectations' in Keynes rather than elsewhere, it is essential first to see exactly what this 'method of expectations' is, and how it is supposed to differ from other approaches.

According to Hicks, the old 'argument' "explains to us the working of the economic system in 'normal' conditions. Booms and slumps, however, are deviations from this norm, and are thus to be explained by some disturbing cause. Such theories therefore ran in terms of deviations: deviations between market and natural rates" (Hicks, 1936, p. 239). By 'argument', as is clear from the foregoing passage, Hicks means the traditional long-period method. Since this standpoint—the method—is something over and above the theory used to explain such normal or long-period values, there is nothing yet in Hicks's passage with which to object. The crucial question is how this old 'argument' is related to the 'method of expectations'. Hicks begins to answer as follows: "the present theory" he writes "breaks away from the whole of this range of ideas" (Hicks, 1936, p. 239). Notice that for 'theory' here, should be read instead 'the method of expectations' (which for the moment Hicks is ascribing to Keynes). So then, Hicks's 'method of expectations' is to be understood as an alternative to the traditional long-period method. This accords with what has already been argued in the previous chapter.

In the next stage of his argument Hicks sets out the characteristic feature of this new method in terms of the 'dating' of commodities: "define supply as that amount of a commodity which sellers are willing to offer *at a particular date* in the market conditions *of that date*" (1936, p. 239, italics added). It is thus clear, that the 'method of expectations' is exactly the same thing as the method of intertemporal equilibrium; except for terminological differences, there is a one-to-one correspondence between these two conceptual frameworks.

However, the next issue is rather more contentious. When Hicks explains in his review of the *General Theory* why the traditional method (i.e. the old 'argument') breaks down, he does so in the following manner:

> It is no longer allowed that ordinary economic theory can give a correct analysis of even normal conditions; the things it leaves out of account are too important. But if there is no norm which we have understood, it is useless to discuss deviations from it (p. 239).

Now, quite apart from the extent to which this statement may or may not reflect the ideas of Keynes (a question to which the discussion will return), and also quite apart from how all of this was seen to affect the meaning of 'static' and 'dynamic' branches of economic theory, there is much here in need of clarification. At one level the passage seems to be saying that demand-and-supply theory does not provide a satisfactory explanation of 'normal' values because it leaves out of account uncertainty and expectations. This, of course, is an argument that is reflected in the modern idea that the forces of demand-and-supply are 'kept at bay' by uncertainty and expectations. Yet the passage says much more, because there is supposed to be 'no norm' at all. *The long-period method of considering deviations between market and natural prices is gone*, or so Hicks seems to be arguing. For the reader who is left wondering about the reasons for its departure, since it is not sufficient to point to a state of 'imperfect understanding' as the cause, Hicks provides two clues. The first is that the prevailing marginalist theory (demand-and-supply) was ill-fitted to the study of anything other than the "norm of the static state" (p. 239) and the second is that "several lines of inquiry have pointed this way in recent years" (p. 239). It would seem obvious to take up each of these two clues in turn.

The first has a familiar ring to it, for it is precisely the reason that Hicks advanced for abandoning the traditional long-period method because of capital theory problems (see above, Chapter VIII, Section D). But in this case, as then, it is difficult to find any validity in his reason; for the problem with Hicks's interpretation in this case derives from exactly the same source as the problem with his argument with respect to capital. It is that the 'quantity of capital' is a problem about marginalist theory rather than one of the traditional long-period method. Furthermore, it is quite apparent that the problems Hicks mentioned in the first part of the passage just quoted are also in the realm of theory not method. An argument for altering the method of analysis because the theory built within it is inadequate is misplaced.

It might also be mentioned here that the problems of the demand-and-supply theories of capital built within the traditional long-period method are of a different nature (one should say of a different order of magnitude) than those which arise from the introduction of uncertainty and expectations. The inadequacy of marginalist theory which stems from the problem of capital is a logical inadequacy—unless capital can be expressed as an homogeneous quantity independently of the rate of profit (which only a one-commodity world assumption would achieve) the theory is inconsistent. The inadequacy which derives from the treatment of uncertainty is, at most, an empirical or applied inadequacy—certain elements which are important in the real world have been left out of account. There is nothing to say that the theory would break down if they were taken into account. Indeed, we have already seen in Chapter V just how important these factors were in the analysis of deviations from long-period positions.

The first clue, then, would seem to be a false lead, as there is no necessary reason to abandon the method if the theory faces problems. But what of the second clue? Are there reasons for dropping the traditional method in the earlier literature 'pointing in this direction'? To resolve this issue it will be useful to start with the literature to which Hicks refers in this regard: the "writings of the econometrists" and the work "in Swedish economics" (p. 240).

The 'Swedish School' to which Hicks alludes, however, offers no real advance on the case that Hicks had presented for himself. In fact, it has already been shown that these writers also argued for the inclusion of uncertainty and expectations into a formal intertemporal demand-and-supply equilibrium framework on the grounds of greater 'relevance'. Lindahl, for example, spoke of the need to bring the theory of value "into closer contact with reality" (Lindahl, 1939, p. 271; see also p. 60 and p. 65) by introducing 'time' into economics via the medium of the method of intertemporal equilibrium. Likewise, Myrdal had argued in *Monetary Equilibrium* that his main purpose was "to include anticipations in the monetary system" (Myrdal, 1939, p. 32), so as to impart to it an "element of greater realism" (p. 43, but see also Lundberg, 1964).

In sharp contrast to these writers (who were, at least, talking about the same thing as Hicks—*viz.* the method of intertemporal equilibrium) are the writings of Hicks's "econometrists". Most of these authors were, in fact, scarcely able even to agree on what 'dynamic' economics (as Hicks was later to christen intertemporal approaches) was, or should be about. The one of their number to whom Hicks refers (Roos, 1934) does no more than state that "an accurate dynamic conception should consider economic phenomena and functions in the process of change and the interrelations of these changes in the course of time" (p. 7) and that "risk must play an important rôle" (p. 7). There is scarcely any 'dynamic' theory with which such a broad description would conflict. Indeed, these 'econometrists' and their early writings produce no reasons at all for the abandonment of the traditional long-period method; a fact which is brought into sharp relief when it is recalled that the two writers to whom these 'econometrists' were most indebted, Irving Fisher and H. L. Moore, both were practitioners of that traditional method. The second clue, therefore, like the first, is also a false lead.

At this point it would seem obvious to return to Keynes, for it just might be that Hicks found the 'method of expectations' in the *General Theory* and that its origin may be firmly fixed in that book. Unfortunately, on Hicks's own authority (Hicks, 1977), this was not the case. Traces of the 'new' method are to be found in Hicks's "Suggestion for Simplifying the Theory of Money" of 1935 (in Hicks, 1967) where it was argued that "the essence of the method I am proposing is that we should take the position of an individual *at a particular point of time*" (p. 64, italics added). In fact, the same idea was clearly enunciated by Hicks in an unpublished paper as early as 1932. There he wrote that "a full equilibrium in the modern sense . . . allows for the influence of future prices on action as well as present prices" (Hicks, 1977, p. 138). This idea, as was shown in the previous chapter, appears to have come direct to Hicks from Hayek.★ Furthermore, it seems likely that the idea

---

★ In the omitted portion of the passage from Hicks's 1932 paper just quoted, he cites Hayek's "Das intertemporale" (Hayek, 1928). There is also a reference there to Knight's *Risk, Uncertainty and Profit*. Yet this work would not seem to have been couched within the framework of the intertemporal method. For example, Hicks's view is hard to reconcile with Knight's stated aim. "The argument of the present essay," wrote Knight, "will center around the general idea of normality . . . the aim will be to bring out the content of the assumptions or hypotheses of the historic body of economic thought referred to by the classical writers as 'natural price' theory" (Knight, 1971, p. 18). These references made by Hicks to virtually any work which dealt with uncertainty and expectations are really no more than a reflection of an inconsistency in

of connecting this notion with uncertainty and expectations was given a further impetus by Hicks's later contact (in 1934) with Myrdal's *Monetary Equilibrium* (see Hicks, 1977, p. 143 and 1963, pp. 308–309). The inescapable conclusion, therefore, is that the 'method of expectations' had its genesis in a train of ideas which developed quite independently of any ideas which may or may not be found in Keynes's *General Theory*.★ From what was said in Chapters VI and VII above, it should be clear that this train of thought was not running along parallel tracks to that of Keynes.

We are now in a position to draw together some threads of the argument outlined thus far concerning the impetus to the change from the traditional long-period method of economic analysis to the method of intertemporal equilibrium. An effort has been made to establish the following points. First, that there is nothing intrinsically 'static' about the long-period method. Secondly, that in the versions of demand-and-supply theory built within the framework of the traditional long-period method there is a *logical* problem concerning the definition of a quantity of capital; a problem which is insoluble in *any* multi-commodity model of demand and supply. Thirdly, that this problem, although being one of theory and not method, formed part of Hicks's case for abandoning that method. Fourthly, that in this respect, uncertainty and expectations as treated by the 'method of expectations' captures only a part of the impetus which led Hicks to the method of intertemporal equilibrium. Fifthly, that the 'method of expectations' was evolved by Hicks under influences which were entirely extraneous to the *General Theory* (and, for that matter, to the *Treatise on Money*, as we shall see in the next chapter).

It remains, now, to establish that Keynes's treatment *does not*

★ This includes the *Treatise on Money*, which Hicks did not, it appears, read until *after* his 1932 paper (1977, p. 7: "at that point (but not earlier) I did go to the *Treatise on Money*"). See also Hicks, 1963, p. 309 and Hicks, 1965, p. 64 for Hicks's view of how his thoughts had developed independently of the *General Theory*.

---

the reasons Hicks advances on this score for the abandonment of the traditional long-period method, and which were hinted at in the previous chapter. For if the treatment of uncertainty and expectations has a history as old as economics itself, then there is no basis for the change in method that Hicks has sponsored on these very grounds.

correspond to the 'method of expectations', and that this treatment is amenable to the traditional long-period method. These two questions will form the subject matter of the next two chapters. However, before proceeding, it is essential to establish a negative point which was mentioned in Chapter V above: namely that the heralding of the intertemporal equilibrium method on the basis of the mere existence of uncertainty and expectations would enforce an interpretation of the hsitory of economic thought which would stress the lack of any possibility for an analytical treatment of these phenomena in the entire literature of the long-period method, and that such an interpretation is unacceptable.

B.   STATICS AND DYNAMICS

A common feature of those works which advocate the use of the method of intertemporal equilibrium is that they argue that this method has a monopoly on the treatment of uncertainty and expectations. The 'stringing together' of short-period positions in sequence over time is contrasted by the writers of such works with the method of earlier theorists by arguing that any other method must operate 'out of time' (see for example, Hahn 1952).* The chief consequences of this type of opinion have been twofold. The first is apparent in the tendency, commented upon in the previous chapter, to seek the origin of the notion of intertemporal equilibrium in any work which seems to deal with time and/or uncertainty and expectations. The second is that this argument paints a picture of the history of economics uncoloured by the presence of a potentially viable apparatus for the treatment of these phenomena *until* the emergence of the notion of intertemporal equilibrium. Indeed, the first argument is no more than a direct consequence of the second. However, against both views quite powerful counter arguments can be mounted. It will be sufficient to show that the first argument is unsound, since in so doing the works mentioned, com-

* It is perhaps also worth recording that Marget (1966), though wrong on so many points concerning the interpretation of Keynes, mounts a powerful assault against this position (cf. vol. II, pp. 368–403 and all the detailed footnotes thereto, and vol. II, p. 409, n.10).

pleted entirely within the framework of the traditional long-period method, will negate the second.

The work of three writers—Hawtrey, Knight and Robertson—would seem to hold the key to the argument in question. For all of these writers dealt, though in rather different ways, with uncertainty and expectations in the theoretical setting provided by marginalist economic analysis. This fact alone seriously impairs the implicit historical position that Hicks takes with respect to the emergence and origin of the notion of intertemporal equilibrium (as distinct from the consideration of short-period deviations). However, to resolve the argument, one needs to ask if any of these writers shared with Hicks the conceptual framework of the notion of intertemporal equilibrium. On this point it is possible to be brief, for the answer is implied by what has already been said in Chapter V above.

Knight, for example, whose *Risk, Uncertainty and Profit* Hicks has explicitly suggested as a progenitor of the notion of intertemporal equilibrium (see Hicks, 1977, p. 138) seems never, in fact, to have operated within that conceptual framework. Aside from the passage from *Risk, Uncertainty and Profit* quoted in n.*, p. 147, throughout the whole of his theoretical work Knight adhered faithfully to the framework of the traditional long-period method.

The same applies to Dennis Robertson, whose name has also been mentioned by Hicks in connection with the emergence of the notion of intertemporal equilibrium. In the new preface to his fellowship dissertation, Robertson wrote of himself as "one . . . drenched with the vision of eternal ebb and flow" (Robertson, 1948, p. xiv); and he spoke to his students in the following terms as late as the mid-1950s:

> [Long-run value is] . . . a norm around which actual value oscillates, as a pendulum does about a vertical line, or a 'sine curve' about a horizontal one, so that . . . whenever it diverges from it a force, . . . is at work tending to bring it back again (Robertson, 1963, p. 93).

All of this affirms the framework of the traditional long-period method. Robertson's entire output cannot be read, especially in view of what was said above in Chapter V, in any other way.

Finally, Hawtrey likewise saw no barrier in principle to the construction of a model dealing with uncertainty and expectations within the traditional framework of considering deviations between market and natural values; this much was made quite clear in Chapter V above.

Were it not for the fact that Hicks's views about uncertainty and expectations (and 'statics' and 'dynamics') are so widely held by contemporary theorists, it might be thought that all of the above somewhat belabours the obvious point that the notion of intertemporal equilibrium has no monopoly on the treatment of uncertainty and expectations or has exclusive claim to being 'dynamic' analysis. After all, both John Stuart Mill and Marshall frequently turned their attention to such issues; Marshall even asserting it to be the whole basis of his work.

C. THE SIGNIFICANCE OF THE GENERAL THEORY

A point has now been reached where some general conclusions may be drawn from the discussion contained in the first part of this study. In fact, an interpretation of the *General Theory* emerges from what has necessarily been a lengthy discussion that can be captured in very simple terms. It is that Keynes's departure from the pre-1936 'orthodoxy' involved a change in *theory* and not the abandonment of the traditional long-period *method*. At this level, the essential novelty of the *General Theory* must be regarded as being embodied in Keynes's alternative explanation (grounded on the principle of effective demand) of the permanent and systematic forces that act in market economies to determine the levels of output and employment. This position departs radically from the orthodox marginalist explanation of value and distribution, the basic tenet of which is that under the operation of the forces of demand and supply there will be a long-run tendency towards the full employment of labour.

In this regard, two further arguments have been advanced. On the one hand, it was noted that the application of the principle of effective demand does not depend essentially on the disappointment of expectations. Consequently, since uncertainty and expectations are not central to Keynes's positive contribution, it was argued that they were better left to one side. On the other hand, it was noted that Keynes's alternative theory of output and employment was at odds with the premise of the orthodox marginalist explanation of value and distribution—the concept of capital as a 'factor of production' whose proportion to labour (and other 'factors') in the production of commodities varied inversely with the rate of interest (profit). These considerations, together with the observation that while Keynes's positive theory constituted a satisfactory alternative to the marginalist position it did not provide in itself a suitable basis for a critique of the internal logic of that theory, led to the conclusion that the more recent criticism of marginalist theory developed by Piero Sraffa could be used to complete this 'negative' task.

However, to this straightforward argument the foregoing discussion suggests that a number of corollaries may be added, not all of which need be mentioned again. The most important of these is that Keynes's contribution has been found to be quite compatible with the economic theory developed by the old Classical Economists. We propose now to consider the extent to which these conclusions are reflected in the transition between Keynes's *Treatise on Money* (which he regarded as a contribution to the orthodox position) and the *General Theory*.

PART TWO

THE *TREATISE ON MONEY* AND THE *GENERAL THEORY*

X. THE METHOD OF ANALYSIS IN THE *TREATISE* AND THE *GENERAL THEORY*

Though the 'methods' that are used in the *Treatise on Money*, and in the *General Theory* are different . . . [there can be] . . . no question that, as between his two works, Keynes was moving in the direction of the new method . . . the Temporary Equilibrium method (Hicks, 1965, p. 77).

It is often said that the development of Keynes's economic thought can be represented as a case of one man's struggle "to escape from the confusions of the quantity-theory" (*J.M.K.*, vol. VII, p. xxxiv); an escape which, one cannot deny, Keynes effected with some finesse in the *General Theory*. But what is important about this view, and why it is mentioned here, is that it indicates strongly that it is at the level of what has been referred to throughout this study as *theory* that one ought to seek the elements of change that separate Keynes from the orthodox position.* In contrast to this, however, is the view that gains expression in Hicks's remarks quoted above. The suggestion there is that it is the level of *method* that embodies the significant element of the change between the *Treatise* and the *General Theory*. However, if the *Treatise* is to be regarded as part of the orthodox position then there would appear to be little force in this argument; at least from the point of view adopted

---

* Despite this, at the level of *theory* there remains a tendency to stress continuity (especially with respect to the transition between the *Treatise* and the *General Theory*). Such a tendency, I would argue, may be found in Leijonhufvud, 1969, pp. 20–24; Hicks, 1967, Ch. 11 *passim*; Hicks, 1977, p. 148; Moggridge, 1976, Chapters 4 and 5 (despite the latter's insistence on the importance of 'change and continuity' in Keynes's thought, p. 76).

in Part I above (which was not, it must be recalled, strictly concerned with the distinctions between the *Treatise on Money* and the *General Theory*).

In this chapter it will be argued that the *Treatise on Money* and the *General Theory* are one at the level of method. In the next chapter it will be shown that they are analytically distinct at the level of theory. Indeed, it will be found that the *Treatise on Money* is so deeply entrenched within the framework of the traditional long-period method that, from this point of view, the continuity between the two books can scarcely be separated from the general continuity, up to that time, in economic thought as a whole. However in the next chapter, when the theoretical structure of each work is compared, change, not continuity, will be of striking significance.

However, before confronting questions of method proper there is a 'negative' task to be undertaken; that of dispelling any remaining suspicion that the distinction between 'decisions to save' and 'decisions to invest' was a particularly significant element in the change between the *Treatise* and the *General Theory* (or even particularly significant in the *General Theory* itself). This issue, it will be recalled, was discussed in a more general framework at the beginning of Chapter VI above.

A. SAVING AND INVESTMENT: DIFFERENT DECISIONS OR NEW THEORY OF EMPLOYMENT?

It has already been argued that the fundamental proposition of the *General Theory*—that saving and investment are brought into equality by variations in the level of income (output)—did not depend on the 'discovery' that decisions to save and decisions to invest were taken by "different people, at different times, and for different reasons".* In fact, this latter doctrine was present in the *Treatise* as well, and it applied as much in the orthodox marginalist argument as it did in the *General Theory*. It is thus desirable to re-affirm this conclusion by showing that it was not this doctrine which took Keynes's economics out the orthodoxy to which it had been confined in the *Treatise* and into the light

---

* For examples of writers who have vented the opposite view, see the references already cited in n.*, p. 83 above.

of the *General Theory*. Instead, the progression which led to the *General Theory* was (as argued previously) connected with Keynes's departure from the orthodox marginalist explanation of the forces that would operate so as to ensure an equilibrium between planned saving and planned investment.

But before undertaking a comparison of the two texts to adduce the evidence of this change, it would not be out of place to indicate briefly first, the role that the 'different decisions' distinction played in the *Treatise vis-à-vis* the *General Theory* and second, the extent to which the distinction was not peculiarly Keynes's and so did not represent a movement away from marginalist economic theory.

The distinction between saving and investment made by Keynes in the *Treatise* is as follows:

> Saving is the act of the individual consumer and consists in the negative act of refraining from spending the whole of his current income on consumption.
>
> Investment, on the other hand, is the act of the entrepreneur whose function it is to make the decisions which determine the amount of non-available output (*J.M.K.*, vol. V, p. 155; see also *J.M.K.*, vol. XIII, p. 19).

Here, then, is the basis for the 'different decisions' interpretation. Keynes himself had made much of the distinction in an extraordinarily long footnote only a page earlier (p. 154, n.1). A little later in the *Treatise* Keynes sets out the distinction in precisely those terms which his subsequent interpretors have sponsored as a fundamental break with tradition:

> the decisions which determine saving and investment respectively are taken by two different sets of people influenced by different sets of motives, each not paying very much attention to the other. [. . .] Not only are the decisions made by different sets of persons; they must also in many cases be made at different times (pp. 250–251).

But to what end does Keynes make this distinction?

On the one hand, of course, it was introduced to show why saving and investment "*often* fail to keep step" (p. 250, italics added) and why "the development of disequilibria between rates of saving and investment . . . is nothing to wonder at" (p. 252). This was no more than one way of demonstrating why the 'credit cycle' was an important problem. Another, not unrelated way, which Keynes also used in the *Treatise*, was to emphasise the 'length' of the short-period; a point to which the discussion will return later. On the other hand, and this is the only extent to which this distinction can be said to 'break' with tradition, it was introduced to dispel any remnants of the idea that capitalists 'automatically' re-invested the entire amount of their savings'.* But even this point, proffered to remove the ambiguity that arose with the appearance of 'hoarding' during trade and credit cycles, 'departs' from the marginalist position only in so far as it describes a case (a short-period case) where the rate of interest did not adjust sufficiently 'quickly' (or 'automatically') to ensure a 'speedy' return to equilibrium (recall n.*, p. 42 above).

In this light, it would seem to be more appropriate to regard this sort of contribution as an elaboration of the orthodox marginalist position rather than a fundamental break from it. Because even if the earlier writers held implicitly the view that equilibrium would re-establish itself 'swiftly', the mechanism by which the adjustment took place was exactly the same—variations in the rate of interest. Remembering what was said in Chapter III about the structure of the long-period method, our conclusion on this point is substantially strengthened; for if earlier writers had over-concentrated their efforts on establishing an adequate (as they thought) long-period theory, it was natural that, sooner or later, someone would want to look more closely at what went on in the short-period. None of the 'second generation' of marginalist writers (one may cite Robertson in particular, though Wicksell and the writers mentioned in Chapter V, Section D could also be included) had any difficulty in accepting the distinction; simply because it entailed no more than a natural extension both of earlier long-period theory of the marginalist school and of the conceptual framework of the traditional method within which that theory had been constructed. But more will be said on this point in the following section.

So, then, even the distinction between saving and investment decisions itself cannot properly be regarded as a fundamental 'break' with the past. As for the *General Theory*, where the distinction is certainly present, it is largely irrelevant. For a substantive theoretical shift had occurred as between the *Treatise* and the *General Theory* with respect to the explanation offered for the mechanism that adjusted saving to planned investment.

---

* See above, Chapter IV, Section C.

The basis of the orthodox marginalist theory was that this required adjustment was achieved through variations in the rate of interest (profit). This, too, was the adjustment mechanism of the *Treatise*. First, Keynes borrowed Wicksell's terminology and argued in his chapter on "The Conditions of Equilibrium" that:

> . . . the natural rate of interest is the rate at which saving and the value of investment are exactly balanced (*J.M.K.*, vol. V, p. 139).

Then in the later, much celebrated, chapter on the *modus operandi* of bank rate, the entire argument was couched in terms of the manner in which the rate of interest influenced 'saving relative to investment'. This, of course, is a strictly neo-'classical' notion. The rate of interest is being viewed in the wholly orthodox way as the balancing factor which brings saving and investment into 'equilibrium'. Further, in the same chapter, one finds Keynes arguing as follows:

> . . . a rise . . . in the market rate of interest upsets the balance between . . . investment and saving, unless a corresponding rise in the natural rate occurs at the same time. *It may do this either by stimulating saving or by retarding investment* (p. 180, italics added).

The paragraph that follows is not without some interest. Keynes argues there that "in the case of saving, the effect of a change in the rate of interest is direct and primary . . . though the amount of the effect may often be quantitatively small in practice, especially over the short period" (p. 180). This 'practical' or empirical qualification to the doctrine that saving was 'primarily' a function of the rate of interest, was replaced by the altered theoretical proposition that saving was a function of income in the *General Theory*. More will be said on this in the next chapter where, since it is very much a question of theory, it more appropriately belongs.

All of this is straightforward marginalist theory applied to an 'analysis of deviations' of the form examined in Chapter V above. The argument may be simply depicted using the following familiar diagrams. (The reader should note that in Fig. 1 we are not concerned with convergence properties, so the magnitude of the elasticities of the functions involved is not relevant.) At A, the system is in equilibrium with the market rate of interest and the natural rate of interest equal ($r_m = r_n$). A disequilibrium between saving and investment of CB, entails a market rate of r_m ($>r_n$); this retards investment by increasing the cost of production of new investment goods and stimulates saving so that there

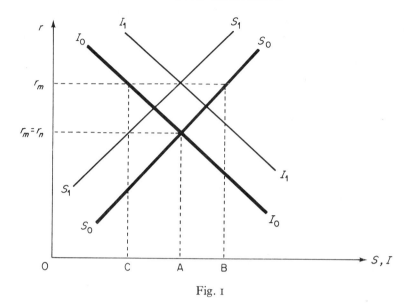

Fig. 1

is an 'excess supply' of saving of CB. [Unless the natural rate rises to r_m (which requires, say, a change in technique) so that the demand and supply curves shift bodily to, let us say, I_1I_1, S_1S_1, the balance between saving and investment is upset. Needless to say, a rise of r_n to *exactly* the correct level would be extremely fortuitous.] Without the appropriate banking policy, variations in the rate of interest (sparked by the imbalance of saving and investment) will, 'at long last' as Keynes put it, return the system to A. This occurs as long as the 'excess demand', $I(r_m)-S(r_m)$, is a continuous and inverse function of 'price' (rate of interest). This can be illustrated diagramatically as shown in Fig. 2.

In the *General Theory*, as already shown, the principle of effective demand provides a long-period theory of output that departs radically from the above ideas. In that book saving and investment are brought into equality by changes in the level of income. There is a rather long passage in Keynes's subsequent paper on "Alternative Theories of the Rate of Interest" in which these points are clarified. It is sufficiently important to quote at length:

> The theory of the rate of interest which prevailed before (let us say) 1914 regarded it as the factor which ensured equality between saving and investment. It was never suggested that saving and investment could be unequal. This idea arose (for the first time so far as I am aware) with

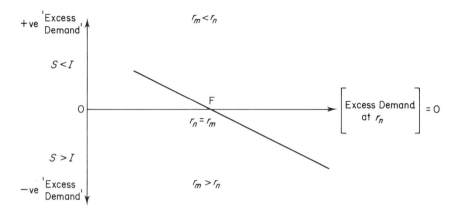

Fig. 2

certain post-war theories. In maintaining the equality of saving and investment, I am therefore, returning to old-fashioned orthodoxy. The novelty in my treatment of saving and investment consists not in my maintaining their necessary aggregate equality, but in the proposition that it is, not the rate of interest, but the level of incomes which . . . ensures this equality. (*J.M.K.*, vol. XIV, p. 211).*

Thus our argument is complete. There is nothing especially unorthodox about the distinction between acts of saving and acts of investment, but there is a great difference between the postulated marginalist adjustment mechanism of the *Treatise* and the principle of effective demand. If distinguishing between investment and saving 'decisions' helped Keynes in any significant way towards the *General Theory*, then it helped him, as he often said himself, back to the 'old-fashioned orthodoxy' where saving and investment were equal. Keynes had discovered along the way, however, that they were brought into equality by variations in the level of income rather than by variations in the rate of interest. It is the appearance of this latter doctrine in the *General Theory* which strikingly distinguishes it from the *Treatise*, not the presence of the 'different decisions' argument. (It is also worth mentioning again here, the fact that a failure to view Keynes's *General*

---

* It is difficult to see why Keynes omits to mention Wicksell in the third sentence, as Kahn's translation of *Interest and Prices* appeared in 1936 and one assumes that Keynes had read the manuscript of the translation well before that date.

Theory in this way obscures the target of Keynes's critique—the orthodox marginalist theory of distribution.)

When one reflects on the fact that apart from Keynes, Wicksell and Robertson (at least) all worked with this supposedly fundamental distinction, it is all the more remarkable that Keynes, alone among them, produced a new *theory* of the adjustment mechanism (and hence a new theory of employment). Had noticing the distinction between 'acts' of saving and 'acts' of investment been sufficient, economics would have had a correct theory of employment very much sooner than 1936. But this was certainly not enough, and it took Keynes's *General Theory* to show that the rate of interest [profit] had nothing whatsoever to do with 'adjusting' saving to investment.

This highlights, of course, the distance Keynes had travelled since 1926, the year in which, as he claimed subsequently, Robertson's *Banking Policy and the Price Level* 'emancipated' him from all that had gone before (see letter to Robertson, 13 December 1936, in *J.M.K.*, vol. XIV, p. 94 and also the *Treatise* in *J.M.K.*, vol. V, p. 154, n.1). In 1936 Robertson, whom Keynes was only too willing to acknowledge as his 'parent' (*J.M.K.*, vol. XIV, p. 202, n.2), was still *trying* to be 'classical' (like Wicksell in *Interest and Prices* according to Keynes). Keynes, on the other hand, had cast off his skin "like a good snake" (*J.M.K.*, vol. XIV, p. 95). It is perhaps worth mentioning that Keynes was prone (perhaps overly so) to exclude Robertson from his definition of 'classical' economists. There is the famous footnote in his "Alternative Theories" (*J.M.K.*, vol. XIV, p. 202, n.2) where Keynes excludes *both* Robertson and Hawtrey from this category; and yet, in the article itself, delivers decisive blows to the theory of interest (i.e. of saving and investment) adopted by both. Furthermore, in the letter to Robertson already cited in this note, Keynes tends to play down the differences between them by writing: "both our minds have been changing continously and enormously, though on parallel lines that all but, yet don't quite, meet, over the last eleven years. . . . The last thing I should accuse you of is being classical or orthodox" (*J.M.K.*, vol. XIV, p. 94).

B. THE CONCEPTUAL FRAMEWORK OF THE *TREATISE ON MONEY*

Returning to the conceptual framework (i.e. method) within which Keynes made propositions of pure theory, it is now necessary to examine first (in the present section) the method of analysis adopted in the *Treatise* and second (in the Section D below, this chapter) the method of the *General Theory*. Here again, the evidence seems to re-inforce the interpretation already offered in Chapter VI.

In the long run, said Marshall, persistent causes dominate completely; market prices may deviate from natural, or long-period 'normal', prices temporarily, but not permanently. This, together with the general rate of profit, provided the conceptual framework of the traditional long-period method. Long-period positions were the centres of 'repose and continuance' of the system towards which market prices 'continually gravitate'. It is within this framework, though with a somewhat more explicit concern for strictly short-period questions than was usual among nineteenth century writers,* that Keynes's *Treatise* is written. Although explicit statements of this method of analysis will not be found in anything like the precise form in which they appear in the writings of the nineteenth century economists, with whom we were concerned in Part I, the overriding impression obtained in reading the *Treatise* is of the perpetual ebb and flow of actual values about their natural level. Indeed, it is possible to go still further and argue that it is only within this framework that the *Treatise* can be correctly interpreted.

To substantiate this argument, it will be sufficient to take three examples from the *Treatise* (from the pure theory part) and to examine them for the presence, or otherwise, of the traditional *method* (as to the

---

* It is, in fact, arguable that this was the reason for Keynes's emphasis on the 'different decisions' position in the *Treatise*. With respect to an earlier 'lack of emphasis' on short-period issues, for example to what Ricardo called his predisposition to 'underestimate temporary effects', see Ricardo's letter to Malthus quoted at the beginning of Chapter I of this study. (Recall that a caveat applies to the interpretation of 'lack of emphasis', firstly because of the fact that for three-quarters of the nineteenth century there was no consensus about the appropriate long-period theory so that one should not be taken by the absence of much explicit discussion of short-period issues and secondly, because such questions as those to which Keynes addressed himself in the *Treatise* were in no way ruled out by earlier theory).

theory which they expound, an examination of this will be left until the following chapter).

Firstly, consider the celebrated Fundamental Equations which express, respectively, the 'formula' for determining the price level of consumption goods and the 'formula' for determining the price level of output as a whole.*

$$P = \frac{E}{O} + \frac{I'-S}{R} \tag{1}$$

$$\pi = \frac{E}{O} + \frac{I-S}{O} \tag{2}$$

Embedded in each of these equations is the idea that actual values deviate from 'equilibrium' values according as saving exceeds, or falls short of the value of new investment. If, in each equation, the first term is viewed as depicting the centre of 'repose and continuance' and the second term as expressing the manner in which 'deviations' arise, the framework of the traditional long-period method is arrived at immediately. For if, in each, only the first term is relevant (that is, if saving equals investment), then there is a ruling general rate of profit and the price level corresponds to what Keynes called the 'rate of efficiency earnings' (*J.M.K.*, vol. V, pp. 122–124). If, on the other hand, the second term is also relevant (that is, if saving and investment are unequal), a disturbance arises such that:

> entrepreneurs will tend . . . to alter the total volume of employment which they offer . . . upwards or downwards, according as [the difference between investment and saving is] positive or negative (*J.M.K.*, vol. V, p. 136).

If, as a second example, the manner in which Keynes elucidates the rise of an inequality between saving and investment is considered, the traditional method is found to be expressed in a quite familiar fashion:

> Following Wicksell, it will be convenient to call the rate of interest which would cause the second term of our fundamental equation to be zero the *natural* rate of interest, and the rate which actually prevails the *market rate* of interest. . . . Every departure of the market rate from the natural rate tends . . . to set up a disturbance of the price level by causing the second

---

* See the appendix to this chapter for definitions and derivation of these equations.

term of the fundamental equation to depart from zero (*J.M.K.*, vol. V, p. 139, italics in original).

Here the idea of deviations between market and natural rates is the standard fare of the traditional long-period method. Indeed, the argument is couched in the very language used in the literature of economics from Adam Smith and Ricardo right down to Marshall. Furthermore, again in the customary language, Keynes argues:

> the *long-period* . . . *norm* of the purchasing power of money is given by the money rate of efficiency earnings of the factors of production; whilst the *actual* purchasing power *oscillates* below or above this . . . level according as the cost of current investment is running ahead of, or falling behind, savings" (vol. V, 137, italics added).*

It is in the light of the conceptual framework that stands behind passages such as these (the traditional long-period method) that it is possible to argue that, in a very broad sense, in the *Treatise* Keynes filled the gap, which he felt had been left by Marshall, that comprised a series of questions of an essentially short-period character. Moreover, his answers were, as will be shown in the next chapter, based essentially on marginalist economic theory.

It is perhaps worth mentioning, in order to prevent this assertion from being misunderstood, that this *does not* mean that Keynes was adhering to a strictly monetarist, or quantity-theory, line. In fact, in so far as the *Treatise* deals with positions of the system where saving and investment are not equal, he was anything but a monetarist. It is true, however, that if the system were in 'equilibrium' (as defined in the *Treatise*) the quantity theory dogma held; it was one of the real theoretical breakthroughs of the *General Theory* to show that even in 'equilibrium' (the new *General Theory* 'equilibrium', of course) the quantity theory did not hold. The fact that it appears to hold by chance—the 'chance' being realised by a fluked full-employment long-period position which might, though would not *in general*, be generated by the operation of the principle of effective demand—has led to some interesting misinterpretations. More will be said on this point, which is really only peripheral to the central thesis of the present study, in the next section of this chapter.

---

* 'Oscillation' is just like the 'perpetual ebb and flow' of Cantillon; Keynes uses this terminology as well (*J.M.K.*, vol. V, pp. 201–202).

Finally, take as a third example Keynes's discussion of the credit cycle. Again, the conceptual framework of the traditional long-period method permeates almost every sentence. It is sufficient to quote just a few to demonstrate this. Keynes speaks, for example, of the 'appropriateness' of the designation of 'credit cycle' for those disturbances where "we have an *oscillation* about an *unchanged* position of equilibrium and not a transition from one position of equilibrium to another" (*J.M.K.*, vol. V, pp. 233–234, italics added). Elsewhere he argues that:

> Booms and slumps are simply the expression of the results of an oscillation of the terms of credit about their equilibrium position (*J.M.K.*, vol. V, p. 165).

In fact, the whole of Book Four of the *Treatise* ("The Dynamics of the Price Level"), and not simply that part of it which relates specifically to the credit cycle, runs in terms of deviations from a long-period 'norm'. The way Keynes poses the general problem in Chapter 16 ("The Classification of the Causes of a Disequilibrium of Purchasing Power") reflects this framework:

> "Assume a state of equilibrium in which the price level corresponds to the cost of production . . . [and] . . . the cost of investment is equal to that of saving. . . . In what way can this state of equilibrium be upset?" (*J.M.K.*, vol. V, p. 231).

The 'oscillation' about this 'equilibrium' is one such cause; a shift to a new equilibrium (caused, say, by a change in technique) will also generate 'oscillations'.

It might be added that it is not surprising that explicit statements about the character of this traditional long-period method are not easy to find. For Keynes, writing in the 1920s, this was the framework he had been brought up on; Marshall had produced the thinking which defined it almost fifty years before (and others even earlier). Keynes no doubt thought it so obvious as to make a re-writing of it unnecessary. This, incidentally, also helps to explain why Keynes does not trouble himself with writing out in any detail the theory of value (or of capital) in the *Treatise*. If his readers wanted long-period theory, they could go to Marshall's *Principles* and find it.

There is a lesson here in comparative historical analysis which could well be learnt by some of those who undertake comparisons between Wicksell's *Interest and Prices* and the *Treatise* and who are surprised to find 'explicit' capital theory in the former and little (explicitly, that is) in the latter. The two books are of a different generation; when Wicksell wrote, capital theory was a vogue (which is the reason why the 'cumulative process', an essentially *monetary* process, stands him apart from his contemporaries). In the 1920s, in England at least, capital theory was, for the moment, submerged under the weight of authority of Marshall (though this was soon to change). That Keynes should bow to such authority, especially when at this stage he was concerned exclusively with short-period questions, is not at all surprising.

It may be, in regard to the theory of value that, as Shove apparently put it, Keynes had not spent the necessary five minutes over it before the *Treatise* was written. But this in no way militates against the present interpretation—that Keynes had not learnt it is not to say that he was not prepared to adopt it. In fact, when in the next chapter it is argued that the *General Theory* departs from the neo-'classical' theory of value, Shove's remark positively supports this case.

C. THE 'LENGTH' OF THE SHORT-PERIOD

Perhaps the most quoted, though not most quotable,* of Keynes's many quips come from his *Tract on Monetary Reform* where he decided that "in the long-run we are all dead." "Economists", he went on to say, "set themselves too easy, too useless a task if in tempestuous seasons they can only tell us that when the storm is past the ocean is flat again." To this same theme Keynes returned on many occasions in the *Treatise*. Indeed, it has led some to conclude that this tendency reflects a deep-rooted discontent that Keynes felt towards the traditional long-period method. However, Keynes's argument (couched in terms of the 'length' of the short-period) is in rather sharp contrast with the fact that, as had already been argued in Part I, the 'short-period' referred not to an interval of calendar time but to the nature of the causes which operate—the 'fitful and irregular' as distinguished from the 'persistent'. It is, therefore, of more than passing interest to enquire into the reasons for Keynes's position on this point, as there may be an implied criticism of the traditional method embodied within it.

The following passages from the *Treatise* serve as an illustration of the

---

* The most quotable is surely the line Professor Shackle reports in his *Keynesian Kalaeidics*—"equilibrium", Keynes is supposed to have said, "is blither".

cavalier manner in which Keynes presented his case. Keynes writes, for instance:

> It may, indeed, be conceded that relative price levels in England and France may not be appreciably different now from what they would have been if the disturbances of the wars of Napoleon had never occurred. . . . But however this may be, it is above all with short-period consequences that we are concerned in some of our most practically important enquiries (*J.M.K.*, vol. V, p. 83).

And again:

> A 'short-period', it would seem, thinks nothing of living longer than a man. A 'short-period' is quite long enough to include (and, perhaps to contrive) the rise and fall of the greatness of a nation' (*J.M.K.*, vol. VI, p. 141).

To this last passage, Keynes adds the following footnote:

> Adam Smith did not under-estimate the length of short-periods. 'Ninety years', he wrote, 'is time sufficient to reduce any commodity, of which there is no monopoly, to its natural price' (*J.M.K.*, vol. VI, p. 141, n.3).★

But does this show a dissatisfaction with the notion of basing economic theory upon the long-period positions and of viewing actual values as deviations from these positions, or is there something else behind Keynes's statement? The answer to this question, which would be expected from the argument in Part I, is that there is indeed another explanation. It resides not in a dissatisfaction with the prevailing *method*, but with a dissatisfaction (growing, though not to be eliminated finally until the *General Theory*) with the aspects of the prevailing orthodox marginalist theory. These aspects were the quantity theory of money† and, more important in the context of this study, the orthodox theory of employment. ‡

★ The passage from the *Wealth of Nations* occurs in 1. xi, p. 244. In the first edition the 'length' was given by Smith as 100 years!

† Kahn has argued that "Keynes' long struggle over a period of six years to produce a version of the *Treatise* worthy of publication was directed partly to an escape from the stranglehold of the Quantity Theory of Money" (Kahn, 1974, p. 6).

‡ By running a few passages from Joan Robinson's thoughts on this matter together, a picture of Keynes's dissatisfaction on this level emerges. She writes: "There was heavy unemployment in England even before the world slump set in . . . . In this fog Keynes was groping for a theory of employment. He had backed up Lloyd George with a rather vague and half-backed argument [in 1929] . . . . But in his great theoretical *Treatise* his mind . . . failed to produce a theory of employment." (Robinson, 1951–79, vol. III, pp. 92–93).

The thing Keynes seems to have found difficult to accept was the fact that *in the long-period* orthodox marginalist theory worked with full employment *and* the quantity theory. Yet it does not seem necessary to produce a long historical exegesis of how Keynes's discontent developed, as there are passages in the *Treatise* itself which attest to the fact that Keynes was a very uneasy traveller on the orthodox train of theoretical thought which allowed neither for persistent unemployment nor for any theory of a monetary economy in the long-period other than that provided (or, more correctly, not provided) by the quantity theory.

There is, for example, more than a trace of irony at the very end of the *Treatise* when Keynes tries to make himself at home with the fact that, under the quantity-theory, "monetary theory, when all is said and done, is little more than a vast elaboration of the truth that 'it all comes out in the wash'" (*J.M.K.*, vol. VI, p. 366). This doctrine, which the theoretical innovations of the *General Theory* were later to expose, fitted Keynes even in the *Treatise* only partly. It is, in fact, no coincidence that some of Keynes's more celebrated estimates as to the 'length' of the short-period follow hard upon some statement or other about the domain of validity of the quantity-theory.* They are no more than rationalisations of the affliction Keynes was forced to abide as long as he maintained the long-period theory of the marginalist school that lay at the base of the *Treatise*.

An idea of Keynes's unease can be gained by juxtaposing two statements Keynes makes immediately after writing down his 'fundamental equations'. He first writes:

> The reader will have perceived by now that the relationship of the purchasing power of money (or the price level of consumption goods) and of the price level of output as a whole to the quantity of money and the velocity of circulation is not of that direct character which the old fashioned quantity equations, however carefully guarded, might lead one to suppose. (*J.M.K.*, vol. V, pp. 131–132).

But only a few pages further one:

> In the case of equilibrium . . . we can express our conclusions in terms of the usual monetary factors . . . (p. 134).

---

* The passage from the *Tract on Monetary Reform* quoted at the beginning of this section is one such instance.

The equation which Keynes then produces "bears a family relationship to Professor Irving Fisher's familiar equation P.T. = M.V." (p. 135).★ It is probably no exaggeration to say that by the time the *Treatise* was finished Keynes numbered among the 'many' of whom he had spoken (borrowing a saying from Goschen) in the *Tract on Monetary Reform* who could not bear "the relation of the level of prices to the volume of currency . . . without a feeling akin to irritation" (*J.M.K.*, vol. IV, p. 61).

As to the other reason for Keynes's preoccupation with the 'length' of the short-period (*viz.* his dissatisfaction with the full-employment condition of orthodox long-period theory), the *Treatise* again provides evidence to back up the position taken at the beginning of this section. The following passages make it clear that Keynes felt that *persistent* unemployment needed explanation. When exploring the implications of a discrepancy between the market and natural rate of interest in the chapter on the *modus operandi* of bank rate, at one point in the argument Keynes writes:

> a state of unemployment may be expected to ensue *and* to *continue*, until the rise in bank rate is reversed or, by chance, something happens to alter the natural rate of interest so as to bring it back into equality with the new market rate (*J.M.K.*, vol. V, p. 184, italics added).

Keynes continues:

> Finally, under the pressure of growing unemployment, the rate of earnings—*though, perhaps, only at long last*—will fall (p. 185, italics added; see also p. 176l and p. 244).

So, in the *Treatise* at least, it was to the 'length' of the short-period (the 'stickiness' of wages) that Keynes had to look if he was to explain *persistent* unemployment. Only in the *General Theory* where, under the operation of the principle of effective demand, saving may equal investment at any level of employment (not just at full employment as the orthodox theory indicated), was Keynes properly able to explain

---

★ Kahn has also cited this apparent 're-affirmation' of the quantity theory as evidence of Keynes's struggle to escape (Kahn, 1974, p. 6). Furthermore, in Chapter 14 of the *Treatise* Keynes returns to the quantity theory and echoes the criticism he levelled at this theory in the *Tract on Monetary Reform* (in terms of "in the long run we are all dead") in the following passage. "The equation obscures disturbances . . . it is intractable for the task of analysing disturbances . . . due to disparities between the rates of saving and investment" (*J.M.K.*, vol. V, p. 208).

unemployment without resorting to the dubious device of the 'length' of the short-period.*

In regard to the method dimension, then, the *Treatise* is firmly within the conceptual framework of the traditional long-period method. The 'length' of the short-period was introduced into the discussion by Keynes because the theory with which he was forced to exist contained elements which he found increasing need to rationalise (see Milgate, 1983a). But what of the *General Theory*?

D.   THE CONCEPTUAL FRAMEWORK OF THE *GENERAL THEORY*

The upshot of the discussion contained in Section B of Chapter VI above was that the *General Theory* was also written within the conceptual framework provided by the traditional long-period method. Consequently, it does not seem necessary to go over again the arguments and evidence which produced this conclusion, save to say, perhaps, that once the new theoretical structure of the *General Theory* was developed Keynes did not have to rely on 'disturbances' from long-period positions in order to generate an explanation of persistent unemployment. Rather, as Keynes could now argue, "we oscillate . . . round an intermediate position appreciably below full-employment" (*J.M.K.*, vol. VII, p. 254).

However there remain some loose ends, which concern particularly the continuity of method between the *Treatise* and the *General Theory*, which may be usefully tidied up here. The first relates to the language in which Keynes expressed the traditional method as between the *Treatise* and the *General Theory*, and to the more explicit treatment of it offered in the latter. The second relates to the disappearance, in the *General Theory*, of the preoccupation evidenced in the *Treatise* with the 'length' of the short-period. The remainder of this section will be devoted to considering each of these questions in turn.

In Chapter VI, Section B, it was shown that Keynes adopted and

---

* It is perhaps unnecessary to point out that if this interpretation is correct, those who have interpreted the *General Theory* solely in terms of downward wage-inflexibility must be wrong. For this inflexibility, even if a fact of life, *is not necessary* to generate persistent unemployment in the *General Theory* (unlike, of course, the *Treatise* case).

elaborated the notion of the 'economic machine' in exactly the manner in which this concept had been defined (indeed, originated) by the early practitioners of the traditional long-period method; as reflecting the behaviour of certain law-governed, persistent, forces in the operation of a market economy. His objections were directed towards the orthodox marginalist theory which held that these forces tended to produce full employment. This language, together with Keynes's other allusions in the *General Theory* to 'natural' and 'persistent' tendencies, is much more explicitly traditional than any that is to be found in the *Treatise*. This, of course, would seem to support the interpretation offered throughout the whole of Part I of this study. It attests, in particular, to the view taken there that the single, most important, contribution of the *General Theory*, resides in its presentation of the correct *long-period* theory of employment. Because it is in these terms only that Keynes's more explicit concern with the traditional long-period method in the *General Theory* can be explained. It is no coincidence that in those places where Keynes did elaborate the analytical aspects of this traditional method, he was usually in the process of explaining the long-period side of his theory of employment.*

The disappearance from the *General Theory* of references to the 'length' of the short-period seems, similarly, to accord with the central argument being put here. There is only one passage which could even approximately be construed as a return to this curious preoccupation. It occurs at the end of Book One of the *General Theory* and echoes, or so it might be thought, the 'too useless a task' charge Keynes had levelled in the *Tract on Monetary Reform:*†

> It may well be that the classical theory represents the way in which we should like our economy to behave. But to assume that it *actually* does so is to *assume our difficulties away* (*J.M.K.*, vol. VII, p. 34 italics added).

It is not hard to see how this passage *might* be interpreted. It comes hard-on-the-heels, so to speak, of Keynes's praise of Malthus—to whom most of Keynes's readers would have attributed a concern for short-period questions. Moreover, the use of the term 'actually' would have conjured up the distinction between 'natural' and 'actual' values

---

* The passage quoted at the beginning of this section is one example.
† There is, however, a vestige of the argument in Keynes's thoughts on mercantilism (*J.M.K.*, vol. VII, p. 343, n.3).

made by the traditional long-period method. But I would argue for a different rendering of the meaning of this passage.

In the first place, when Keynes referred to the "great puzzle of effective demand with which Malthus had wrestled" (*J.M.K.*, vol. VII, p. 32) he did not seem to regard this as a great *short-period* puzzle only. It was, in Keynes's opinion, "fundamental" to the economics which had been taught, "for more than a century" (p. 32). But if fundamental, it must apply to the general description of long-period 'normal' conditions. (It is useful to reflect upon Keynes's distinction between voluntary and involuntary unemployment in this regard, because by arguing that the first category covers 'frictional' unemployment, this distinction widens the domain of operation of the principle of effective demand beyond the traditional neo-'classical' idea that unemployment was a *deviation* from 'normal' long-period conditions, and hence was only a short-period ('frictional') phenomenon. The terminology 'frictional' and 'persistent' as applied to unemployment is but another reflection of the long-period side of the principle of effective demand.)

As to the use of the term 'actually', this applies not to the distinction between natural and market prices, but to the distinction (to which Keynes is here referring) between a theory designed to depict an imaginary world and one which tries to explain the operation of an actual market economy.*

To summarise the drift of the argument so far in this chapter, then, it may be said that the *Treatise* and the *General Theory* are one at the level of method. This conclusion seems to be reinforced, first, by the fact that Keynes's 'length' of the short-period arguments were dropped the moment that he was in possession of an adequate explanation of persistent, long-period, unemployment and, second, by the fact that the differences of theory (rather than of method) between the two books is reflected in the more explicit concern with strictly long-period issues

---

* This, incidentally, is the crux of Meek's idea (1965, p. 10 *et seq.*) that the post-*General Theory* era has seen the decline of the concept of the economic machine. The decline has come from an attempt to side-step the solution of the problems which arise in an actual economy by arguing in terms of 'optimal' economic strategies—not to solve the problem of reality, but to change the actual system so as to bring it nearer to what it 'should' be. So when Meek speaks of a 'decline', he does not mean (nor, therefore, does his argument conflict with that of the present study) that the traditional method has outlived its usefulness.

in the *General Theory*. This much of the comparative examination of these two books would, therefore, seem to support what was said in Part I about the nature of Keynes's departure from his predecessors.

E. 'CAUSAL SEQUENCES' AND 'DISEQUILIBRIUM'

This brings us to the final issue of substantial importance with which this chapter must deal. It has to do with the interpretation (for the moment, from the point of view of method) which is to be assigned to Keynes's use of the notions of 'causal sequences' and 'deviations' from long-period centres of gravitation of the system. This leads directly to the question of assigning a meaning to Keynes's idea of 'equilibrium' and 'disequilibrium'. The reader will appreciate that these are much more than questions about semantics. In the recent theoretical literature on 'Keynesian' economics, that works within the framework of the method of intertemporal equilibrium (usually adopting quite specific variants of a 'temporary equilibrium' system), 'sequence in time' and 'disequilibrium' have very particular definitions which are, by association, and quite incorrectly, assigned to Keynes's usage of a similar terminology. It would therefore seem appropriate to dwell a little on Keynes's usage of similar terms.

Take as a starting point the following passage from the *Treatise*, where Keynes first talks about 'causal processes':

> The fundamental problem of monetary theory is not merely to establish identities . . . . The real task is to treat the problem dynamically, analysing the different elements involved, in such a manner as to exhibit the *causal process* by which the price level is determined, and *the method of transition from one position of equilibrium to another*.
>
> The forms of the quantity theory, however, on which we have all been brought up . . . do not, any of them, have the advantage of separating out those factors through which, in a modern economic system, the *causal process* actually operates during a period of change" (*J.M.K.*, vol. V, p. 120, italics added).

Two things emerge from this passage. On the one hand, the reference to a 'causal' analysis (especially in the second paragraph) seems to be an allusion to Keynes's belief, expressed explicitly a few pages further on, that the equations of the quantity theory were mere identities ("truisms which tell us nothing in themselves" (p. 125)) which did not permit an adequate analysis of cause and effect, whereas the Fundamental Equations did allow for this.* On the other hand, 'causal process' seems to refer to the behaviour of the system when saving and investment are out of step. This is made clearer when Keynes, two chapters later, returns to elaborate the implications of a discrepancy between saving and investment and does this by moving "first forwards, and then backwards, in the causal sequence" (p. 163; see also pp. 164–167).

When Keynes speaks of causal 'sequence' or 'process', therefore, he does so in a wholly traditional manner. That is, his argument runs in terms of the *deviation* of actual (or market) values from 'equilibrium' (long-period normal) counterparts. The 'equilibrium', of course, is not the thing that is to be regarded, as it is under the method of intertemporal equilibrium, as a sequence in time of short-period positions; but the *disturbance* has a sequential character to it. It goes without saying, that if other disturbances occur during the process of adjustment, the sequential process will itself be interrupted. This, of course, is just a reflection of the fact that it is well not to overstate the purely cyclical character of a disturbance (cf. *J.M.K.*, vol. V, p. 250).

This traditional way of looking at things is the same both in the case where an 'oscillation' occurs about an *unchanged* position of equilibrium and in the case where an 'oscillation' is due to the requirement that the system *moves from one position of equilibrium to another*.† These notions are maintained in the *General Theory*, even though, from the point of view of theory, the 'equilibrium' there has rather different characteristics.‡ It is worth pointing out, in addition, that in Keynes's hands the gravitation process itself received more detailed attention than had been

---

* Of course, it was for this purpose that they were explicitly designed (even though Keynes was prone to refer to them as just other forms of the quantity equations, *J.M.K.*, vol. V, p. 125 and p. 198). Keynes spoke of one of their advantages as residing in the fact that they constituted "a much more powerful instrument of analysis . . . when we are considering what kind of monetary and business events will produce what kind of consequences" (p. 198).

† It should be mentioned, though this will be discussed in the next chapter, that the disturbances of which Keynes speaks in the *Treatise*, while looking to be of two different types (a simple oscillation about an unchanged equilibrium and the transition to a new equilibrium), may be regarded, analytically, as one. Whatever the initiating cause, a discrepancy between saving and investment manifests itself as a divergence between the market and natural rates of interest.

‡ See, for example, *General Theory* (*J.M.K.*, vol. VII, pp. 48–50), and the discussion there about the transition from one state of long-term expectations to another.

accorded to it previously. In the *Treatise*, of course, this elaboration was undertaken within an orthodox theoretical setting; something which was to change in the *General Theory*. Nevertheless, specific causes of 'disequilibrium' were outlined (in Book Four of the *Treatise* and Chapter 22 of the *General Theory* for example), and the manner in which such disturbances would work themselves out, if uninterrupted, was discussed at length.

There is something of an instructive contradiction between the traditional framework of these tasks, which Keynes regarded as a useful method of describing the 'characteristics of disequilibrium' as well as providing a way of discovering the "*dynamical* laws governing the passage of a monetary system from one position of equilibrium to another" (*J.M.K.*, vol. V, p. xvii, italics added), and the idea propagated by Hicks (among others) that 'dynamics' (as distinct from the theory of capital accumulation) involves a need to date every commodity and to work within the framework of intertemporal equilibrium. There is just no evidence that in the passage from the *Treatise* to the *General Theory* Keynes had simultaneously followed Hicks's course.

APPENDIX: KEYNES'S FUNDAMENTAL EQUATIONS: DEFINITIONS AND DERIVATION

(a)   Certain Definitions

   i. E = money income (= Σ earnings) (= cost of production)
thus, E = Rent + Interest + Wages (W) + 'normal' entrepreneutial reward

  ii. Q = profits ('windfalls') = E (actual) − E (definition above)

 iii. $S = \Sigma_i\,(E_i$ − current consumption of the ith individual)
thus, $E = S$ + current consumption

 iv. $I = S + Q$ (I = value of current I, not rate of current I)
thus, iii and iv together imply, $E = I − Q$ + current consumption

  v. O = output = Available output + Non-available output
= R (flow of liquid goods and services) + C (net flow of increments to capital goods and loan capital)
Note: a.   Current consumption = $R\pm$ ($\mp$ changes in Hoards)
             b.   Current Investment = $C\pm$ ($\pm$ changes in Hoards)

 vi. K = stock of real capital = Fixed K + Circulating K + Loan K

(b) The Price Level of Consumption Goods

i. I' = income earned in the production of investment goods

thus, $E - I'$ = cost of production of current output of consumption goods

$E - S$ = current expenditure on consumption goods (recall that $O = R + C$)

ii. P = price level of consumption goods

thus, $P.R$ = current expenditure on consumption goods

$E.\dfrac{C}{O} (= I')$ = cost of production of new investment goods

Now, $P.R = E - S$

$$= \frac{E(R + C)}{O} - S$$

$$= \frac{E}{O} \cdot R + I' - S$$

$$P = \frac{E}{O} + \frac{I' - S}{R} \qquad (1)$$

iii. W = rate of earnings per unit human effort ($\frac{1}{W}$ = labour power of money)

iv. W_1 = rate of earnings per unit of output (rate of efficiency earnings)

v. e = coefficient of efficiency

thus, $W = eW_1$

Equation 1 then becomes,

$$P = W_1 + \frac{I' - S}{R}$$

$$= \frac{1}{e} W + \frac{I' - S}{R} \qquad (1a)$$

(c) The Price Level of Output as a Whole

i. P' = price level of new investment goods (assumed given)

ii. π = price level of output as a whole

iii. I = value of new investment (as distinct from I')

Now,

$$\pi = \frac{P.R + P'C}{O}$$

$$\pi = \frac{E - S + I}{O}$$

$$\pi = \frac{E}{O} + \frac{I - S}{O} \tag{2}$$

Or,

$$\pi = \frac{1}{e} W + \frac{I - S}{O} \tag{2a}$$

(d)   A Modification

   i. Q_1 = profit on consumption goods
  ii. Q_2 = profit on investment goods
 iii. Q = total profit = $Q_1 + Q_2$

Now, we obtain

$$Q_1 = P.R - \frac{E}{O} \cdot R$$
$$= E - S - (E - I')$$
$$= I' - S$$

and

$$Q_2 = I - I'$$

so that,

$$Q = Q_1 + Q_2 = I - S$$

Re-writing equations 1 and 2 we obtain

$$P = W_1 + \frac{Q_1}{R} \tag{1b}$$

$$\pi = W_1 + \frac{Q}{O} \tag{2b}$$

XI. THE THEORETICAL SYSTEM OF THE *TREATISE VERSUS* THE *GENERAL THEORY*

in his great theoretical *Treatise* [Keynes] . . . failed to produce a theory of employment (Joan Robinson, 1951–1979, vol. III, p. 93).

The respective theoretical systems that underlie the *Treatise* and the *General Theory* are most obviously distinguished by the theory of employment (and thereby the process through which saving and investment are brought into 'equilibrium') that each adopts. For although it is true, as Joan Robinson's remark suggests, that the *General Theory*'s principle of effective demand is not present in the *Treatise*, there is a theory of employment there, but it is the orthodox marginalist theory of employment.

In this chapter these theoretical properties of the *Treatise* model will be clarified in order to highlight its contrast with the new theoretical system Keynes evolved in the *General Theory*.

A. THE NATURAL RATE OF INTEREST AND THE LEVEL OF EMPLOYMENT: MARGINALIST THEORY

Before looking directly at the *Treatise*, however, it would not be out of place to indicate very briefly the aspects of theory that need to be established as being part of the *Treatise* model in order to enable us to conclude that it represents a contribution to the 'analysis of deviations' based upon orthodox marginalist theory.

The principal idea of the marginalist orthodoxy was that relative prices are the 'balancing factors' that ensure equilibrium between demand and supply (see Chapter IV, Section B above). In particular, the rate of interest adjustment mechanism operates to equalise saving and investment. As was shown in Chapter IV, it is this proposition that underlies the marginalist notion that in long-period equilibrium, where saving equals investment and the natural rate of interest equals the market rate of interest, full employment prevails. Furthermore, in equilibrium, prices correspond to costs of production and, specifically, 'factors' receive payment equal in value to their 'marginal contribution' to production. All of this was shown in some detail in Chapter IV above, so it is not necessary to cover that territory again.

B.   THE THEORETICAL STRUCTURE OF THE *TREATISE ON MONEY*

The question of what constitutes the characteristics (in terms of the level of employment) of the saving-investment equilibrium of the *Treatise* revolves around three issues of theory. Firstly, the analytical meaning of the distinction between the 'natural' rate of interest and the 'market' rate made in the *Treatise* (*J.M.K.*, vol. V, p. 139); secondly, the implications of Keynes's use of a rate of interest adjustment mechanism to establish equilibrium between saving and investment; and thirdly, whether it is possible to give a precise meaning to one of Keynes's stated 'conditions of equilibrium'—that the equilibrium price level corresponds to the 'rate of efficiency earnings' (*J.M.K.*, vol. V, p. 122, *et passim.*). In considering these issues in turn, it will be argued in this section that each of the three is no more than a *Treatise* variation on marginalist theory; where in long-period equilibrium only full employment is possible.

Consider first the 'natural' versus 'market' rate of interest distinction. In the *Treatise* Keynes seems initially to introduce this terminology as a matter of convenience: "Following Wicksell, *it will be convenient* to call the rate of interest which could cause the second term of our second fundamental equation to be zero the *natural rate* of interest" (*J.M.K.*, vol. V, p. 139, opening italics added). It is not obvious from this that Keynes meant to *define* the natural rate in the same, precise, way in which Wicksell had defined it (as the real return to capital in production); for inasmuch as Wicksell also associated the natural rate with a stable price level it *could* be argued that it was in this sense only (i.e. without the implication of it extending to the theory of capital and employment) that Keynes adopted it in the *Treatise*.* Because it is certainly true that when the second term drops out of the second fundamental equation there is a stable price level for output as a whole.

However, closer inspection of other parts of the *Treatise* helps both to overcome Keynes's obscurity on this point† and to indicate that an interpretation of the type just suggested does not seem appropriate.

To begin with, Keynes did go on to *define* the natural rate of interest more concretely as the rate at which "saving and the value of investment are exactly balanced" (vol. V, p. 139). And since the value of investment is nothing but the value of the increment of *real* capital (p. 117),‡ there is nothing to suggest that Keynes could possibly be saying anything different here about how the natural rate of interest is determined than Marshall had already said when he argued, *using traditional marginalist theory*, that the rate of interest (profit) was the price paid for the use of 'capital' or for the command over 'investible resources' in any market.§ The natural rate of Wicksell is just this equilibrium rate (i.e. the long-period equilibrium rate of return to capital in production); determined in marginalist theory by technological and psychological considerations (Robertson's 'productivity and thrift', 1963, p. 388).

Furthermore, Keynes recognises that in a *Treatise* 'natural rate of interest equilibrium' there will be full employment—this, of course, being the fundamental proposition of the orthodox theories of capital and employment. For example:

---

* For example Hayek (1931–1932), in his review of the *Treatise*, complained that Keynes had not based his discussion of the natural rate of interest on any thorough 'capital theory'.

† It is ironic to find Keynes complaining of Wicksell's obscurity over this issue (*J.M.K.*, vol. V, p. 176); the very point at which Keynes himself was less than perspicuous!

‡ We have left out loan capital (i.e. the net balance of claims on money) so, in effect, we are simplifying the discussion by assuming a closed economy (cf. *J.M.K.*, vol. V, p. 117).

§ When Keynes later tried to describe and outline the 'classical' theory of interest in the *General Theory* he chose words which, if cited without a reference, could easily be mistaken as having come from the *Treatise* (see *J.M.K.*, vol. VII, p. 165; but see also pp. 175–176).

in equilibrium . . . the factors of production are *fully*-employed (*J.M.K.*, vol. V, p. 132, italics added.)

or again (when the market rate of interest is greater than the natural rate):

> a state of *unemployment* may be expected to ensue, *and to continue*, until the rise in bank rate [market rate★] is reversed, or by chance, something happens to alter the *natural rate* of interest so as to bring it back to *equality* with the new *market* rate (vol. V, p. 184, italics added.)†

From this it is possible to conclude that the theoretical structure of Keynes's natural rate/market rate distinction is no more than a version of the same distinction made in neo-'classical' theory. It embodies the essentials of the orthodox marginalist theories of capital and employment even if these are not always clearly and explicitly stated.‡

Fortunately, however, this is not all the evidence that exists to support the case that the *Treatise* model (and especially the characteristics of its 'equilibrium') is just a variant of neo-'classical' theory. Perhaps even stronger evidence resides in the mechanism of adjustment between saving and investment that Keynes used in the *Treatise*. This was entirely 'orthodox', with the rate of interest "influencing the rate of investment *relative* to that of savings" (*J.M.K.*, vol. V, p. 171, italics added). This is just one way of saying that the excess demand (or supply) for 'savings in general' is reduced by variations in the rate of interest (the mechanism was outlined in Figs 1 and 2 of the previous chapter):

> a rise . . . in the market rate of interest upsets the balance between . . . investment and saving, unless a corresponding rise in the natural rate occurs at the same time. *It may do this either by stimulating saving or by retarding investment* (vol. V, p. 180, italics added.)

While it is not necessary to go over again the arguments concerning the orthodox flavour of this aspect of *Treatise* theory, there is a related

---

★ The true market rate will be some conglomeration of bank and bond rates. Keynes, however, tended to use 'market' rate as synonymous with 'bank' rate in those cases (for example, in this passage) where a precise definition did not impinge upon the validity or force of the argument. The exact definitions may be found in *J.M.K.*, vol. V, p. 179. See also n.†, p. 69 above.

† See also *J.M.K.*, vol. VI, pp. 184–186.

‡ Cf. *J.M.K.*, vol. V, p. 274 where some obscurity still remains to be cleared away.

point upon which some comment is in order. It concerns an *empirical* qualification Keynes makes in the *Treatise* which might be mistaken for a theoretical change concerning the mechanism by which saving and investment are brought into equilibrium:

> In the case of saving, the effect of a change in the rate of interest is direct and primary and needs no special explanation, *though the amount of the effect may often be quantitatively small in practice, especially over the short period* (vol. V, p. 180, italics added.)

Hicks (1937), for example, erected the whole of his 'Keynes and the Classics' interpretation on the view that in the *General Theory* income was brought in to replace the rate of interest in the 'savings function' for a particular case where the effect of a change in the rate of interest on savings was 'quantitatively small' (Hicks, 1937, p. 129 and p. 132) but where the effect of a change in income was not insignificant.* Moreover, in conjunction with the *Treatise* definition of saving (*J.M.K.*, vol. V, p. 154), in terms of the proportion of *income* not consumed, there is not a little temptation to see this as the beginnings of the principle of effect demand.† This, however, would be quite wrong. A practical qualification does not change the general (abstract) theoretical relationship. It may go some way to dispelling such mistaken ideas if it is noted again here that Marshall made exactly the same qualification:

> considering . . . a large . . . market for capital, we cannot regard the aggregate supply of it [i.e., savings in general*] altered quickly and to a considerable extent by a change in the rate of interest (Marshall, 1961, p. 534).

It would be an intrepid historian of economic theory, indeed, who would conclude from this that Marshall had abandoned the orthodox marginalist rate of interest adjustment mechanism. There is no reason why things should be any different in Keynes's case just because he changed the theoretical system in a later book.

---

* It is not surprising, therefore, that he called this "Mr. Keynes's *special theory*" (Hicks, 1937, p. 133, italics in original.)

† One recent interpretation of the *Treatise* never discusses the role (the crucial role in terms of the *Treatise vis-à-vis* the *General Theory*) of the rate of interest (Mehta, 1977, pp. 205–209).

‡ Marshall used this terminology only a page earlier (p. 533); it is clear that this is what he meant by the 'supply of capital' in this passage.

This brings us to the last of the three issues (mentioned at the beginning of this section) around which the interpretation of the theoretical characteristics of the *Treatise* equilibrium revolve:

> [when] saving and . . . investment are exactly balanced, . . . the price level of output as a whole . . . exactly corresponds to *the money rate of the efficiency earnings of the factors of production* (*J.M.K.*, vol. V, p. 139, italics added.)

This, it would seem, must be interpreted to mean that price equals cost of production (p. 111) but it is not clear whether the statement also embodies the familiar 'marginal conditions' of neo-'classical' theory. However, while there is no direct evidence in the *Treatise* which would permit us to draw any inference about the latter possibility, indirectly, of course, from the arguments of this and the previous chapter, we should not be surprised to find this to be the case. Even stronger evidence to support this, however, is to be found in the fact that the term 'rate of efficiency earnings' was commonly used to describe the process by which competition was seen to determine the level of 'normal' wages by orthodox neo-'classical' theorists (especially those in Cambridge; see, for example, Pigou, 1929, p. 349). The term, in fact, belongs to none other than Marshall:

> The tendency of [competition] . . . to cause . . . earnings to find their own level, is a tendency to equality of efficiency-earnings (Marshall, 1961, p. 549.)

For Keynes (so familiar with Marshall's language and its theoretical implications) to have chosen the expression *without* being aware of what Marshall meant to be conveyed by it seems an unlikely possibility. The fact that he did not explicitly separate his usage from that of Marshall would appear to indicate that he was prepared to accept the latter's theory that went with it.

Thus the general conclusion that emerges from the arguments offered in this section is that there can be no doubt about the orthodox nature of the theoretical system which lies at the base of the *Treatise*'s analysis of deviations.

C.   THE PRINCIPLE OF EFFECTIVE DEMAND

In the *General Theory*, as already shown in Chapter VI, the principle of effective demand overthrew all of this. It simultaneously replaced the orthodox marginalist theory of employment and capital, to which the *Treatise* is tied, with the new theory of employment that is embodied in the proposition that variations in the level of output (employment) ensure that saving and investment are equalised. Since it has been shown already how fundamentally this theoretical system was in opposition to the then orthodox marginalist theory (in Chapters VI and VII above), no more need be said to enable us to draw the conclusion that the *General Theory* and the *Treatise* differ at the same level of *theory* as that which separates the *General Theory* from the pre-1936 orthodoxy. Nevertheless, there are some points relating to how Keynes viewed the theoretical system of the *Treatise* by the time he had finished the *General Theory* which, for the sake of completeness, should now be mentioned.*

The first of these relates to Keynes's view of the concept of the 'natural' rate of interest used in the *Treatise*:

> it was a mistake to speak of the natural rate of interest [in the *Treatise*] . . . for at *every* rate of interest there is a level of employment for which that rate is the 'natural' rate, in the sense that the system will be in *equilibrium* with that rate of interest and that level of employment (*J.M.K.*, vol. VII, p. 242, Keynes's italics omitted, the additional italics are ours.)

This passage, from the *General Theory*, says no more than that since the principle of effective demand determines the level of output and employment (i.e. the 'equilibrium' of saving and investment) the rate of interest, or more properly the natural rate of interest, has nothing to do with the basic theoretical mechanism which is at work. The level of employment is determined irrespective of the rate of interest (p. 242.) Thus:

> I am now no longer of the opinion that the concept of a 'natural' rate of interest, which previously seemed to me a most promising idea, has anything very useful . . . to contribute to our analysis (vol. VII, p. 243.)

It is interesting to note that this implies that it is possible, according to the theoretical structure of the principle of effective demand, for there

---

* These points simply reflect Keynes's view of the theoretical aspects of the pre-1936 orthodoxy which we have discussed already (Chapters VI and VII). However, it did not seem appropriate in that more general discussion to cite in support of the argument those specific remarks that Keynes made about the *Treatise* as part of that orthodoxy.

to be *persistent* unemployment when the interest rate is *either* high *or* low. With the rate of interest thus divorced of its marginalist associations, it is clear that certain 'problems' must be faced in reconstructing economic theory in terms of the contribution of the *General Theory*, because it is then obvious that the 'marginal efficiency of capital' theory of investment cannot be retained. Furthermore, the result implies also that there may be persistent unemployment when the wage-rate is either high or low.

The second point to be mentioned in connection with Keynes's post-*General Theory* views of the *Treatise* has a bearing upon the 'change of definition of terms' interpretation of the whole of Keynes's work (this view, as already noted in Chapter V, Section D above, found its most active supporter in Dennis Robertson). In particular, according to this view, all that needs to be done to get from the *Treatise* to the *General Theory* is to change the definition of income (to include 'windfalls'—the *Q*—of the *Treatise*). Now, it has been argued already (in Chapter V) that changing definitions only affects the way in which a *given* mechanism of adjustment is represented and that it does not affect the mechanism itself (a point which Keynes never conveyed successfully to Robertson). This fact is brought into sharp relief when it is realised that even on the *Treatise* definitions of saving and investment* the replacement of the orthodox rate of interest adjustment mechanism by the principle of effective demand would lead to very different conclusions than those derived from the orthodox approach. Keynes argued as much in the *General Theory*:

> "In my *Treatise on Money* I defined what purported to be a unique rate of interest . . . which, in the terminology of my *Treatise*, preserved the equality between the rate of saving (*as there defined*) and the rate of investment. [. . .]
> I had, however, overlooked the fact that in any given society there is, *on this definition*, a *different* natural rate of interest for each hypothetical level of employment" (vol. VII, p. 242, italics added.)

This leaves only one last source of confusion to expose. It is necessary to understand properly what it means to say, as some writers have said, that the *Treatise* represents a 'dynamic' analysis of 'disequilibrium'

---

* Which are, of course, slightly different from those of the *General Theory* (see *J.M.K.*, vol. VII, pp. 60–61 and pp. 77–80 for the differences).

while the *General Theory* is 'comparative statics' (cf. e.g. Shackle, 1967, p. 162). Fortunately, the analytical categories of *theory* and *method* which have been applied in the present re-examination of Keynes render this task straightforward.

Under the traditional long-period method there are two tasks to be performed. Firstly, the explanation of the persistent tendencies of the system (i.e. the provision of a *long-period* theory for the determination of the magnitudes of, and interrelationships between, the principal variables which define the object of the analysis) and, secondly, the analysis of deviations (i.e. the provision of an explanation of those temporary forces which interfere with the 'gravitation' of the system towards its long-period position). These are the only meanings that can be assigned to the inadequate terminology embodied in the idea of 'comparative statics' versus 'disequilibrium analysis'. For the *Treatise* is concerned with the analysis of deviations while the *General Theory* is concerned with statements of tendency about the persistent forces at work in the system. But to suggest that the latter concern is somehow 'pedestrian' or even a 'regression' (cf. e.g. Shackle, 1967, p. 148) is evidence of an analytical confusion. The analysis of deviations makes no sense in the absence of a 'long-period' theory.

D.   FROM THE *TREATISE* TO THE *GENERAL THEORY*

The theoretical transition from the *Treatise* to the *General Theory* outlined above, together with the argument of the previous chapter, reinforce the central conclusion of Part I of this study: the analysis of both the *General Theory* and the *Treatise on Money* is conducted within the framework provided by the traditional long-period method while the theoretical system of the *General Theory* departs from the marginalist orthodoxy (of which the *Treatise* was a part) by offering a new theory of employment which conflicts with the then prevailing theory of capital and of employment (and hence, of value) conducted in terms of demand-and-supply.

As has been argued, while this implies that Keynes's theory of output (employment) is not compatible with the neo-'classical' theory of value, it means also that to furnish a complete description of the determining circumstances for all the constituent elements of the object of the analysis (and not just of the levels of output and employment) it is necessary to find compatible theories of value and distribution with which to supplement Keynes's principle of effective demand. It is here that the theoretical system of the old Classical Economists seems to offer the greatest promise of success. Of course, in such a reconstruction new issues and problems, of both theory and method, would be raised. For example, the whole question concerning the implications of the fact that the 'natural' tendency of a market system is towards structural unemployment would have to be faced squarely. But although there would be new problems, it does appear that this approach provides a stronger basis from which to proceed than that provided by orthodox marginalist analysis.

Appendix 1. NATURAL PRICES, PERSISTENT FORCES AND THE CONCEPT OF SELF-ADJUSTMENT

A. NATURAL PRICES: ANALYTICAL AND ETHICAL ASPECTS

The concept of natural price (and, therefore, the traditional long-period method) emerged in part under the influence of the writings of the Natural Law philosophers on the early 'scientific' works in economics. However, the influence from this quarter fostered, at least in the early days of economics, a confusion between the purely analytical device of examining natural or long-period normal constructs and the ethical implications of the doctrine of 'natural law' as used, for example, in the Scholastic literature (see Robbins, 1952, pp. 44–49 on this point). It would not seem out of place, therefore, to stress in this appendix the ethical neutrality of the traditional long-period method.

Adam Smith himself was not always innocent of assigning an ethical content to the traditional method (as noted by Meek, 1965, pp. 4–6).* In a detailed consideration of this habit of Smith, Lionel Robbins was led to conclude that: "it is quite true that Adam Smith . . . had certain theological leanings, and from time to time [clothed] his results in the language of Deistic philosophy . . . . But this has no more to do with the fundamental validity of his argument than the theological language in which from time to time Newton was apt to refer to the universe, has

---

* "[God] created the machine of the Universe so as at all times to produce the greatest quantity of happiness" (*Moral Sentiments*, as quoted in Meek, 1965, pp. 4–6).

to do with the validity of his system of natural movements" (Robbins, 1952, pp. 24–25).* However, among the nineteenth century writers few would appear to have subscribed to this mistaken opinion. Wicksell, for instance, was perfectly clear on the necessary distinction between the 'analytical' and the 'ethical' aspects of the concept (see e.g. Wicksell, 1901, vol. I, p. 5) as, indeed, was Marshall who wrote that "it is sometimes *erroneously* supposed that normal action in economics is that which is right morally" (Marshall, 1961, p. 35, italics added). Keynes commented favourably on this aspect of Marshall's method in the following terms: "there is, I think, no passage in his works in which he links economic studies to any ethical doctrine in particular" (*J.M.K.*, vol. X, p. 170). If Palgrave's *Dictionary of Political Economy* may be taken as summarising the consensus of opinion on this issue at the beginning of this century, then it would appear that much had been done to expose the false association between ethical doctrines and the examination of natural or long-period normal positions. The entry under 'Political Economy' (written by W. E. Johnson) states that "the confusion between scientific law and ethical law no longer prevails. In this connection the term normal has replaced the older word natural . . . [and we] understand by the expression *normal* something which presents a certain empirical uniformity or regularity" (1963, vol. III, p. 139, italics in original).

This is not to say that once an explanation of the forces determining the outcome of these 'natural tendencies' has been provided an author cannot at that stage make some personal judgement (an ethical statement, so to speak) about the 'desirability' of this outcome. But such judgements are not contingent upon the abstract notion of 'natural tendencies', rather they derive from the results these 'tendencies' produce. That is, they are made on the basis of theory not method. This point has been expressed aptly by Meek:

> The economy may work . . . in a law-governed way . . . but what is law-governed is not necessarily good. Whether the [economy] ought to be left alone or not is something which can properly be decided only after the

---

* Robbins continues: "In my judgement it is an error to judge the positions adopted in the *Wealth of Nations* by reference back to the *Theory of Moral Sentiments* rather than by examining the merits of the arguments by which they are supported in the contexts in which they appear" (1952, p. 25). See also Keynes's similar argument on this point in *J.M.K.*, vol. IX, p. 279.

manner of its operation, and the results it produces, have been thoroughly analysed (Meek, 1965, p. 8).

A clear example of this is provided by the Classical economists advocacy of *laissez-faire* in the case of trade policy (as pointed out by Keynes, *J.M.K.*, vol. IX, p. 279). The conclusion that bounties on the importation of wage-goods (and, in particular, on the importation of corn) were not 'desirable' was based on a theoretical argument that can be seen in its simplest form in Ricardo's writing. According to his theory, 'profits depend on high or low wages' so that a bounty on corn imports raises wages and hence lowers profits. But the latter provide the mainspring for accumulation (a generally 'desirable' end in Ricardo's mind), so bounties must be eliminated.

B. THE CONCEPT OF SELF-ADJUSTMENT

In a contribution to a series of radio broadcasts, subsequently published in *The Listener* in November 1934 (reprinted in *J.M.K.*, vol. XIII, pp. 485–492), Keynes contrasted the views of orthodox economics with the views of those he chose to label 'heretics' (he allied himself with the heretics of course; p. 489) in terms of a distinction between one group that held that the economic system was 'self-adjusting' (the orthodox school; p. 486) and another that held that there was 'no significant sense' in which the economic system was self-adjusting (the heretics; p. 487). It goes without saying that Keynes was careful to acknowledge that the orthodox school admitted that 'frictions' might give rise to 'temporary' aberrations but nevertheless, if the system was not tampered with, there was an inherent tendency for these disturbances to be eliminated—even if after the lapse of a considerable period of time. (Indeed, the advocacy of State intervention is a theme which runs consistently through Keynes's work from *Indian Currency* through to the celebrated paper "The End of *Laissez-Faire*" in 1926 and on to the *General Theory* itself.) Unfortunately, distinctions such as these are prone to lead to confusion if taken too literally and it is therefore necessary to attempt to be a little more precise about the concept of self-adjustment.

The problem with the literal interpretation of Keynes's argument is as follows. There is, in fact, an important and significant sense in which a capitalist economy is self-adjusting. It is quite clear that according to the traditional long-period method the economy will always *tend* to produce, if left to its own devices so to speak, an objective outcome (see Meek, 1965, p. 6). It is nonsensical to postulate anything else without also taking up the position that economic theory cannot make any general statements at all. If there are systematic forces, however these are described and explained, there is always a 'tendency' towards self-adjustment. Indeed, the 'method dimension' of economic analysis discussed throughout this study is synonymous with 'self-adjustment' in this sense. What then was Keynes driving at in the above quoted remarks?

The meaning of these remarks, and of the many like them in the *General Theory* that refer to 'obstacles to full employment', must be considered carefully. According to orthodox marginalist theory, the *outcome* of the operation of the systematic forces isolated by that theory (demand-and-supply) ensured, in the long-run, the full employment of labour. Now, there are two different grounds upon which Keynes opposed this position. The first is a pre-*General Theory* argument. It held that although orthodox theory stated the long-run 'tendencies' correctly (see e.g. *J.M.K.*, vol. IV, p. 65), the system could still find itself at a point in the trade-cycle where the presence of the long-run 'tendencies' might be so weakly felt that some relief might be afforded by State intervention (see e.g. *J.M.K.*, vol. V, pp. 184–185 on the *modus operandi* of the bank rate and *J.M.K.*, vol. XIII, p. 249 on Hayek's review of the *Treatise*).

The second argument is radically different from this, because it is erected on the basis of the principle of effective demand. It is argued in this context that the orthodox statement of tendency is itself wrong. We may quote Keynes:

> [the orthodox idea] that the aggregate demand price of output . . . is equal to its aggregate supply price for all volumes of output, is equivalent to the proposition that there is no obstacle to full employment. [however] this is not the true law (vol. VII, p. 26).

It would appear to be this second argument that underlies Keynes's remarks to his radio audience.

In the proper sense of the term, therefore, Keynes's own examination of the economy in the *General Theory* presupposes 'self-adjustment'— the problem is that the self-regulating mechanism produces results (like unemployment) that are undesirable.

Appendix 2. NOTES ON 'STOCKS AND FLOWS', 'SUPPLY-PRICE' AND 'QUASI-RENT'

A. 'STOCKS' AND 'FLOWS'

In the foregoing discussion of the marginalist theory of the rate of interest (profit), it was assumed that it was possible to speak of a symmetry between the notions of the 'demand for capital' and the 'demand for investment' (and also of a parallel symmetry between the 'supply of capital' and the 'supply of saving'). Yet in the course of that discussion only passing reference was made to the important distinction between stocks and flows* which is, in this particular context at least, reflected in the commonly held position that it is not possible to relate (in any simple way) the demand for capital and the demand for investment (see e.g. Haavelmo, 1960, p. 216) as the former is a demand for a stock while the latter is a demand for a flow.† It is now necessary to clarify the basis upon which the previous discussion has been conducted.

The fundamental proposition underlying our discussion may be put

---

* See above, Chapter IV, Section B.

† Haavelmo's argument is that "the demand for investment cannot simply be derived from the demand for capital. Demand for a finite addition to the stock of capital can lead to any rate of investment from almost zero to infinity" (1960, p. 216). It is clear, however, that we cannot properly interpret Haavelmo's remarks as disputing the fact that the negative 'slope' of the investment demand function *is implied by* the negative 'slope' of the demand function for capital as a stock (i.e. the negative elasticity of the latter, with respect to variations in the rate of interest, implies the negative elasticity of the former).

simply: if the desired stock of capital varies inversely with the rate of interest (profit)—which, as already shown, is the basic premise of the marginalist theory of distribution—then an inverse relationship also exists between the demand for capital as a flow (investment demand) and the rate of interest. Furthermore, there is always a direct relationship between the actual elasticities of the two demand functions involved.

In the simplest case of all, where the turnover time of capital is equal in all industries (a 'yearly cycle' so to speak) and only circulating capital is used, these relations are revealed in their essence. For here, the actual elasticities of the demand function for capital as a stock and the demand function for capital as a flow (investment demand) are equal (see Garegnani, 1978–1979, pt. I, p. 346). Indeed, the two functions will be identical. However, the presence of fixed capital in production (retaining the 'yearly' production cycle assumption), while it does not alter the basic fact that the elasticity of the demand function for capital implies the elasticity of the demand function for investment, does mean that the respective magnitudes of these elasticities will differ. For in this case the rate of replacement of fixed capital (which depends ultimately upon the rate of depreciation) will be reflected in the 'slope' of the investment demand function.

To illustrate these points, consider an 'increase' in the demand for capital as a stock (from K to $K^\star$) induced by a fall in the natural rate of interest from $r_n (= r_m)$ to $r_n^\star (< r_m)$ where, $r_n^\star = r_n - \triangle r_n$. Of course, whether there is fixed capital or not, as long as there are forces working to lower the market rate of interest in the direction of the new natural rate $r_n^\star$, the demand for investment must increase if the initial stock of capital is to take on the new physical composition compatible with the equilibrium defined by $r_n^\star$. This ensures the validity of the basic relation between the two functions; the negative 'slope' of the demand function for capital implies a negatively 'sloped' investment demand function (see Garegnani, 1978–1979, pt. I, p. 352 for a numerical example illustrating this point). But when fixed capital is present the actual magnitudes of the elasticities will differ between the two functions.

Under the assumption of a constant rate of depreciation δ, $0 < \delta \leqslant 1$, rendering the efficiency of an item of fixed capital independent of its age (see Sraffa, 1960, p. 64), we will have $\varepsilon_{\mathrm{ID}} = \varepsilon_{\mathrm{KD}} \cdot \frac{1}{\delta}$ as the relation between the magnitudes of the two elasticities. Notice that if $\varepsilon_{\mathrm{KD}}$ is less than zero so too is ε_{ID}. If $\delta = 1$ the whole capital stock is used-up each 'year' and we are back in the circulating capital case.

B.   SUPPLY-PRICE

In Chapter II, Section D, long-period positions were defined in terms of a uniform rate of profit on the *supply-price of capital*. It did not then seem particularly essential to embark upon a discussion of the precise meaning which was to be attached to this phrase as such a discussion would have diverted attention from the main problems there at issue (*viz.* the characteristics of the analytic technique that has been referred to as the traditional long-period method). Nevertheless, for the sake of completeness, such a discussion may now be presented.

Marshall (to whom we owe the term) defines supply-price as follows:

> the price required to call forth the exertion necessary for producing any given amount of a commodity, may be called the *supply-price* for that amount during the same time. (Marshall, 1961, p. 142, italics in original.)

Next, for Marshall, the *supply-price of capital* "represents a postponement of enjoyment or a waiting for it" (1961, p. 233, italics in original) and this is equal, in equilibrium, to the rate of interest (profit). Now it will be clear that this is not the same sense in which this term was employed in Chapter II, Section D, above.

In everyday language the sense in which it is there used is as follows: the *aggregate* value of the various pieces of capital equipment used in the production of a given output.* But this will not really do as a technical definition (though, it is all that is needed to follow the argument in

---

* We may say 'unit of output' without upsetting our definition or, for that matter, anything we shall say in this note. However, it should be made absolutely clear that we are making no reference to 'marginal' units of output here (or, for that matter, 'average' costs as the traditional theory of the firm calls them). In short, the definition of supply-price which we must settle upon has to be clearly distinguished from the meaning that term acquires in the marginalist theory of value and distribution. Our 'everyday' definition seems to be in full accord with that given in Palgrave's *Dictionary* (1963, vol. III, p. 488). Johnson's definition runs there as follows: "the supply-price of a commodity is found by adding together the prices which have to be paid to the different agents which contribute to the production of a *unit* of the commodity." The italicised 'unit' reflects the fact that by its use Johnson, following Marshall, means 'marginal' unit.

Chapters II and III above). There are too many things left unsaid. Let us therefore be more specific.

First, we may specify what is meant by 'aggregate value' very easily. It is the sum of the products of price and quantity for all those commodities which appear as means of production. But our second problem is not so straightforward. What is to be understood by the phrase 'pieces of capital equipment used' (or 'commodities which appear as means of production')? Here the everyday meaning which we might attach to such a phrase leads us astray. For by it we *do not* mean to include *all* those commodities used as means of production. Those which must be explicitly excluded are those commodities (used as means of production) which would not, at normal prices, be reproduced. It seems hardly necessary to add that the supply-price of capital cannot be determined independently of relative prices and the rate of profit. This, however, should not be thought thereby to exclude items of fixed capital; rather what has been excluded are those items which might be referred to as 'obsolete machines'. This accords with our earlier definition of the dominant technique and conforms with Marx's equivalent idea of the means of production associated with the 'socially necessary technique'.

However, what has been excluded from our definition of the supply-price of capital is the value of any obsolete machines, earning a quasi-rent but not reproduced at normal prices, used in production. This accords with Sraffa's argument that "land [and] obsolescent instruments have the properties of non-basics" (1960, p. 78).

C. QUASI-RENT

This is a convenient place to take up another point of definition; this time of the term *quasi-rent*.

Marshall (from whom, again, this term derives) defines it in the following way:

> "the term *quasi-rent* will be used in the present volume for the income derived from machines and other applicances for production made by man" (Marshall, 1961, p. 74, italics in original.)

The following may help to clarify this definition. Consider a simple circulating capital system of the following type (recall Chapter III, Section A, for the notation):

$$(1 + \pi)\Sigma_j k_{ij}p_j + \omega l_i = p_i y_i \qquad\qquad i,j = 1 \ldots n$$

According to Marshall's definition, total quasi-rent in industry i is:

$$Qi = \pi\,(\Sigma_j k_{ij}p_j)$$

This is just total profits in industry i:

$$P_i = p_i y_i - \Sigma_j k_{ij}p_j - \omega l_i$$

However, we have used the term quasi-rent not in Marshall's sense but in Sraffa's sense: "quasi-rent . . . is received for those fixed capital items which, having been in active use in the past, have now been superseded but are worth employing for what they can get" (1960, p. 78). Sraffa's definition captures more clearly that quasi-rent (unlike value) arises from scarcity alone. If an item (q) is being used as current means of production in some industry i, but is not reproduced at normal prices, we may write:

$$(1 + \pi)\,\Sigma_j k_{ij}^1 pj + \omega l_i^1 + \varrho_1 q_1 = p_i^1 y_i$$

$$(1 + \pi)\,\Sigma_j k_{ij}^h p_j + \omega l_i^h + \varrho_h q_h = p_i^h y_i$$

We assume that there are h different varieties of q currently used (in the case of land, where the same argument applies as in the case of an obsolete machine, it would be land of h different fertilities) and that there exists $g, g = 1 \ldots h$, such that $\varrho_g = O$. This ensures uniformity of the rate of profit. Total quasi-rent, on Sraffa's definition, is

$$Q_i = \overset{\Sigma}{_h}\,\varrho_h q_h$$

(This, it will be recalled, is not part of the supply-price of capital.)

REFERENCES

Arrow, K. and Hahn, F. (1971). *General Competitive Analysis*. Edinburgh: Oliver and Boyd.

Bagehot, W. (1873). *Lombard Street*, 3rd edn. London: H. S. King.

Barker, T. (1980). "The Economic Consequences of Monetarism". *Cambridge Journal of Economics*, vol. IV, December.

Baumol, W. J. (1977). "Say's (at least) Eight Laws, or what Say and James Mill may really have meant". *Economica*, vol. XLIV, May.

Birck, L. V. (1927). "Theories of Overproduction". *Economic Journal*, vol. XXXVII, March.

Blaug, M. (1968). *Economic Theory in Retrospect*, 2nd edn. London: Heinemann (1st edn, 1962).

Bleaney, M. (1976). *Underconsumption Theories*. London: Lawrence and Wishart.

Bliss, C. J. (1974). *The Re-appraisal of Keynes's Economics: An Appraisal*. University of Essex Discussion Paper, no. 55.

Bliss, C. J. (1975). *Capital Theory and the Distribution of Income*. Amsterdam: North-Holland.

Böhm-Bawerk, E. von. (1899). *Capital and Interest*, in three volumes. Illinois: Libertarian Press (1959).

Bonar, J. (1922). *Philosophy and Political Economy*, 3rd edn. London: Allen and Unwin (1st edn, 1893).

Brown, M. *(et al.)*. (1976). *Essays in Modern Capital Theory*. Amsterdam: North Holland.

Bukharin, N. (1972). *Imperialism and the Accumulation of Capital*. New York: Monthly Review Press (first published, 1924).

Cannan, E. (1893). *A History of Theories of Production and Distribution from 1776 to 1848*. New York: Kelley (reprinted, 1967).

Cantillon, R. (1755). *Essai sur la Nature du Commerce en Général* (H. Higgs, ed.). London: Frank Cass (1959).

Clark, J. B. (1891–2). "The Statics and Dynamics of Distribution". *Quarterly Journal of Economics*, vol. VI.

Clark, J. B. (1899). *The Distribution of Wealth*. London: Macmillan.

Clifton, J. A. (1977). "Competition and the Evolution of the Capitalist Mode of Production". *Cambridge Journal of Economics*, vol. I, June.

Clower, R. W. (1965). "The Keynesian Counter-revolution: A Theoretical Appraisal", as reprinted in Clower (1969).

Clower, R. W. (ed). (1969). *Monetary Theory*. Harmondsworth: Penguin.

Corry, B. A. (1959). "Malthus and Keynes". *Economic Journal*, vol. LXIX, December.

Debreu, G. (1959). *The Theory of Value*. New Haven: Yale University Press.

Dixit, A. (1977). "The Accumulation of Capital Theory". *Oxford Economic Papers*, vol. XXIX.

Dobb, M. (1937). *Political Economy and Capitalism*. London: Routledge and Kegan Paul.

Dobb, M. (1973). *Theories of Value and Distribution Since Adam Smith*. Cambridge: Cambridge University Press.

Eagly, R. V. (1974). *The Structure of Classical Economic Theory*. Oxford: Oxford University Press.

Eatwell, J. (1975a). "Mr. Sraffa's Standard Commodity and the Rate of Exploitation". *Quarterly Journal of Economics*, vol. LXXXIX, November.

Eatwell, J. (1975b). *Scarce and Produced Commodities*. Unpublished Ph.D. Thesis, Harvard University.

Eatwell, J. (1977). "The Irrelevance of Returns to Scale in Sraffa's Analysis". *Journal of Economic Literature*, vol. XV, March.

Eatwell, J. and Milgate, M. (eds) (1983). *Keynes's Economics and the Theory of Value and Distribution*. London: Duckworth.

Edgeworth, F. Y. (1925). *Papers Relating to Political Economy*, in three volumes. New York: Frankling (reprinted, 1970).

Eshag, E. (1963). *From Marshall to Keynes*. Oxford: Blackwell.

Fetter, F. W. (1904). *Principles of Economics*. New York: Century Company.

Fetter, F. W. (1927). "Interest Theory and Price Movements". *American Economic Review, Papers and Proceedings*, vol. XVII, March.

Fisher, I. (1896). *Appreciation and Interest*. London: Macmillan.

Fisher, I. (1930). *The Theory of Interest*. London: Macmillan.

Friedman, M. (1980). "Response to Questionnaire on Monetary Policy". *Memoranda on Monetary Policy*. London: HMSO.

Garegnani, P. (1958). *A Problem in the Theory of Distribution from Ricardo to Wicksell*. Unpublished Ph.D, Cambridge.

Garegnani, P. (1960). *Il Capitale Nelle Teorie Della Distribuzione*. Milan: Giuffre.

Garegnani, P. (1964–65). "Note su Consumi, Investmenti e Domanda Effettiva". *Economia Internazionale*.

Gargenani, P. (1970a). "Heterogeneous Capital, the Production Function and the Theory of Distribution", reprinted in Hunt and Schwartz (1972).

Garegnani, P. (1970b). "Reply to Bliss". *Review of Economic Studies*, vol. XXXXVII.

Garegnani, P. (1976). "On a Change in the Notion of Equilibrium in Recent Work on Value: A Comment on Samuelson". In M. Brown (1976).

Garegnani, P. (1978–1979). "Notes on Consumption, Investment and Effective Demand". *Cambridge Journal of Economics*, vols II and III, December 1978 and March 1979.

Garegnani, P. (1979). "A Reply to Joan Robinson". *Cambridge Journal of Economics*, vol. III, June.

Grandmont, J-M. (1977). "Temporary General Equilibrium Theory". *Econometrica*, vol. XLV, April.

Green, R. (1982). "Money, Output and Inflation in Classical Economies". *Contributions to Political Economy*, vol. I, March.

Groenewegen, P. D. (1973). "A Note on the Origin of the Phrase 'Supply and Demand". *Economic Journal*, vol. LXXXIII, June.

Haavelmo, T. (1960). *A Study in the Theory of Investment*. Chicago: Chicago University Press.

Haberler, G. (1958). *Prosperity and Depression*, 4th edn. London: George Allen and Unwin.

Hahn, F. (1952). "Expectations and Equilibrium". *Economic Journal*, vol. LXII, December.

Hahn, F. (1965). "On Some Problems of Proving the Existence of an Equilibrium in a Monetary Economy", as reprinted in Clower (1969).

Hahn, F. (1973). *On the Notion of Equilibrium in Economics*. Cambridge: Cambridge University Press.

Harrod, R. (1937). "Mr Keynes and Traditional Theory". *Econometrica*, vol. V, January, as reprinted in Harrod (1972a).

Harrod, R. (1948). *Towards a Dynamic Economics*. London: Macmillan.

Harrod, R. (1972a). *Economic Essays*, 2nd edn. London: Macmillan.

Harrod, R. (1972b). *The Life of John Maynard Keynes*. Harmondsworth: Penguin (first published, 1951).

Hawtrey, R. G. (1913). *Good and Bad Trade*. New York: Kelley (reprinted, 1970).

Hawtrey, R. G. (1923). *Currency and Credit*, 2nd edn. London: Longmans and Green.

Hawtrey, R. G. (1937). *Capital and Employment*. London: Longmans and Green.

Hayek, F. A. (1928). "Das intertemporale Gleichgewichtssystem der Preise und die Bewegungen des Geldwertes". *Weltwirtschaftliches Archiv*, July.

Hayek, F. A. (1929). *Monetary Theory and the Trade Cycle*, translated 1933. London: Joanthan Cape.

Hayek, F. A. (1931–32). "Reflections on the Pure Theory of Money of Mr. J. M. Keynes". *Economica*, vols XI–XII, August 1931 and February 1932.

Hayek, F. A. (1932). "Dr Hayek on Money and Capital: A Reply". *Economic Journal*, vol. XLII, June.

Hayek, F. A, (1935). *Prices and Production*, 2nd edn. London: Routledge and Kegan Paul (1st edn, 1931).

Hayek, F. A. (1936). "The Mythology of Capital". *Quarterly Journal of Economics*, vol. L, February.

Hayek, F. A. (1940). "Review of Lindahl's *Studies in the Theory of Money and Capital*". *Economica*, New Series, vol. VII, August.

Hayek, F. A. (1941). *The Pure Theory of Capital*. London: Macmillan.

Hicks, J. R. (1935). "Wages and Interest: The Dynamic Problem", as reprinted in Hicks (1963).

Hicks, J. R. (1936). "Mr Keynes's Theory of Employment". *Economic Journal*, vol. XLVI, June.

Hicks, J. R. (1937). "Mr Keynes and the 'Classics'". *Econometrica*, vol. V, April as reprinted in Hicks (1967).

Hicks, J. R. (1946). *Value and Capital*, 2nd edn. Oxford: Clarendon Press (1st edn, 1939).

Hicks, J. R. (1963). *The Theory of Wages*, 2nd edn. London: Macmillan (1st edn, 1932).

Hicks, J. R. (1965). *Capital and Growth*. Oxford: Clarendon Press.

Hicks, J. R. (1967). *Critical Essays in Monetary Theory*. Oxford: Clarendon Press.

Hicks, J. R. (1973a). *Capital and Time*. Oxford: Clarendon Press.

Hicks, J. R. (1973b). "The Austrian Theory of Capital and its Rebirth in Modern Economics", in Hicks and Weber (eds) (1973).

Hicks, J. R. (1977). *Economic Perspectives*. Oxford: Clarendon Press.

Hicks, J. R. and Weber, W. (eds) (1973). *Carl Menger and the Austrian School in Economics*. Oxford: Clarendon Press.

Hull, C. H. (ed) (1899). *The Economic Writings of Sir William Petty*, in two volumes. New York: Kelley (reprinted, 1963).

Hunt, E. K. and Schwartz, J. (eds) (1972). *A Critique of Economic Theory*. Harmondsworth: Penguin.

Jevons, W. S. (1875). *Money and the Mechanism of Exchange*. London: H. S. King and Company.

Jevons, W. S. (1884). *Investigations in Currency and Finance*. New York: Kelley (reprinted, 1964).

Jevons, W. S. (1871). *The Theory of Political Economy* (R. D. C. Black, ed.). Harmondsworth: Penguin (1970).

J.M.K., see Keynes, J. M.

Johnson, H. G. (1951–2). "Some Cambridge Controversies in Monetary Theory". *Review of Economic Studies*, vol. XIX.

Juglar, C. (1889). *Des Crises Commerciales et de leur Retour Périodique*, 2nd edn, republished by Gregg Press, Farnborough, 1968 (1st edn 1862).

Kahn, R. F. (1931). "The Relation of Home Investment to Unemployment". *Economic Journal*, vol. XLI, as reprinted in Kahn (1972).

Kahn, R. F. (1954). "Some Notes on Liquidity-preference", *Manchester School*, September, as reprinted in Kahn (1972).

Kahn, R. F. (1972). *Selected Essays on Employment and Growth*. Cambridge: Cambridge University Press.

Kahn, R. F. (1974). *On Rereading Keynes*. Oxford: Oxford University Press.

Kaldor, N. (1939). "Speculation and Economic Stability". *Review of Economic Studies*, vol. VII, October.

Kaldor, N. (1955–56). "Alternative Theories of Distribution". *Review of Economic Studies*, vol. XXVIII, as reprinted in B. McCormick and E. Smith (eds): *The Labour Market* (Harmondsworth, Penguin, 1968).

Keynes, J. M. (1973–to date). *The Collected Writings of John Maynard Keynes*. London: Macmillan. Abbreviated throughout this study to *J.M.K.*

Keynes, J. Neville (1917). *The Scope and Method of Political Economy*, 4th edn. reprinted, New York: Kelley (1963).

Klein, L. R. (1968). *The Keynesian Revolution*, 2nd edn. London: Macmillan (1st edn, 1966).

Knight, F. (1915–16). "Neglected Factors in the Problem of Normal Interest". *Quarterly Journal of Economics*, vol. XXX.

Knight, F. (1917–18). "The Concept of Normal Price in Value and Distribution". *Quarterly Journal of Economics*, vol. XXXII.

Knight, F. (1921). "Cost of Production and Price over Long and Short Periods". *Journal of Political Economy*, vol. XXIX, April.

Knight, F. (1935). "The Ricardian Theory of Production and Distribution", in two parts. *Canadian Journal of Economics and Political Science*, vol. I, February and May.

Knight, F. (1971). *Risk, Uncertainty and Profit* (1921). Chicago: University of Chicago Press.

Koopmans, T. (1957). *Three Essays on the State of Economic Science*. New York: McGraw-Hill.

Kregel, J. A. (1973). *The Reconstruction of Political Economy*. London: Macmillan.

Laidler, D. (1972). "Thomas Tooke on Monetary Reform". In M. Peston and B. Corry (eds): *Essays in Honour of Lord Robbins*. London: Weidenfeld and Nicholson.

Lange, O. (1942). "Say's Law: A Restatement and Criticism". In Lange *et al.* (eds): *Studies in Mathematical Economics and Econometrics in Memory of Henry Schultz*. Chicago: University of Chicago Press.

Lavington, F. (1921). *The English Capital Market*. London: Methuen.

Lavington, F. (1922). *The Trade Cycle*. London: P. S. King and Son.

Leijonhufvud, A. (1968). *Keynesian Economics and the Economics of Keynes*. Oxford, Oxford University Press.

Leijonhufvud, A. (1969). *Keynes and the Classics*. London: IEA.

Lindahl, E. (1929a). "Prisbildningproblemets uppläggning från kapitalteoretisk synpunkt". *Ekonomisk Tidskrift*, as translated in Lindahl (1939).

Lindahl, E. (1929b). "Review of Myrdal's Dynamic Pricing". *Economic Journal*, vol. XXXIX, March.

Lindahl, E. (1930). *Penningpolitikens Medel*, as translated in Lindahl (1939).

Lindahl, E. (1939). *Studies in the Theory of Money and Capital*. New York: Kelley (reprinted, 1970).

Lundberg, E. (1937). *Studies in the Theory of Economic Expansion*. New York: Kelley (reprinted, 1964).

McCulloch, J. R. (1864). *Principles of Political Economy*, 5th edn. Edinburgh: Adam and Charles Black (1st edn, 1820).

Machlup, F. (1977a). *Essays on Hayek*. London: Routledge and Kegan Paul.

Machlup, F. (1977b). "Hayek's Contribution to Economics". In Machlup (1977a).

Malinvaud, E. (1953). "Capital Accumulation and the Efficient Allocation of Resources". *Econometrica*, vol. XXI, April.

Malinvaud, E. (1960–61). "The Analogy between Atemporal and Intertemporal Theories of Resource Allocation". *Review of Economic Studies*, vol. XXVIII.

Malinvaud, E. (1977). *The Theory of Unemployment Reconsidered*. Oxford: Blackwell.

Malthus, T. R. (1820). *Principles of Political Economy*, 1st edn, as partly reprinted in Ricardo (1951–1973), vol. II (all page references are to Malthus's text).

Malthus, T. R. (1827). *Definitions in Political Economy*. New York: Kelley (reprinted, 1971).

Marget, A. (1966). *The Theory of Prices* (1938–1942), in two volumes. New York: Kelley.

Marshall, A. and M. P. (1879). *The Economics of Industry*. London: Macmillan.

Marshall, A. (1920). *Industry and Trade*, 3rd edn. London: Macmillan (1st edn, 1919).

Marshall, A. (1923). *Money, Credit and Commerce*. London: Macmillan.

Marshall, A. (1926). *Official Papers by Alfred Marshall*, edited by J. M. Keynes. London: Macmillan.

Marshall, A. (1961). *The Principles of Economics*, 9th (variorum) edn (C. W. Guillebaud, ed.) in two volumes. London: Macmillan (1st edn., 1890). Unless otherwise stated, all reference are to vol. I: 'Text'.

Marx, K. (1963). *Theories of Surplus-Value* (1856), in three volumes. Moscow: Progress Publishers.

Marx, K. (1967). *Capital* (1867), in three volumes. New York: International Publishers.

Marx, K. (1971). *A Contribution to the Critique of Political Economy*. London: Lawrence and Wishart.

Marx, K. (1975). *Wages, Price and Profit*. Peking, Foreign Languages Press.

Massie, J. (1750). *An Essay on the Governing Causes of the Natural Rate of Interest* (J. Hollander, ed.). Baltimore: Johns Hopkins (1912).

Meek, R. L. (1965). *The Rise and Fall of the Concept of the Economic Machine*. Leicester: University of Leicester Press.

Meek, R. L. (1973a). *Studies in the Labour Theory of Value*, 2nd edn. London: Lawrence and Wishart (1st edn, 1956).

Meek, R. L. (ed.) (1973b). *Turgot on Progress, Sociology and Economics*. Cambridge, Cambridge University Press.

Mehta, G. (1977). *The Structure of the Keynesian Revolution*. London: Martin Robertson.

Milgate, M. J. (1977). "Keynes on the 'Classical' Theory of Interest". *Cambridge Journal of Economics*, vol. I, September.

Milgate, M. J. (1979). "On the Origin of the Notion of 'intertemporal equilibrium'". *Economica*, vol. XLVI, February.

Milgate, M. (1983a). "Keynes and Pigou". *Contributions to Political Economy*, vol. II, March.

Milgate, M. (1983b). "The New Keynes Papers". In Eatwell and Milgate (1983).

Milgate, M. and Eatwell, J. (1983). "Unemployment and the Market Mechanism". In Eatwell and Milgate (1983).

Mill, James (1844). *Elements of Political Economy*, 3rd edn. New York: Kelley (reprinted, 1965).

Mill, J. S. (1874). *Essays on Some Unsettled Questions of Political Economy*, 2nd edn. (1st edn., 1844). New York: Kelley.

Mill, J. S. (1871). *Principles of Political Economy* (Ashley, ed.). New York: Kelley (1st edn., 1848).

Misselden, E. (1622). *Free Trade*. New York: Kelley (reprinted, 1971).

Modigliani, F. (1944). "Liquidity Preference and the Theory of Interest and Money". *Econometrica*, vol. XII.

Modigliani, F. (1963). "The Monetary Mechanism and its Interaction with Real Phenomena". *Review of Economics and Statistics*, vol. XLIII.

Modigliani, F. (1977). "The Monetarist Controversy or, Should We Forsake Stabilisation Policies?" *American Economic Review*, vol. LXVII.

Moggridge, D. E. (1973). "From the *Treatise* to the *General Theory*: an Exercise in Chronology". *History of Political Economy*, vol. V.

Moggridge, D. E. (1976). *Keynes*. London: Fontana.

Morishima, M. (1977). "Pasinetti's *Growth and Income Distribution Revisited*". *Journal of Economic Literature*, vol. XV, March.

Myrdal, G. (1939). *Monetary Equilibrium*. New York, Kelley (reprinted, 1965; Swedish original, 1931).

Neisser, H. (1934). "General Overproduction: A Study of Say's Law of Markets". *Journal of Political Economy*, vol. XLII, August.

Nuti, D. M. (1970). "'Vulgar economy' in the theory of distribution". *De Economist*, vol. CXVIII, as reprinted in Hunt and Schwartz (eds), 1972.

Ohlin, B. (1937a). "Some Notes on the Stockholm Theory of Savings and Investments: Part I". *Economic Journal*, vol. XLVII, March.

Ohlin, B. (1937b). "Some Notes on the Stockholm Theory of Savings and Investments: Part II". *Economic Journal*, vol. XLVII, June.

Ohlin, B. (1937c). Alternative Theories of the Rate of Interest: I". *Economic Journal*, vol. XLVII, September.

O'Leary, J. J. (1942). "Malthus and Keynes". *Journal of Political Economy*, vol. L, December.

Opie, R. (1931). "Marshall's Time Analysis". *Economic Journal*, vol. XLI, June.

Palgrave, R. I. (1963). *Dictionary of Political Economy* (1894–1899), in three volumes (H. Higgs, ed.). New York: Kelley.

Pasinetti, L. L. (1969). "Switches of Technique and the Rate of Return in Capital Theory". *Economic Journal*, vol. LXXIX.

Pasinetti, L. L. (1974). *Growth and Income Distribution*. Cambridge: Cambridge University Press.

Patinkin, D. (1965). *Money, Interest and Prices*, 2nd edn. New York: Harper and Row (1st edn, 1955).

Patinkin, D. (1976). *Keynes's Monetary Thought*. North Carolina: Duke University Press.

Patinkin, D. and Leith, J. C. (eds) (1977). *Keynes, Cambridge and The General Theory*. London: Macmillan.

Pigou, A. C. (1929). *Industrial Fluctuations*, 2nd edn. London: Macmillan.

Pigou, A. C. (1936). "Mr. J. M. Keynes's General Theory of Employment, Interest and Money". *Economica*, vol. III, February.

Pigou, A. C. (1937). "Real and Money Wage Rates in Relation to Unemployment". *Economic Journal*, vol. XLVII, September.

Pigou, A. C. (1944). *Lapses From Full Employment*. London: Macmillan.

Pigou, A. C. (1950). *Keynes's General Theory*. London: Macmillan.

Pigou, A. C. (ed.) (1966). *Memorials of Alfred Marshall* (1921). New York: Kelley.

Ricardo, D. (1951–1973). *The Works and Correspondence of David Ricardo*, in eleven volumes, edited by P. Sraffa with the collaboration of M. Dobb. Cambridge, Cambridge University Press.

Robbins, L. (1930). "On a Certain Ambiguity in the Concept of Stationary Equilibrium". *Economic Journal*, vol. XL, June.

Robbins, L. (1952). *The Theory of Economic Policy in English Classical Political Economy*. London: Macmillan.

Robertson, D. H. (1937). "Alternative Theories of the Rate of Interest: II". *Economic Journal*, vol. XLVII, September.

Robertson, D. H. (1938). "Mr. Keynes and 'Finance'". *Economic Journal*, vol. XLVII, June.

Robertson, D. H. (1947). *Money*, 4th edn. London: Nisbet and Co. (1st edn. 1922).

Robertson, D. H. (1948). *A Study in Industrial Fluctuation*. London: L. S. E. Reprint Series (no. 8).

Robertson, D. H. (1949). *Banking Policy and the Price Level*, 3rd edn. London: Staples Press (1st edn, 1926).

Robertson, D. H. (1951–2). "Comments on Mr. Johnson's Notes". *Review of Economic Studies*, vol. XIX.

Robertson, D. H. (1952). *Utility and All That and Other Essays*. London: George Allen and Unwin.

Robertson, D. H. (1963). *Lectures on Economic Principles* (1957). London: Fontana.

Robertson, D. H. (1966). *Essays in Money and Interest* (J. R. Hicks, ed.). London: Fontana.

Robinson, E. A. G. (1936). "Mr Keynes on Money". *The Economist*, February.

Robinson, E. A. G. (1947). "J. M. Keynes: Obituary". *Economic Journal*, vol. LVII, March.

Robinson, J. (1947). *Essays in the Theory of Employment*, 2nd edn. Oxford: Blackwell (1st edn, 1937).

Robinson, J. (1951–1979). *Collected Economic Papers*, in 6 vols. Oxford: Blackwell.

Robinson, J. (1971). *Economic Heresies*. London: Macmillan.

Robinson, J. (1973). *Introduction to the Theory of Employment*, 2nd edn. London: Macmillan (1st edn, 1937).

Robinson, J. (1979). "Garegnani on Effective Demand". *Cambridge Journal of Economics*, vol. III, June.

Roos, C. F. (1934). *Dynamic Economics*. Indiana, Principa Press.

Samuelson, P. A. (1943). "Dynamics, Statics and the Stationary State". *Review of Economics and Statistics*, vol. XXV, February.

Samuelson, P. A. (1968). "What Classical and Neo-Classical Monetary Theory really was". *Canadian Journal of Economics*, vol. I, no. 1 as reprinted in Clower (1969).

Samuelson, P. A. (1971). "Paradoxes of Schumpeter's Zero Rate of Interest". *Review of Economics and Statistics*, vol. LIII.

Say, J-B. (1880). *A Treatise on Political Economy*, translated from the 4th edn. New York: Kelley (reprinted, 1971).

Schumpeter, J. (1934). *The Theory of Economic Development*. Havard: Harvard University Press.

Schumpeter, J. (1954). *History of Economic Analysis*. London: George Allen and Unwin.

Shackle, G. L. S. (1967). *The Years of High Theory*. Cambridge: Cambridge University Press.

Shove, G. (1933). "A Review of Hicks' *Theory of Wages*", as reprinted in Hicks (1963).

Sismondi, J. C. L. (1819). *Nouveaux Principes d'Economie Politique*, in 2 vols. Paris: Delaunay.

Smith, A. (1776). *An Inquiry into the Nature and Causes of the Wealth of Nations* (Cannan, ed.) in two volumes. London: Methuen (references are to book, chapter and page).

Solow, R. M. (1980). "On Theories of Unemployment". *American Economic Review*, vol. LXX.

Sowell, T. (1972). *Say's Law: An Historical Analysis*. Princeton: Princeton University Press.

Sowell, T. (1974). *Classical Economics Reconsidered*. Princeton: Princeton University Press.

Steuart, J. (1767). *An Inquiry into the Principles of Political Oeconomy* (Skinner, ed.) in two volumes. London: Oliver and Boyd (1966).

Sraffa, P. (1932a). "Dr Hayek on Money and Capital". *Economic Journal*, vol. XLII, March.

Sraffa, P. (1932b). "A Rejoinder". *Economic Journal*, vol. XLII, June.

Sraffa, P. (1960). *Production of Commodities by Means of Commodities*. Cambridge: Cambridge University Press.

Steiger, O. (1971). *Studien zur Entstehung der Neuen Wirtschaftslehre in*

Schweden. Berlin: Dunker and Humblot.

Steiger, O. (1976). "Bertil Ohlin and the Origins of the Keynesian Revolution". *History of Political Economy*, vol. VIII.

Stigler, G. J. (1965). *Essays in the History of Economics*. Chicago: University of Chicago Press.

Sweezy, P. (1946). "Keynes the Economist". In S. Harris (ed): *The New Economics*. London: Dobson.

Turgot, A. R. J. (1973). *Reflections on the Formation and Distribution of Wealth*. In Meek (ed.) (1973).

Uhr, C. G. (1973). "The Emergence of the 'New Economics' in Sweden: A Review of a Study by Otto Steiger". *History of Political Economy*, vol. V.

Walras, L. (1874–77). *Elements of Pure Economics*, translated by W. Jaffé. London: George Allen and Unwin (1954).

Whitaker, J. K. (1971). "The Schumpeterian Stationary-state Revisited". *Review of Economics and Statistics*, vol. LII.

Wicksell, K. (1898). *Interest and Prices* (1898), translated by R. F. Kahn. New York: Kelley (reprinted, 1965).

Wicksell, K. (1901). *Lectures on Political Economy*, in two volumes (L. Robbins, ed.). London: Routledge and Kegan Paul (1934).

Wicksell, K. (1954). *Value, Capital and Rent*. New York: Kelley (reprinted, 1970).

Wicksell, K. (1969). *Selected Papers on Economic Theory* (1959) (E. Lindahl, ed.). New York, Kelley.

Winch, D. (1966). "The Keynesian Revolution in Sweden". *Journal of Political Economy*, vol. LXIV.

INDEX

A

Accumulation:
  and employment, 39
  and rate of profit, 49 & n
  see also 40, 90
Anticipations, *see* Expectations
Arrow, K., 127
Austrian theory of capital, 45, 140; *see also* Period of production
Automatic forces, 110, 158; *see also* Market mechanism, Self-adjustment
Average period of production, 44n, 45, 137

B

Bagehot, W., 19, 25
Bank Act (1844), 99n
Bank rate, *modus operandi* of, 170; *see also* 69n
Banking school, 64–68, 75
Banking system, 70, 71, 109
Barker, T., 110 & n
Baumol, W., 47n, 57, 58
Birck, L. V., 54n
Blaug, M., 40, 46n, 47 & n, 52
Bleaney, M., 52, 54n
Böhm-Bawerk, E. von, 22, 42, 59, 129, 137
Bonar, J., 21n
Bond rate, 69n
Bootstraps theory of interest, 95n
Budget deficit. *See* Government expenditure
Bukharin, N., 50
Bulls and bears, 94 & n

C

Cannan, E., 25
Cantillon, R., 20, 165n
Capital:
  Austrian theory of, 45, 140
  criticisms of orthodox marginalist theory of, 6, 117n, 132, 137, 145; by Keynes, 111–122; by Sraffa, 138, 140; equivalent to a critique of orthodox theory of employment, 6, 123–124
  as factor of production, 6, 44, 132, 151
  glut of, 50
  marginal efficiency of, 91–93, 105, 106
  mobility of, 24n
  physical composition of, 42
  and time, 129, 139–140
  Walras' theory of, 45 & n, 137 & n
Capital, demand for:
  relation to demand for investment, 92, 96, 115, 116n, 181, 193–5
  function of rate of interest, 40, 80, 92
  stock and flow aspects of, 42 & n, 193–5
  see also 43, 69, 128–129
Capital, quantity of:
  average period of production measure, 44n, 45, 137
  basis of orthodox marginalist theory of distribution, 42–43, 44, 128
  basis of orthodox marginalist theory of employment, 6, 96, 181
  problems of measurement of, 117n, 137, 145; in classical *v.* marginalist theory, 39, 44
  in value terms, 44, 146, 181

Capital, theory of:
  equivalent to theory of employment (in marginalist economics), 96, 181; Keynes opposes, 96–97, 117, 121, 151
  problems of equivalent to problems of theory of employment (marginalist theory), 123–4; see also Employment
  role of time in, 129, 139–140
Capital, value of, depends on rate of profit, 44, 146; see also 181
Capital market, 109, 126n, 183
Capitalist economy, defined, 10
Carver, T. N., 93n
Cassel, G., 93n
Clark, J. B., 21, 32, 42, 137
Classical Economics:
  Keynes's definition of, 13, 36, 40; see also 114–115
  our definition of, 13, 36–40; Keynes's criticisms of, 46, 51n, 98–101, 124
  lacks a theory of output, 39, 51–52, 55, 101
  and orthodox marginalist theory, 45
  role of demand and supply in, 47n, 62
  structure of, 36–40
Classical dichotomy, 27, 45, 58; see also Monetary Forces
Clifton, J., 24n
Competition, 184; operation of ensures uniformity of rate of profit, 23–24
Consumption:
  function of level of income, 82n
  unproductive (Malthus), 50
Corn economy, 38 & n
Corry, B., 46n, 52
Credit, 65; effect of contraction of, 72
Credit cycle, 158, 166
Crises:
  Marx on, 55 & n, 61–2
  over-investment theory of, 70n
Crowding out, 79, 109
Cumulative process (Wicksell), 58, 68–71
Currency school, 64–68, 75

D
Debreu, G., 10, 127, 134
Deistic philosophy, 189 & n

Demand and Supply:
  basis of marginalist theory, 4, 6, 41–46, 119–120, 128–129, 140
  in Classical Economics, 47n, 62
  in orthodox capital theory, 146; see also Capital, demand for
  see also 37, 145
Depression of trade, 72
Disequilibrium:
  between saving and investment, 70, 80–81, 86n, 87n, 182–183; see also Saving and Investment
  and equilibrium, 2, 4, 69–70, 136, 166, 175–176
  role of, in General Theory, 2, 4, 87n
  role of, in Treatise on Money, 157–166, 175–176
Distribution:
  Classical theory of, 37–38; relation to theory of value, 37
  Keynes opposes marginalist theory of, 96–97, 101, 103, 151; see also, Effective demand, principle of
  Marginalist theory of, 41–42; criticisms of, 5, 44, 140–141, relation to theory of employment, 6, 96
  premises of marginalist theory of, in the analysis of saving and investment, 41–42, 166–167, 180, 181–182
  see also Capital, Factors of production
Dixit, A., 127, 128, 140
Dobb, M., 52, 62, 100
Dynamic analysis, 32–33, 126, 129–130, 135, 143, 147, 149–151, 176

E
Eatwell, J., 108n
Economic machine, 87, 172: see also 189n
Edgeworth, F., 13, 35, 45
Effective demand, 48, 54, 71, 105
Effective demand, principle of:
  defined, 77–84, 114, 116, 165, 184–187
  as a long-period theory of output, 84–91
  relation to marginalist theory of distribution, 96–97, 101, 103, 125, 151
Effectual demand, 50, 54; in Smith, 47n

Employment:
   Classical approach to, 39, 56–57
   long-period theory of (Keynes),
      84–91, 96–97, 103, 151
   marginalist and Keynes's theory
      contrasted, 3, 96–97
   marginalist theory of, relation to
      theory of distribution, 6, 96;
      relation to theory of capital,
      123–124, 181
   see also Keynes, Output
Equilibrium:
   between saving and investment; in
      marginalist theory, 41–42, 58,
      69–70, 87n, 179–180; in Treatise
      on Money, 80–81, 157–162,
      181–183; in General Theory, 81,
      82–85, 86n, 165, 185, 187; see
      also Saving and Investment
   and disequilibrium, 2, 4, 69–70, 74,
      136, 166, 175–176
   at full employment (marginalist
      theory), 2, 7, 41, 43, 78, 169
   at less than full employment (Keynes),
      3, 78, 85, 87n; see also 80
   general, 102
   intertemporal, 12–13, 85, 97,
      125–142; see also Intertemporal
      equilibrium
   long-period, 12, 69, 85
   notion of, 4, 69; change in, 127–129
   temporary, 113n, 127n, 130, 155, 174
   variations in rate of interest establish,
      69–70, 181–183
Eshag, E., 93, 94n, 116n
Expectations:
   disappointment of, as friction, 113 &
      n.
   method of, 112, 143, 144–149; see also
      Intertemporal equilibrium
   see also 90–91, 102, 126
Ex ante/Ex post, 78, 135–136

F
Factors of production:
   capital and labour as, 6, 41, 44, 57,
      96–97, 132, 151
   full employment of, 57, 92
Fetter, F. W., 129
Fisher, I., 128, 137, 147
Forced saving, 27n, 71n

Frictions:
   interfere with normal operation of
      market mechanism, 1, 4, 63,
      72–73, 74–75, 85, 104, 108
   examples of: money wage, 97n,
      104–111, 171n; real wage, 107;
      rate of interest, 93, 108n;
      uncertainty and expectations,
      90–91, 94–95, 113 & n
Fullarton, J., 64
Full capacity;
   defined, 39 & n
   relation to full employment; in
      Classical economics, 39; in
      marginalist economics, 41; in
      Keynes, 90
Full employment:
   in Classical economics, 39, 46, 51n,
      57, 84
   in marginalist economics, 41, 43, 46,
      57–58, 75, 84, 110–111
   deviations from, 71–72
   and Say's Law, 46, 57
   tendency towards, 4, 7, 43, 57, 72, 92,
      110; disputed by Keynes, 82, 84,
      109, 110, 170, 172
Full utilisation, 39
Fundamental equations (Keynes), 80,
      81, 164, 169, 176–178

G
Garegnani, P., 5, 11, 31n, 35, 39, 42,
      44n, 45 & n, 52, 53n, 78n, 88n, 96,
      99n, 100, 101, 113, 126n, 137n
Glut, general:
   James Mill denies, 48
   Marx on, 55
   Ricardo-Malthus controversy over, 45,
      49–54; Keynes's assessment of,
      46
Gold, 70
Goschen, H., 170
Government expenditure:
   and employment, 79–82
   financing of, 109; see also Crowding
      out
   and general level of prices, 79, 109
   and wages, 109
Grandmont, J. M., 127
Green, R. H., 64n
Groenewegen, P. D., 47n

H

Haavelmo, T., 193 & n
Haberler, G., 54n, 68n, 70n, 72n, 85n, 104, 106n
Hahn, F. H., 13, 127n, 149
Harrod, R., 78n, 85n, 95;
  correspondence with Keynes, 112, 118–121
Hawtrey, R., 71–72, 150
Hayek, F. von., 14, 68n, 71n, 82n, 147 & n, 181n; on intertemporal equilibrium, 127–140
Hicks, J. R.:
  his IS-LM model, 2, 85n, 183
  on method of expectations, 144–149
  on money wage inflexibility, 108
  on statics and dynamics, 32n, 129
  on stationary state hypothesis, 29n, 31n, 141–142
  on temporary equilibrium, 4, 129–130, 155
  see also 102, 104, 112
Hilferding, R., 61n
Hoarding, 27n, 48n, 73
Hull, C. H., 21n
Hume, David, 64

I

'Imperfectionists', 109
Interest:
  bootstraps theory of, 95n
  monetary *v.* real phenomenon, 98–101, 116
Interest, rate of:
  bank and bond rates, 69n
  as conventional phenomenon, 96
  effects of decline in money wage on, 106 & n
  effects of monetary policy on, 96; *see also* Bank rate
  and investment, 79–80, 92–93, 193–195
  Keynes's criticisms of 'classical' theory of, 111–122
  liquidity-preference theory of, 91, 93–96, 111–122
  market: in Wicksell, 14, 69, 136, 179, 180–181; in *General Theory*, 14–15, 185; in *Treatise on Money*, 115n, 159–161, 180–182

rigidity of, 93, 108n
  and supply of savings, 82n
  and rate of profit, 14, 98–101
  variations of, ensure balance between saving and investment, 43, 82, 103, 136, 158, 180; criticised by Keynes, 93–95, 103, 106n
  see also Saving and investment
Intertemporal equilibrium:
  method of, defined, 12–13, 127–129; origin of, 129–136; reasons for emergence of, 136–140
  and method of expectations, 143–145
  see also, 85, 97, 125, 143, 150, 174
Investment:
  in Classical economics, 39, 51
  demand for: as function of rate of interest, 42, 43n, 79–80, 93, 193–195; inelasticity of, 43n, 93; relation to demand for capital, 80, 92
  and employment, 79–80
  as a flow, 42, 115 & n, 193–195
  marginal efficiency of capital theory of, 91–93, 105, 106
  marginalist theory of: and theory of value and distribution, 42–44; premises of, 43, 166–167, 180, 181–182
  planned *v.* actual, 39; *see also Ex ante/ex post*
  public *v.* private, 79, 109; *see also* Crowding out
  and saving, *see* Saving and Investment.

J

Jevons, W. S., 21, 28, 42, 59
Johnson, H., 85n, 93
Johnson, W. E., 190
Juglar, C., 61n

K

Kahn, R., 78–82, 113, 170n
Kaldor, N., 43, 95n
Keynes, J. M.:
  and Classical economics, 98–101, 124, 188; his definition of, 13, 36, 40, 51n
  criticisms of theory of interest, 103, 111–122

criticisms of Marshall, 115, 118
criticisms of Pigou, 106–107
criticism of quantity theory, 165
criticisms of Ricardo: on full
    employment, 40; on glut
    controversy, 45, 50–51; on rate of
    interest, 98–101; soundness of,
    46, 50–51, 98–101
fundamental equations, 80, 81, 164,
    169, 176–178
liquidity preference theory, 91, 93–96,
    103, 111, 112, 113
on long-period method, 96–87, 97,
    125, 171
on long-period unemployment, 85–88,
    163–167, 171–174
and marginalist theory of distribution,
    96–97, 101, 103, 151
on money wages, 104–111, 170
on natural rate of interest, 115n,
    159–161, 164–165
on output and unemployment, 84–91,
    173, 184–187
principle of effective demand, 77–84,
    96–97, 101, 103, 114, 116, 125,
    151, 165, 184–187
on saving and investment: in *Treatise
    on Money*, 156–162, 180–182; in
    General Theory, 78, 82, 83, 88,
    103, 184–187
on Say's Law, 46
short-period assumption (in *General
    Theory*), 89–90
see also, 1, 2, 3, 7, 13, 27n, 35, 66, 89n,
    141, 144, 145, 148 & n
'Keynesian economics', contemporary
    position of, 2–5, 125–126, 188
Klein, L., 46n, 79n
Knight, F., 23n, 32, 44, 116n, 137n,
    147n, 150
Koopmans, T., 127
Kregel, J., 83n

L
Labour:
    demand for, 43; and money wages,
        105–111; and real wages, 43,
        107
    as factor of production, 6, 41, 44, 57,
        96–97, 136, 151
    full employment of, 41, 43, 46, 57–58,
        75, 84, 110–111; see also Full
        employment
    less than full employment of, 71–72,
        82, 84, 109, 110, 170, 172; see also
        Unemployment
    market, 43
    supply of, 43; and real wages, 107
Lacking, 73
Laidler, D., 64n
Laissez-faire, 104, 191–192
Land, 196
Lavington, F., 25, 71, 72–73, 94
Leijonhufvud, A., 3, 79n, 87n, 97n,
    104n, 155n
Leith, J. C., 79n
Lindahl, E., 127, 134–135, 146
Liquidity preference, 91, 93–96, 103; as
    alternative theory of interest,
    112–113; as critique of earlier
    theories, 111–113
Long-period method:
    defined, 12, 20
    Keynes on, in *Treatise on Money*,
        163–171; in *General Theory*,
        86–87, 97, 171–174
    monetary forces under, 26–28, 60–61,
        65, 170–171
    movement away from, 3, 4, 125–126,
        136–140, 141–143, 145, 148–149
    and natural price, 19–23, 128,
        189–191
    and self-adjustment, 23n, 191–192
    and stationary state hypothesis,
        28–33, 138–139
    see also 32–34, 85
Long-period position:
    defined, 12, 14, 20–22
    as centre of gravitation, 9n, 20, 22, 26,
        33
    characterised by full employment, 2,
        7, 41, 43, 78, 169; see also Full
        employment
    characterised by less than full
        employment, 3, 39–40, 78, 85,
        87n; see also Unemployment
    and general rate of profit, 14, 20–22,
        23–26, 29–30, 128
    and short-period position
        distinguished, 12, 34, 57, 60–61,
        63, 69, 74–75
    see also, Equilibrium

M

McCulloch, J. R., 38, 49n, 56n

Machlup, F., 130n

Malinvaud, E., 125, 127, 134 & n

Malthus, T. R.:
and Ricardo, 48–54
and Sismondi, 54 & n
on saving and investment, 51–52
see also 45, 46n, 47, 163n, 172–173

Marget, A., 68n, 93, 149n

Marginal efficiency of capital, 91–93, 105, 106

Marginal productivity:
of capital, 116; relation to marginal efficiency of capital, 116–117
as theory of distribution, 131–132
see also Distribution

Marginal propensity to consume, 82, 105

Marginalist theory, 35; structure of, 41–46; Keynes and, 96–97

Market clearing, 41

Market economy, 10

Market mechanism:
and frictions, 1, 4, 63, 72–73, 74–75, 85, 104, 108
orthodox view of, and Keynes's view of contrasted, 3–4

Market price, see Price, market

Marshall, A.:
definition of normal price, 24, 25, 60, 128, 163, 190
on demand for money, 94
on frictions, 30–31, 74, 111
Keynes criticises, 115, 118
on stationary state hypothesis, 29, 30, 31 & n, 151
on value of capital, 44
see also 13, 28, 36, 40, 42, 43n, 45, 59 & n, 105, 115, 165, 183, 195–196

Marshall, M. P., 25, 74, 111

Marx, K.:
definition of prices of production, 25
on glut controversy, 50, 54, 61
on Currency school-Banking school debate, 64n, 75n
see also 6, 10, 12, 13, 21n, 26n, 48n, 54, 99n

Massie, J., 20

Meek, R. L., 21, 23, 173n, 189 & n, 190

Mercantilism, 21, 47

Mehta, G., 183n

Method of analysis:
criterion for judging, 9n
defined, 5, 11
see also 7; Intertemporal equilibrium, Long-period method

Method of expectations (Hicks), 112; see also Intertemporal equilibrium

Milgate, M., 76n, 107

Mill, James, 13, 47–48

Mill, J. S.:
on Currency school-Banking school debate, 67–68
on relation between long-period and short-period theory, 74–75
on stationary state hypothesis, 32–33, 151
see also 11, 13

Misselden, E., 21n

Mixed economy, 10

Modigliani, F., 2, 85 & n, 88n, 104, 109n, 110

Moggridge, D., 79n, 83n, 85n, 155n

Monetarism, 109, 165

Monetary forces:
classical dichotomy, 27, 45, 57–58
and real forces, 26, 57
see also 26–28

Monetary policy, 96, 99, 109

Money:
demand for, 112; for transactions purposes, 65, 94; for precautionary purposes, 94; for speculative purposes, 94
idle, 48n
Keynes on, see Interest, Keynes, Liquidity preference
Marx on, 55
as medium of exchange, 47, 48
neutrality of, 27
quantity theory of, 27, 48, 63–68, 155, 165, 169–170; Keynes criticises, 165; long run v. short run aspects, 65–68, 169–170, 174–175; J. S. Mill on, 67–68; Wicksell on, 63–68
Ricardo on, 28, 98–100
supply of 112; effects of increase in, 64–65, 109; see also Price level
velocity of circulation of, 65, 66, 169
see also 93, 147

Moore, H. L., 147

Multiplier, 78–80, 114
MV=PT, 64, 170
Myrdal, G., 127, 135–136, 146, 148

N
Natural Law, 21, 189
Natural Price, *see* Price, natural
Natural tendencies, 87
Neisser, H., 54n
Neoclassical economics, *see* Marginalist
    theory
Newton, I., 189
Non-basic commodities, 196
Normal conditions:
    defined, 14, 24
    and natural price, 19–23
    see also 173; Long-period position
Nuti, D. M., 100

O
O'Leary, J. J., 46n
Opie, R., 22, 31n
Orthodox economics, *see* Marginalist
    theory
Output:
    long-period theory of, in marginalist
        economics, 57; in Keynes, 84–91,
        103, 151, 173
    and quantity of money, 68
    and investment, 80
    no theory of in Classical economics,
        39, 51–52, 55, 101
    theory of, and saving-investment
        process, 39, 51–52, 103
Over-investment, 70n
Over-production, 47, 52, 53, 55, 75; *see
    also* Glut
Own rates of interest, 132, 133, 142
Oxford, 119n

P
Palgrave, R. H. I., 11
Parsimony, 51–52
Pasinetti, L., 78n, 91, 101n, 113
Patinkin, D., 3, 77, 78, 79n, 104n
Period of production, 44n, 45, 137
Petty, W., 21
Pigou, A. C., 2, 13, 36, 40, 85n, 88
Pigou effect, 106n
Population, Malthusian theory of, 37, 40
Preferences, 41

Principle of effective demand:
    defined, 77–84, 114, 116, 165,
        184–187
    as a long-period theory of output,
        84–91
    relation to marginalist theory of
        distribution, 96–97, 101, 103,
        125, 151
Productivity and thrift, 95, 181
Propensity to save, 106n
Price:
    flexibility, 42
    present *v.* future, 147
    of production (Marx), 25, 161
Price, market:
    defined, 21
    and demand and supply, 47n
    relation to natural price, 61, 145, 173
Price, natural:
    defined, 19–20
    of labour, 37
    and long-period method, 19–23,
        189–191
    and price of production, 25
    relation to market price, 61
Price level, 66, 70, 79, 164–166, 169,
    170
Profit:
    as surplus, 38
    as windfall, 14, 177–178, 187
Profit, rate of:
    Classical theory of, 37–38
    determined by competition of capitals,
        49 & n, 99 & n
    general, 14, 23–26, 44, 128: and
        definition of long-period method,
        20–22, 128
    marginalist theory of, 42–45; *see also*
        Capital, Distribution
    relation to rate of interest, 14, 98–101
    relation to wage, 37, 99n, 191
    Ricardo-Malthus dispute over, 49–51
Psychology, 41, 85
Public works, 79, 81

Q
Quantity theory of money, *see* Money
Quasi-rent, 196–197

R
Real balance effect, *see* Pigou effect

Real forces, and monetary forces distinguished, 26, 57; see also Productivity and thrift
Realisation problem, 55
Reswitching, 44n
Reverse capital-deepening, 44n
Ricardo, D.:
  on employment, 40, 51
  on long-period v. short-period questions, 1, 2, 21
  debate with Malthus, 48–54
  on monetary theory, 28, 98–101
  on natural v. market price, 21, 24
  'saving is spending', 39–51
  on Say's Law, 47, 49
  on value and distribution, 36–39
  see also 6, 10, 13, 14, 20, 30n, 36, 45, 59, 163n, 191
Rigidities, see Frictions
Robbins, L., 29n, 32, 46n, 189
Robertson, D. H., 23n, 26n, 27, 30, 68n, 73–74, 83n, 95, 150, 162, 181
Robinson, E. A. G., 77, 83n
Robinson, Joan, 24n, 27, 80–81, 88n, 95, 98n, 113, 179
Roos, C. F., 147

S
Samuelson, P. A., 26n, 29n
Saving:
  depends on rate of interest, 82n, 159, 182–183
  depends on income, 82n, 106n, 183
  and spending, 39, 51
  planned v. actual, 41
  see also Thrift
Saving and investment:
  analysis of, as theory of output, 39, 51–52; in marginalist theory, 41, 42, 43, 46, 82, 103
  analysis of, and theory of value and distribution, 166–167, 180, 181–182
  different decisions, 83–84, 156, 162; no distinction in Classical economics, 51–52
  equalised at full employment, 41, 42, 43, 46
  equalised at less than full employment, 78, 81
  equalised by variations in level of

income, 78, 82, 83, 88, 103
  equalised by variations in rate of interest, 43, 103, 159–162, 180–182
  temporary maladjustment between, 53–55; admitted by Kahn, 78–81; admitted by Keynes, 156–162, 180–182; admitted by Ricardo, 56
Say, J. B., 46–47
Say's Law:
  in Classical economics, 46–57, 98; does not imply full employment, 57
  in marginalist economics, 57–58
  see also 45, 48, 66
Scholastics, 189
Schumpeter, J. A., 2, 14n, 29n, 46 & n, 52, 54n, 55n, 61n, 68n, 85n, 88n
Self-adjustment, 23n, 191–192
Short-period:
  assumption of in General Theory, 89–90
  length of, 22, 26, 157, 167–171, 172–173
  monetary theory in, 60–63
  and long period theory, 34, 57, 58, 60–61, 63, 69
  relegation of Keynes to, 2, 3, 4, 84–85, 90, 93, 97, 104n
Short-period position, 12, 127
Shove, G., 139
Sismondi, J. C. L., 47, 54, 61n
Smith, A.:
  and long-period method, 19–21, 128, 189
  on rate of profit, 49 & n
  saving is spending doctrine, 50–51, 53 & n, 99n
  see also 6, 10, 14, 36, 37, 47, 59
Solow, R. M., 110
Sowell, T., 47n, 54n, 55n
Sraffa, P., 5, 6, 27n, 37, 38n, 100, 131–132, 138, 140, 152, 196, 197
Static conditions, 32, 117n, 126, 129, 133n, 143, 149–151
Stationary state, 28–33, 117n, 138–139, 141–142, 145
Steiger, O., 138
Stigler, G. J., 47n
Stocks and flows, 42, 92, 193–195

Substitution, 40, 43–44
Supply and demand, *see* Demand and
   supply
Supply-price, 131, 195–196
Surplus, 38, 100
Swedish school, 127, 134–136, 146
Sweezy, P., 107

T

Tatonnement, 59
Taussig, ., 93n
Technology, 41, 85
Temporary equilibrium, 113n, 127n,
   130, 155, 174
Thrift, 95, 181
Time, 129, 139–140, 146
Tobin, J., 3, 110
Tooke, T., 64, 65
Trade cycle, 72–73, 86, 158
Turgot, A. R. J., 20

U

Uncertainty, 73, 90–91, 94–95, 102,
   126, 146
Underconsumption, 54, 61n
Unemployment:
   as long run phenomenon, 8, 85–91,
     173
   as short run phenomenon, 2–4, 68,
     84–85
   involuntary *v.* frictional, 89n, 173
   structural, 89

'Unobtrusive postulate', 43n
Unproductive consumption, 50
Utility maximisation, 41

V

Value, theory of:
   Classical, 36–37, 38, 39
   Marginalist, 125, 151
Velocity of circulation, 65, 66, 169

W

Wage labour, 10
Wage, money:
   effects of reductions in, 105–111
   inflexibility of, 97n, 104–111, 171n
Wage, real:
   and employment, 40, 43, 107
   and rate of profit, 37, 191
   rigidity of, 107
   subsistence, 37
Walras, L., 14, 22, 26n, 32, 42, 45 & n,
   58, 127, 137 & n
Whitaker, J. K., 29n
Wicksell, K.:
   cumulative process, 68–71
   on natural rate of interest, 14, 59, 65,
     69, 136
   on quantity theory of money, 63–68
   see also 22, 25, 28, 42, 44, 58, 61n,
     83n, 97, 127, 129, 161, 162, 164,
     165, 167